JERK

Twelve Steps to Rule the World

by

Christopher Surdak

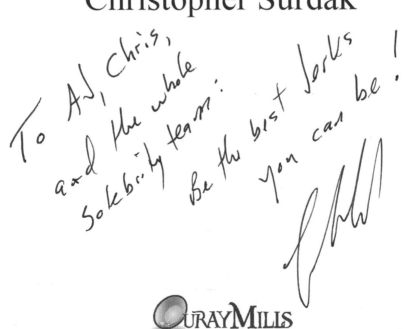

To AJ, Chris, and the whole Sokebrity team: Be the best Jerks you can be!

OURAYMILLS
OMNIMEDIA

Printed in the United States of America

First Edition Paperback:
ISBN-13: 978-09977693812
ISBN-10: 0997693819
eBook ISBN: 978-0-9976938-0-5

Cover Photos by SF Photography
Cover Art by Kaitlyn Buchanan

Dedication

I dedicate this book to my aunt Margaret Ann and Uncle George Mitchell, without whose love and support this book would never have happened. You were all the support that I had in the hardest and most challenging time of my life and I can never thank you enough.

Jerk is also dedicated to my parents, Cynthia and Walter Surdak, Jr., who taught me that if you want something badly enough and if you work for it long and hard enough, you might still get it anyway. ;-)

And to my wife Jeanne and our daughter Ryleigh. When you truly care about someone, sleep is optional.

Christopher Surdak, June, 2016

Falling leaves abound,

Grass slumbers awaiting 'likes,'

Ho! Spring jerks to life!

Foreword

In the 1990s I was a new breed of consultant helping organizations develop a newfangled type of data structure called a data warehouse. Integrating information from the far reaches of an organization and structuring it specifically to generate previously unforeseen insights gave rise to an insatiable corporate craving for evermore broader, faster and more detailed information. Coupled with the internet's limitless ability to create and move information, the Dark Ages of Data were over and the information arms race was underway.

By the turn of the century, a new realization of the power and value of information had emerged.

This trend, known as Big Data, started to take hold. But despite what the vendors all told us, Big Data challenges and opportunities were not just about the size of one's database. Instead they were multifaceted. In 2001, I characterized Big Data as consisting of three dimensions of magnitude: *volume, velocity* and *variety*. The ability to solve this three-dimensional riddle created competitive separation in every sector, and still does today.

Around the same time, bad people bashed big planes into big buildings. 9-11 was not only a domestic security wake-up call, it was a data security wakeup call as well. In addition to the horrendous loss of life, many companies also lost the lifeblood of their business: their information. I wondered how this loss affected their balance sheets and how insurance claims for these lost information assets were being handled. After cracking open my yellowed college accounting books and perusing the balance sheets of information product companies like Experian, TransUnion and ACNielsen, to my great surprise I realized that information is not a balance sheet asset, although it clearly meets the criteria. To add insult to injury, the U.S. insurance industry immediately updated commercial general liability policy standard to *exclude* information from these policies. And not to be outdone, the accounting standards aristocracy updated a key standard to *disallow* the capitalization of electronic data.

I had mistakenly believed information was a recognized asset. This fueled my desire to further develop and advocate the concept of "infonomics" which I had conceived a few years prior. Even though information was denied asset class status, it was imperative that organizations *measured, managed and monetized* it as if it were an actual asset.

Over the next decade and a half, we have seen the introduction of business models, products and services to capitalize on the value of information. Look no further than the smart phone, Google, Facebook, LinkedIn, Uber, Airbnb and the multitude of companies selling or bartering with information assets while thumbing their noses at accountants and tax collectors who are steeped in antiquated notions of information. Companies positioning themselves to collect and analyze large amounts of data stood to gain in power and wealth at the expense of those who did not value data in the same way.

Today, Big Data now seems almost passé. It's as they say, "the new normal." We talk about machine learning, smart machines, intelligent enterprises, digital business, and autonomous devices ("internet of things") in almost a mainstream vernacular. These disruptors jerk their chosen industry through the clever use of a new intersecting set of wealth-generating concepts, namely, what Gartner refers to as the "Nexus of Forces": mobile, social, cloud and information.

In *Jerk* Chris Surdak describes how and why this new breed of company is able to cause the disruption that it does. He explains why their success isn't just certain, it is inevitable. And he describes how existing capital-centric companies can change their strategy and tactics embrace our new information-centric world, and beat the "Jerks" at their own game. If your business is going retrograde because it's failing to treat information as an asset, this book just might jerk you into the 21st century.

Jerk is a mind blowing tour of the new world we live in. It explains how we got here, where we are likely to go, and why this change is happening. It provides a structure for understanding this world, and points to new innovations, challenges and choices we will face in the near future.

I hope you find *Jerk* to be entertaining, enlightening, and just a bit scary. I sure did!

Douglas Laney

VP & Distinguished Analyst, Chief Data Officer Research and Advisory

Gartner

Table of Contents

SECTION I: Going Backwards to Go Forward

"The farther backward you can look, the farther forward you are likely to see."-
Winston Churchill

"Study the past if you would define the future."- Confucius

"History is the fiction we invent to persuade ourselves that events are knowable and that life has order and direction."-
Bill Watterson as Calvin in 'Calvin and Hobbes'

This first section is about the past, the present and our future. I firmly believe that to understand where you are going you must understand where you are starting from. And to understand today's world, we must first understand how we got here, to the world we all know today.

You may or may not be a fan of history, but for the latter sections of this book to make sense, I urge you to join me on a bit of an exploration of the past.

Chapter One: Why Jerk?

"A person with a new idea is a crank until the idea succeeds."-
Mark Twain

*"In my opinion, we don't devote nearly enough scientific
research to finding a cure for   jerks."- Bill Watterson as
Calvin in 'Calvin and Hobbes'*

I always knew I wanted to be a serial author; to me it seemed an
idyllic way to earn a living. Write one book, have it do well, fly
around talking about it, and the follow-on books simply write
themselves. Many of the people I admire seemed to have done the
same. Steven Covey, Tom Peters, and Peter Drucker jump
immediately to mind. To a casual observer, it seemed easy. Why in
the world didn't everybody do that?

Sometimes, reality can be hard. And in this case, the reality was
nothing like I had thought it would be.

Even so, once I finished the manuscript of my first book, *Data
Crush*, I immediately started planning book two. When I approached
my editor about book two she was initially less than enthused. She
reinforced that I had to do more to push *Crush* before moving on to
the next one (she was still not too familiar with my multi-threaded
nature). She wondered if the content would be 'fresh' and 'relevant'
(I've come to know that this is editor-speak for, 'What the hell are
you talking about?')

But the main thing she held on to was the name. As with my first
book, which did not start out as *Data Crush*, coming up with a good
name seems to be the most important part of publishing. And in her
mind, *Jerk* was not a bell-ringer.

Sometimes I can let things slide, and I'm usually open to other
people's points of view. If all of us always agreed about everything,
none of us would ever learn anything. But as for the title of this

book, I was adamant it be called *Jerk*. Nothing else would really fit. If you're reading this now, it is only because I made some pretty good arguments about why *Jerk* should be called *Jerk* and not something else. Thanks for your support!

No, Really, Why *Jerk*?

As with many words in the English language, 'jerk' has a number of meanings. In addition to its familiar and common uses, jerk is a term used by physicists. Jerk is the third derivative of the equation of motion; it is a change in acceleration over time. If velocity is a change in position over time, and acceleration is a change in velocity over time, jerk is a change in acceleration over time. It's the sensation you feel the moment you step on the gas in a powerful car. It's what you feel the instant you slam on the brakes shortly thereafter. It's that sickening bounce you sometimes feel when an old elevator suddenly starts or stops, and it's the feeling you get the instant something smacks you upside the head – by surprise. In physics, jerk represents an extremely rapid change in condition – violent, uncontrolled and difficult to contain.

$$\vec{j} = \frac{\delta \vec{A}}{\delta t} = \frac{\delta^2 \vec{V}}{\delta t^2} = \frac{\delta^3 \vec{S}}{\delta t^3}$$

Rate of Change in Acceleration
Second Derivative of Velocity
Third Derivative of Position
Figure 1.1: The Mathematical Equation for Jerk

Like that one cousin, coworker or friend of yours who 'just ain't right,' jerk can be powerful, annoying and destructive. Jerk can rip the teeth off of gears in machinery, burn out circuits in electronics, and make a nuclear reactor spin out of control. Jerk can destroy the best-engineered, most thoughtfully designed systems our society can create.

The same can be said of the new wave of companies entering every segment of our society. These companies seek to destabilize existing businesses and systems. They look for companies that believe they are too big to fail, and then beat them because of their bigness. They hunt down sacred cows and slaughter them. They dive right into seas of regulations and bureaucracy and then simply deny that they exist. They use data to cause jerk in existing, stable industries. And so the title *Jerk* seemed apropos.

Jerk is the encore to my first book, *Data Crush*, which was the culmination of six years of effort in trying to come to terms with the changes that new technologies were bringing to our world. In the late 'oughties' there was a perfect storm of new technologies that stood to change our daily lives. Smart phones, cloud computing, social media and broadband communications were each revolutionary in their own way. But taken collectively, they impact every aspect of how we work, play, and interact with one another.

Data Crush attempted to make sense of these technological forces. I'm happy to report that the feedback has been extremely positive. While writing *Data Crush* I was a little worried that the material, advice and guidance that I provided might grow stale quickly. Because of this, I strove to understand the social, technical and business forces at play so that the resulting advice was fundamental.

More important than the positive reviews is that, three years after writing *Data Crush*, pretty much all of my predictions and forecasts have proven to be correct. I don't think there's any magic to that, it's just sound engineering and scientific principles applied to the things going on around us. I've used the same approach in writing *Jerk*. I hope this book stands the test of time as well.

Enough Already! What about *Jerk*?

I came up with the title *Jerk* based upon my own experience with Internet startups in the late 1990s. Back during Internet Bubble 1.0, nearly everyone was getting into the startup game. After the economic boom cycle following the end of the Cold War, people had way more money than sense. That, plus the potential upside coming from discovering and infiltrating this brand-new frontier (more about this later) meant that it was pretty easy to land investment capital. In fact, during my first-ever meeting with real, bona fide angel investors, in December of 1999 I saw just how easy it was to get investment capital at the peak of the bubble. I sat over dinner with two brothers, wealthy from Wall Street commissions and eager to become billionaires, and gave these two strangers the 'elevator pitch' about my idea. After 20 minutes, the two brothers excused themselves and went to the washroom together. Five minutes later they returned to the table, handed me a check for $250,000 and said "We're in."

Man, I miss those days.

Unfortunately, my startup at that time fell victim to the same bubble burst that practically killed off an entire generation of tech workers. Nine months after receiving that check, I found myself tearing down ridiculously expensive office furniture, hand loading it onto a U-Haul truck, driving it across Lower Manhattan, carrying it up five stories, and reassembling it in the offices of the other startup that had bought the furniture from us for five cents on the dollar. For me, the year 2000 was a rollercoaster ride, and I learned to take my humble pie with a healthy side order of sheepishness.

Sock Puppets to the Rescue

Like every startup in history, we had a business plan. We didn't just have a business plan, we had a gorgeous, compelling, well-thought-out business plan. It was foolproof, or so we thought. Having a completely ridiculous business plan was key during Bubble 1.0. It had to show what in those days was called 'the hockey stick.' The hockey stick was a model (in Microsoft Excel, naturally), that showed a revenue curve shaped just like a hockey stick. After initially slow growth, the company's revenue would suddenly take off, almost vertically, as more and more users consumed more and more of our offering.

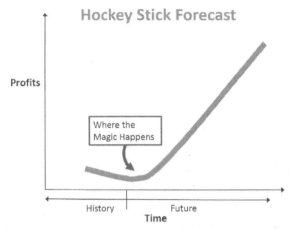

Figure 1.2: Startup funding in the 1990s demanded a 'hockey stick' business plan

Back then, nobody cared if the model and its assumptions were patently absurd. No, just have a hockey stick revenue chart and people would throw money at you like you were a hobo at a Bernie Sanders rally. Perhaps one of the most famous (at the time) examples of this was Pets.com, the company made famous by its dog-sock-puppet mascot. Pets.com was a direct-to-home retailer for pet food, modeled after Amazon.com. They promised fast delivery, convenience and low prices, all at the same time.

Now, in my old rocket scientist days we had a saying used by NASA folks: Fast, Good, Cheap – pick any two. So, when I saw Pets.com take off and become an overnight, multi-billion-dollar sensation, I figured something was amiss. It crashed right after the bubble burst, despite having, and delivering for a time, a hockey-stick revenue stream. What people realized shortly thereafter is that, according to Pets.com's own model, it would have had to capture something like 110 percent of the total pet food market in the United States to break even.

Figure 1.3: The Pets.com sock puppet, the only valuable part of their company

Ah, a fool and his money …

But What About Now?

If a hockey-stick-shaped curve for revenues and customer adoption was outlandish back then, is it any different now? There are two reasons why the answer is emphatically Yes.

First, almost two billion people have access to the Internet today. They live in it and depend upon it. Many are addicted to it. So, if you have a good idea, you can sell it to one quarter of humanity, instantly.

Second, as I discussed in *Data Crush,* we now live in a world where practically anything and everything that you need to run a business is available instantly, in the cloud, pay-as-you-go, with little or no fuss. Anyone can start a new company at almost no cost and then readily scale up and out to meet changes in demand. Indeed, these days it's hard for a startup company to receive funding if they haven't already created a revenue stream, because there's just no excuse for not getting there on your own.

This means there are effectively no barriers to entry anymore for *anyone* with a good idea. Today, not only do you not need to sit at dinner with rich people trying to get access to their capital, you don't even really need capital. You can just try out your new idea, for nearly no cost, and if people like it you're an instant success.

So, in the world of the 'tensies,' new companies don't grow, or expand, or accelerate – they jerk. They take off. They go all hockey-stick and explode, just like we forecasted back in Internet 1.0, only 20 years prematurely. Companies like Uber, Airbnb, Lyft, and Doctor On Demand jerk because the economic and social barriers to user adoption and growth have evaporated. Now, if a company has a good idea and people learn about it, that company finds itself filling a vacuum of need and desire as fast as the Internet can carry it. This is why they are disruptive. This is why they succeed wildly. This is why they Jerk.

And this is just the beginning. By 2015 there were more than a billion people connecting to the Internet primarily via their smartphones. We use them 24 hours a day, 365 days a year, and most of us would be lost without them. Smartphone users will double in number by 2020, while total Internet users will exceed four billion. Five years after that, these numbers will almost double again, and almost all of humanity will be interconnected digitally, with smartphones as our primary portal to our digital existence.

By mid-2015 smartphone users had downloaded more than 150 billion apps. These apps provide all manner of tools, distractions and capabilities, almost instantly and at nearly zero cost to the user. Today, if your organization makes a cool app and releases it to the world, you have instant access to more than a billion new customers. This represents a digital lottery where everyone and anyone is encouraged to play, because the costs are so low and the rewards are astronomically high.

Worldwide Internet Users

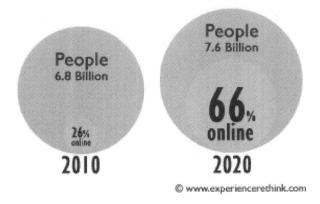

© www.experiencerethink.com

Figure 1.4: Forecasted growth in Internet Users by 2020

Neo, It... Is... Inevitable

Shout out to the movie *The Matrix*. Indeed, Jerk is the inevitable
result of the disappearance of barriers to entry and the ability to
access billions of customers, instantaneously. With this, a new and
successful idea doesn't just grow or accelerate, it jerks. It takes off
and becomes wildly successful because there are no longer any
restraints against such explosive growth. To the contrary, rapid
growth feeds upon itself, just like a snowball rolling down a
mountain or the latest off-color tweet from a Kardashian. In this
environment, small, nimble organizations appear out of nowhere,
create entirely new products or services serving entirely untapped
markets, and become billionaires. Or they can take control of
existing mature markets, virtually overnight.
Jerk explains how these upstarts achieve their dramatic wins. These
companies, these Jerks, search for mature industries with closed
minds, closed markets and overconfident executives. They then
apply the Digital Trinity of Mobility, Social Media and Predictive
Analytics to rip, tear and burn out old paradigms. More on this later.

In this book you will see how rapid, unanticipated changes are
tearing existing business models apart. Previously powerful

corporations are being eclipsed by these new upstarts, these Jerks. Entire industries are being disrupted, seemingly overnight. A dozen or so people, living in a shipping container in Lagos or Cairo or Mumbai, can create a business like Uber in a matter of months or even weeks. Their business may be one that is technically illegal in many jurisdictions, breaks every tradition set by two centuries of capitalism, and does what existing players will not do, and this is why they win. When they do, they win big, and many of them create billions of dollars in market value in mere months. Companies like Uber aren't one-offs. They're not special, unique or unusual. They're the new normal in a world reorienting around information, rather than capital.

Denial: Not Just a River in Egypt

Over the course of the last three years I have worked with thousands of executives, legislators, judges and other leaders. The vast majority of them have told me, "That stuff doesn't apply to me." Or, "Our business or industry is different." Or, "We're too big to be affected by those changes." A couple of years ago I would try to plead my case that these people were not protected from the changes all around them. They weren't special, they weren't unique. They weren't little snowflakes. But by now I've reached the point where if I run into denial I usually just bid the person adieu, and hope that they don't run out of soma.

Believing that you're invulnerable *is* a large part of your vulnerability! If you believe this to be true of your business, you're helping to seal your own fate. The Ubers of the world are coming to get you, and no one is safe. These new players follow a formula, and if there is a formula to be followed, *anyone* can do so in *any* industry. This is the essence of *Jerk*. The recipe follows.

Figure 1.5: The seven stages of grief, or dealing with bad news

How This Book Is Organized

Jerk has four parts. First, I provide a little historical context. How did we get to where we are today, and how is it possible that all of this change is predictable, even inevitable? Part Two will lay out what I call the 'Dirty Dozen of Being a Jerk,' or the 12 things that Jerks do in order to create, well, jerk. These 12 things represent the formula for jerking an existing company, industry, meme, policy and so on. Follow these 12 steps and you can Uber any organization in any industry with surprising ease and speed.

Part Two will show that Jerks follow a discernable pattern. There are consistencies in how they do what they do, and where they choose to do it. How and why they succeed is knowable and can be replicated anytime, anywhere, by anyone. This represents both the threat to any existing player in any market, and the opportunity for anyone trying to be a Jerk with their new product or service. Indeed, it's somewhat scary that these changes can happen so easily and quickly, and yet that's what the realities of our New Normal dictate.

Part Two gives examples of companies causing Jerk in different industries. Time and again I have heard how a given industry or business is somehow safe from these changes. The range of my examples should put this delusion to rest. You will see that no existing organization is safe from Jerk. No company is too big, no market is too protected, no regulatory structure is too strong to avoid being disrupted. The forces creating Jerk are structural and touch every nook and cranny of our society. It is inevitable that this will happen to your organization. It's simply a matter of time, and a matter of how *your* use of the Digital Trinity changes *your* expectations and behaviors in our New Normal.

Lest you despair the future of your business after these first two sections, Part Three of *Jerk* lays out the counter-formula to Jerk. What things must an existing organization do to survive in the face of this onslaught, and how might you put these same forces to work to your advantage? These six responses, which I call the 'Digital Dashpots,' can help existing companies slow down the onslaught of Jerks, and buy them some time. Trust me, the changes won't be easy, necessarily so, but if you want a fighting chance at this you need to count more on fighting and less on chance.

Finally, in Part Four I will provide a story of what living in a world of Jerk might look like by 2025. *Data Crush* closed with a similar set of predictions for the year 2020, and the feedback was that this effort was very useful in making these changes seem real.

In summary, *Jerk* is an exploration of the New Normals of business: constant, endless, boundless disruption. It presents an approach for causing disruption, 'the formula,' and shows how nearly anyone can use the formula to disrupt nearly any industry. *Jerk* will explore how young David's defeat their chosen Goliaths despite seemingly impossible odds. It will also explain why many of the Goliaths contribute to their own downfall. I hope that all of this material shows that if there is a formula for successfully disrupting an existing player in a mature market, then no player in any market is safe from *Jerk*.

It is worth noting that much of this book has been built upon the foundations laid in *Data Crush*. If you haven't read that book, you may find it useful for providing context around concepts I will discuss, such as gamification, contextification, etc. It's a fast read, and may help put much of what you will find in *Jerk* to better use.

All Hope Abandon Ye Who Enter Here?

By now it may seem that I'm painting a rather bleak picture for existing companies. But this is not the case at all. Rather than portraying a digital Dante's Inferno, where existing companies merely wait for their doom, I believe that it is possible for existing, large organizations to out-Jerk the little guys. Extinction is not inevitable. Existing companies can survive, but only if they act quickly, courageously and disruptively. This isn't easy, but it is possible.

Organizations that do this will reap even greater rewards than new competitors because, even today, size *can* matter. After all, many of us know from old holiday gatherings the only thing more disruptive than a little jerk is a really, really big jerk. *Jerk* provides Goliaths with a Philistine's Survival Guide, and examples of how to use it. With that, let's jump right into *Jerk*.

Chapter Summary:

1. Organizations the world over are experiencing dramatic change. These changes may seem to be due to technology, but they are not. The changes around us are social changes, and they impact everything.
2. Society is reorienting towards a new set of rules and a new set of expectations based upon recent technical advances. This wouldn't be possible without technology, but technology is just an enabler.
3. These changes are allowing a new kind of company to enter the market place and take advantage of these new rules and expectations to rapidly dominate existing players.
4. These new rules and expectations are knowable and measurable, which means they can be acted upon.

Chapter Two: An Introduction to Us

"Being powerful is like being a lady. If you have to tell people you are, you aren't."- *Margaret Thatcher*

"If the world was perfect, it wouldn't be."- *Yogi Berra*

The fundamental shift happening today is the change from a world dominated by capital (or money) to one dominated by information. I've been accused of being grandiose in making this statement, but that's not the case. This shift is the primary driver of disruption, conflict and discomfort in today's world. It is also the dominant source of new opportunities.

This chapter looks at how information is replacing capital as the basis of wealth and power. If you're someone who doesn't have time for this, or you don't really care about context, you may want to skip this section. But, given that one of the key concepts of this entire book is that context is now king, you may want to spend a little time here.

From Dukes to Dollars to Digits

To understand why this shift is so fundamental, we need to look at the history of human society. According to historians, our notion of modern human society started around 3,500 BCE, or almost 5,500 years ago. By that time, humans had transformed from being wandering, clan-based hunter-gatherers to localized, communal farmers of flora and fauna. This changed our economy from being based on what you found, caught or collected to being based on what you grew, harvested or mined from underground. As we settled down, our wealth was less dependent on luck and more dependent on location.

All of these resources came from the land and, as a result, land took on ever-increasing importance. If you controlled land you controlled people's ability to create wealth. This gave you power. We created

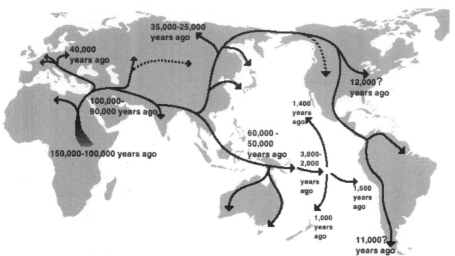

Figure 2.1: Current scientific thinking on human migration across the Earth

the notion of land ownership. We created the concepts of lord and tenant, of king and knave, of sheriff and serf. For the first five millennia of human society, land was the basis of wealth and power in the world.

This political and economic system carried us through the Dark Ages somewhat intact, and provided the early seeds of today's legal and social systems. It was by no means an ideal system as land isn't exactly portable, fungible or easy to make change with (hey brother, can you spare a quarter hectare?), but at the time it was the best we could do.

Then, in 16th century Italy, Westerners started to wake up from the Dark Ages, spurred on by innovations and technologies seeping in from China and other points East. Europe entered the Renaissance, and with this transition came the beginnings of capitalism. The international trade in goods and ideas led to two major disruptions: new sources of thinking and new sources of wealth. It took a while for these disruptions to take hold. But once they did, a revolution was born.

Figure 2.2: Might this Chinese map supposedly from 1418, clearly showing the Western Hemisphere, change how we view the voyages of Columbus?

The Industrial Revolution: A Revolution of Capital

By the 1700s the changes wrought by the Renaissance began to take over the world at large. Merchants who controlled fleets, commerce guilds and money soon became wealthier and more powerful than land owners. Naturally, land owners weren't terribly pleased with this, and they put forth a number of efforts to stem their loss of power. These efforts are known as the American Revolution, the French Revolution, the Franco-Prussian War, World Wars I and II, and so on. Disruption caused by innovation is nothing new.

Land holders, in the form of kings, emperors and so on, put up a good fight. However, as technology advanced, those who had control of the new source of wealth and power in the world (capital) had an enormous advantage over those who controlled the old sources. Democracy and socialism (new forms of political systems), fueled by capitalism and communism (new forms of power systems) took over from feudalism and imperialism.

This change was massively disruptive. In addition to the wars, this shift from land to capital caused the global migration of millions of people, leading to the hodge-podge of races and creeds presently known as the United States. It led to the beginning of the exploitation of the recently rediscovered Western Hemisphere. It led to the explosion in global trade initially sparked by the Columbian Exchange and the global silver-sugar-opium trade. Evolving technology continued to spur on this transition.

To see the level of disruption caused by a shift in wealth and power, one need only pay a little bit of attention to high school history and keep an open mind.

Contemporary Capitalism

So how does this help to understand today's world? For more than 200 years we have been orienting towards this capital-centric society. Our laws, our customs, our education system, our trade, our politics have all aligned with the notion that capital was the new king.

In business, every one of our processes, rules, titles and metrics are designed to control the ebb and flow of capital. In the law, we protect capital ownership, we enforce contracts, we tax commerce as much as, if not more than, we tax land. We educate and train accountants, financial advisors, business people, auditors and attorneys. We create ever more sophisticated means of using capital to create more capital.

Our technologies and innovations continually spurred on this capital orientation. We invented advertising and marketing. We invented stock markets. We invented new technologies such as steel and oil and railroads and electricity. These were all capital-intensive innovations that unleashed the industrial revolution, creating even more capital. This accelerated the shift away from land-centricity and towards capital-centricity.

Along the way we found that in order to better manage capital we had to do a lot of record-keeping. Keeping track of land ownership was relatively easy. After all, it wasn't going anywhere. But capital was rather more mobile than land, and knowing what you had and where it was became critical to the whole capital process. Over time, we innovated around the process of managing capital with banking, cash, stocks, bookkeeping and so on. These innovations to manage capital were the seeds of yet another revolution - the Information Revolution.

Figure 2.3: Accountants keeping books in the early 1900s

The Birth of Our Data-Centric Society

By the mid-20th century the growing scale and scope of capital began to tax our abilities to document and manage it. Bombers, battleships and battalions required enormous amounts of capital inputs and the old double-entry bookkeeping approach created by Muslim traders 13 centuries earlier just couldn't keep up. A World War II battleship had millions of components, each precisely engineered, manufactured and delivered at the right time. Even if you wanted to hire an army of accountants to keep track of it all, there simply weren't enough wing-tips and pocket protectors to go around.

Figure 2.4: Schematic of a World War II B-17 bomber

The demands for better mechanisms of capital control and management during World War II led to the development of the computer. Computers were initially primitive, expensive and huge. They were simplistic, clunky, and the size of entire buildings. In the early days of computers, 'bugs' literally were bugs - insects that crawled into the guts of a computer and caused it to short out.

Despite their limitations, computers were revolutionary. Early computers could perform hundreds of thousands or even millions of calculations overnight, consistently and accurately. A single early computer could do the work of hundreds or thousands of

accountants. In one fell swoop, the seeds of the next revolution in social and economic power were sown as a replacement for armies of slide-rule-carrying geeks.

By the 1980s, advancements in technology allowed computers to sit on people's desks. The PC was not just an advanced typewriter, as many in that era suggested. PCs allowed more and more people to manage capital allocation in ever more detailed ways. Spreadsheets were the real revolution here, as they allowed for the rank and file in an organization to better model, predict and manage the use of capital.

Figure 2.5: The first computer, ENIAC, at my alma mater, The University of Pennsylvania

In the 1990s, most of us in the information technology industry were focused upon deploying a range of new capital-management tools. We used Enterprise Resource Planning (ERP), Customer Relationship Management (CRM), Supply Chain Management (SCM) and other software tools, each designed to help organizations better manage the ebb and flow of capital. During the 1990s, hundreds of billions of dollars were spent globally to implement systems for managing capital. This trend continues today.

The PC Meets Indiana Jones

As we deployed each of these enterprise systems we began to notice a curious thing: information began piling up. Back in the 1990s this was a problem. Computer storage was expensive, and storage capacity limited. Our computer networks were primitive, and no one was sure if TCP/IP or Token Ring was the preferred technology.

I recall upgrading my copy of Microsoft Office while working at Lockheed Martin Astro Space in 1992. I opened the box and found something like 30 3.5-inch floppy disks inside, which collectively held about 40 megabytes of data. That was a vast amount of information in that day, and we joked back then that Microsoft had created yet another version of bloatware with the latest version of Office. I settled in at my desk, and spent the next two working days installing that software onto my IBM PC, powered by the latest Intel 386 microprocessor.

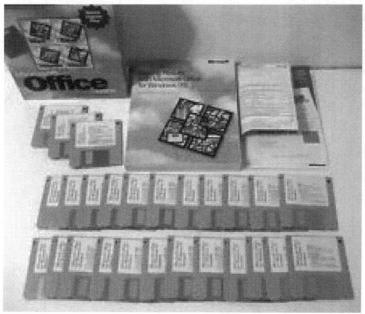

Figure 2.6: Loading Microsoft Office 1995 took a really, really long time

Our new enterprise systems created two or three times that amount of data every day, which was hard to even imagine back then. Storing old data became a real problem, as disks were expensive and prone to failure. As a result, most organizations put old, inactive data onto cassette tapes. Tapes were relatively cheap and compact, and could safely store data for a long time. The problem with tapes is that once information was on one, it was very hard to get it back. You had to find the tape, load it, and then read it for potentially hours to find what you were looking for. Like the ending scene of Raiders of the Lost Ark, many treasures were lost forever on a magnetic tape, stored in a warehouse somewhere.

Data Driven Decision-Making

Around this same time, the quality revolution was occurring in America. This built on J. Edward Deming's work in the 1950s. Companies began to implement information systems for capital management. Statistical analysis was a big part of the quality revolution, and quantifying process performance was viewed as essential for improving process quality. It didn't take long for statisticians to realize that the new information systems were loaded with process data, and old data developed a new-found value to organizations.

By the late 1990s organizations were building systems that could store old data in a format that still allowed for analysis. These systems were called data warehouses, and analyzing old data to search for avenues for improving capital management became known as business intelligence. The thinking was that by analyzing old business data it was possible to find inefficiencies and variability in processes, which would allow for capital to be used more efficiently and effectively. And the faster and more efficiently you managed capital, the more of it you could create and accumulate. The accelerating growth of the global economy through the 1980s and 1990s was a direct result of information technology increasing our ability to manage more and more capital, faster.

Email: The End of the Memorandum

Capital management systems required that managers, accountants and other process participants actually had access to the automated processes. Initially this was achieved with what was called dumb terminals, the chromebooks and netbooks of their day. As the price of PCs fell, individuals could have one on their desk. This greatly expanded their ability to create and consume information. Both terminals and PCs were networked together, so that people could participate in computerized capital management processes. People also found that once they were connected it was easier to share files, models and other content.

My father spent his entire career in information technology, from punch cards to iPads. I remember in the early 1980s, while I was in middle school, my father coming home from work one day very excited. He had just implemented something called 'email' at work. He said it would change the world. I gave him a typical-teen, "yeah dad, whatever," and continued playing games on my Atari 800.

Figure 2.7: The founders of Compaq Computer, with the first 'portable computer'

It turns out my dad was right; email changed everything. Suddenly, computers weren't just about creating and managing information about capital. With email, we started to create information about information. We'd send spreadsheets, notes and papers and other chunks of information back and forth so that we could improve our collective productivity. We invented workflow, which gave people the ability to review and approve what others were saying about or doing with capital. And we began connecting with one another, globally, in entirely new ways.

Email replaced the memo as the standard means of business communication, almost overnight. Armies of stenographers, typists and secretaries (oh, the political incorrectness of it all!) found themselves out of jobs, while executives struggled to type on their new IBM PCs and Macintosh computers. Through the 1980s and 1990s hundreds of thousands of unemployed office workers became familiar with the disruption that would be caused by the information revolution.

In 1998 I worked at Citibank, assisting them in deploying PeopleSoft as their new Human Resources Management System (HRMS). I recall senior executives 'lamenting' how many emails they received every day, as this was the new indicator of their power and influence. One would complain that he received 80 emails a day. His colleague would reply that she received over a hundred a day, and the gauntlet was thrown! While email started out as a novelty for university professors, by the late 1990s it had become the dominant means of interoffice communication.

Thank You Al Gore

By 1990 an obscure American government agency known as the Advanced Research Projects Administration (ARPA) had decided to privatize one of its innovations: ARPANet. This was a project by the U.S. government to build a communications network that was resilient enough to survive an all-out nuclear attack. The thinking was that if America had a suitably robust computer network, we could still destroy the other side of the planet after the Soviets had destroyed our side. Turnabout is fair play, after all.

After privatization, ARPANet became the Internet, and suddenly people everywhere could easily communicate. There was a positive resonance between adoption of the PC and adoption of the Internet. The more there was to do on the Internet, the more you wanted to be there, too. Further, the original purpose of the computer, the better management of capital, began to give way to a new purpose: the creation and management of content.

The Internet swept across the world, changing the way that people interacted with information. When I started college, the library was the only option if you wanted to look something up. By the time I finished my undergraduate degree there was an entirely new way to find things out. You logged into a computer, turned on something called a web browser, and went to a place called a website, perhaps named Yahoo!, and there you could actually find answers to your questions without ever leaving your desk.

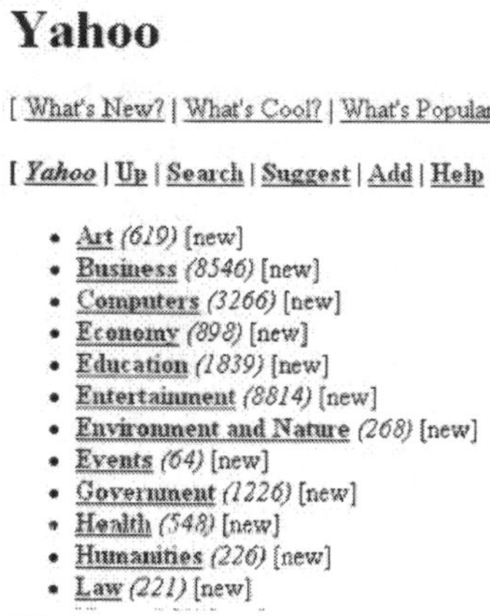

Yahoo

[What's New? | What's Cool? | What's Popular? | A Random Link]

[*Yahoo* | Up | Search | Suggest | Add | Help]

- Art *(619)* [new]
- Business *(8546)* [new]
- Computers *(3266)* [new]
- Economy *(898)* [new]
- Education *(1839)* [new]
- Entertainment *(8814)* [new]
- Environment and Nature *(268)* [new]
- Events *(64)* [new]
- Government *(1226)* [new]
- Health *(548)* [new]
- Humanities *(226)* [new]
- Law *(221)* [new]

Figure 2.8: Yahoo search engine page, radical stuff in 1994

This was radically new stuff! When the PC first came out, people wondered why anyone would want one. With ERP systems for managing capital, email for talking about managing capital, and the Internet for looking up information whenever you wanted to, our information revolution had begun. By the year 2000 enough of us owned and were comfortable with PCs that another new revolution was at hand. We were entering a content revolution, where organizations that assisted in the creation and delivery of content grew in importance.

Searching, Posting and Chatting

By the turn of the century, people were spending more and more time online. We no longer wanted to just work on the Internet, we wanted to play, shop and be entertained. Our use of the Internet grew beyond mere capital management. We started to create information for its own sake. If we wanted to know something, we checked online. If we wanted to buy something, more and more of us shopped online, and if we wanted to meet someone, we started to interact with one another online. The nature of the Internet fundamentally changed from being a business tool to being a connection and content tool.

Many companies attempted to tap into our changing demands, and several companies have become dominant players in today's world. Google, Amazon, Facebook, eBay and others rode the content and connectivity wave and became digital behemoths. These companies monetized content, as they were the first to recognize that information had inherent value, not based on its relationship to capital.

This too was a radical idea. For 50 years companies invested in information technology in order to better manage capital. Suddenly, information was worth owning and managing by itself, because information had value. Indeed, thousands and thousands of investors wondered why anyone would invest in Google, a company that didn't *do* anything. Or invest in Amazon, a company that didn't and couldn't make a profit on its capital. Who would invest in Facebook, a company that simply allowed others to create content? The wave of content companies ignored this disbelief and focused on what they knew would be valuable someday: they facilitated and monetized the creation of content, rather than capital.

The Next Social and Political Revolution

It is increasingly evident today that capital is losing out to information as the basis of wealth and power. Recently, national governments and central banks have implemented *negative* interest rates, in an effort to keep using capital as a means of control. At the same time, information-based companies such as Apple, Google, Microsoft and Facebook are stockpiling billions of dollars in capital, unsure of exactly what to do with it.

Negative interest rates were an unthinkable fiction as recently as the global fiscal meltdown of 2008 and the following Great Recession. Yet they are now becoming a capital management reality because old, capital-centric social structures have no other responses to the changes brought about by the information revolution. Old land-holders built armadas of warships, enormous standing armies and all manner of land-centric bureaucracies in order to keep control of their land in the face of capitalists. Kings, emperors and czars took extreme measures to try to maintain power through the Industrial Revolution. Today's capitalists are forced to do the unthinkable to try to prevent their inevitable loss of wealth and power. The irrationality of negative interest rates simply punctuates the degree to which capital is becoming irrelevant in a world soon to be dominated by information.

People and organizations whose power derived from the control of capital are losing that power. They are being replaced rapidly by those whose power stems from controlling information. When I see disruption in capitalist norms, in the form of formerly impossible fiscal policies, the industrialized printing of fiat currency, or the mass redistribution of capital wealth through liberalized politics, I don't see a world in transition; I see a world in the midst of a revolution. We are surrounded by evidence of this coming change, and the historical parallels are obvious.

For 5,000 years of human history, control of land was the basis of wealth and power in the world. With the Industrial Revolution, capital took over for land, and that transition took 200 years to fully evolve. We are experiencing another revolution in how wealth and power are created in human society. Soon, control of information will replace control of capital as the basis of wealth and power in our world. And this time, the transition won't take 200 years, it'll take 20. And now, in 2016, we're about five years into that transition.

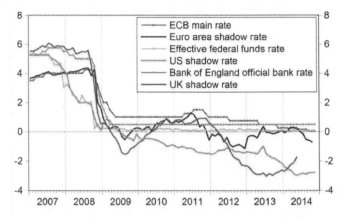

Figure 2.9: Negative interest rates, fiction becomes fact in 2009

Companies that embrace this change will be the next Standard Oil, U.S. Steel, General Electric or AT&T. Those who do not will become any number of other companies, aligned to a land-centric view of society, who have been lost to the sands of time.

Chapter Summary:

1. For the last 200 years human society has oriented towards a capital-centric economy. Before that, society was land-centric and before that it was tool-centric.
2. Society is now reorienting towards a new basis of wealth and power: information.
3. Companies currently growing in importance, influence, wealth and power are information-centric, rather than capital-centric.
4. This reorientation towards information is not only growing or accelerating, it's jerking.

Chapter Three: The Six 'New Normals'

"For creatures such as we the vastness of the universe is bearable only through love."- Carl Sagan

"Happiness isn't good enough for me! I demand euphoria!"- Bill Watterson as Calvin in 'Calvin and Hobbes'

Six forces are driving customer behaviors, expectations and choices in our increasingly information-centric world. These six forces, or Six New Normals, are fundamental. They affect all aspects of society. They influence every purchase that you or your customers make, and they determine who will be the winners and the losers as we transition from capitalism to informationism.

Jerks are following these rules to gain unassailable advantage over traditional competitors, and they're winning because they both understand these factors and live by them. If you want to compete in the coming decades, you need to understand these New Normals, and make them central to your strategies and tactics.

Fair warning: this is a meaty chapter. It covers a lot of ground, ranging far and wide across time, space and your own daily routine. Set aside a bit of time for this one, as you'll want to both read it and digest it. You'll find it worth the effort.

Found in Translation

Shortly after *Data Crush* was released, it was licensed for publication in China. Now, certain business and technical topics translate well between countries and languages; others do not. After the translators finished their work (in a remarkably short time) *Data Crush* was recast as *The New Normal*. The ideas and concepts from *Data Crush* translated quite well, only the name didn't survive the re-edit (noticing a trend with editors and names here?).

What was interesting about this new name is that I had been working on some material around the idea of our New Normal. I'm continually struck by both the speed with which new ideas and technologies are adopted by societies and how we are completely unfazed as we do it. Such easy acceptance of change is not typical of humans.

In most developed countries, if you walk down the street you'll likely notice several people staring at the face of a smartphone. They are slightly hunched over, arms half-cocked, staring intently into their hands like a squirrel contemplating a nut. And they are mesmerized. Transfixed. Completely and totally absorbed by the world in the palms of their hands. I remember not so long ago we used to call that posture the 'Blackberry Prayer,' and that wasn't a compliment. When the Blackberry (the first moderately intelligent phone) came out, early adopters foretold our addiction to smartphones and apps as they prayed into their new digital deity. I recall working for an executive who was an early Blackberry adopter. I had several hour-long conversations with him where he did not once look up from his Blackberry. He talked to me mostly in grunts, harrumphs and half sentences, as though he had just emerged from several hours in an opium den.

Figure 3.1: The 'Blackberry Prayer,' which later became the 'Smartphone Stare'

When only one or two per cent of us were doing the prayer it was annoying, even offensive. Fifteen years later, billions of us have replaced the 'Blackberry Prayer' with the 'Smartphone Stare,' fortifying our diets with massive doses of LED radiation along the way. Today, nearly all of us are doing 'The Stare,' and many of us are annoyed if anyone bothers us to look up from our smartphones. After all, it's important that I see this latest video posted to Facebook by my junior high school sweetheart. Sorry that I almost ran over you and your dog while I was driving and F-bookin'. OMG, LOL.

Humanity has been coming up with new tools for hundreds of thousands of years. Every time we do, it takes us a while to get used to the changes they bring. Initially, only a few of us are willing to open up to the possibilities of new technologies, and often the results are disquieting, obnoxious, or both. The first person to harness fire was probably initially shunned as he inadvertently burned down a few huts.

As each new technology takes hold, it changes how we interact with the world. We have been doing this for a long time. Only now, we go through the process unbelievably – almost irrationally – quickly.

It is not the technical changes that are powerful and disruptive. Rather, it is the social and behavioral changes that they catalyze. These technological advances touch nearly all of us in very deep and personal ways, and they affect how we interact with others.

The six trends of this 'New Normal' are:
1. **Quality**: People expect perfection. Deliver less and they will abandon you.
2. **Ubiquity**: Globalization means everything, everywhere. Anything less is unacceptable.
3. **Immediacy**: Immediate gratification. "There's an app for that." Instantly, or even better: predictively.
4. **Disengagement**: Don't build, don't run, don't outsource, don't care. I only buy a result.
5. **Intimacy**: People hunger for other forms of connectedness. Feeling like part of a community will be even more important as our needs are met more anonymously.

6. **Purpose**: People hunger for and need a sense of purpose.

For your organization to succeed, these six factors must underlie every decision that you make.

Quality

New Normal #1: Quality no longer differentiates; it is simply expected. Deliver less than perfection and you will lose your customers.

 Quality doesn't matter. Customers just expect quality. These statements are inflammatory, because they fly directly in the face of two centuries of Capitalist dogma. Besides, if it's true, this is a huge problem. What we all care about now is how you handle things when perfection is lost. How quickly a company responds to correct the unexpected and the imperfect is how we now measure value.

Most of us are quick to notice when something doesn't work. A device won't turn on, an email doesn't reach your friend, your tablet won't connect to the coffee shop's WiFi, you can't figure out how to print something from Windows 8 (I'm *still* trying to figure that one out), and so on. Whenever something doesn't work, we tend to get pretty agitated pretty quickly. After all, we are extremely busy and don't have time to troubleshoot things when they don't work properly.

What's amazing is not that we easily notice when things go wrong, it's that we pay no attention to all of the things that go right. Throughout your day hundreds or thousands of things go perfectly right and you pay them no mind whatsoever. As someone who has spent a quarter-century trying to make these things possible, it is somewhat disheartening that we engineers have gotten so much right and nobody seems to notice.

For more than half a century, organizations have been focused on improving quality. The quality revolution, started by J. Edward Deming in the 1950s, rode on the wave of mass consumerization that followed World War II. The world's population had finally ridden out both a decade-long depression and a war that claimed millions of lives. With peace came a new prosperity and a new level of production capacity that was idled by the end of the war. People who had lived through years of rationing suddenly had cash to spend and houses to fill. And people were good at it.

Figure 3.2: Windows 8, where the heck is the print button?

Unfortunately, product quality left a lot to be desired. Many products were of poor quality and highly unreliable. To meet the immediate demand, producers cut corners to push products out the door. This was especially true of Europe and Japan. They had their economies razed to the ground during the war. In that environment anything was better than nothing, and all manner of sub-standard products were dumped on the market.

This bothered economist Deming, because it was highly inefficient. Through the 1950s he guided Japan in the use of quality principles such as Statistical Process Control to dramatically improve production quality. By the late 1970s Japanese products were no longer thought of as shabby, but rather some of the world's best.

This was all because of the efforts of a nerdy American economist shunned by executives from his own country.

Figure 3.3: W. Edward Deming, father of the quality revolution

By the 1980s American companies woke up. The Japanese economy experienced remarkable growth as demand for its products soared. Japanese products were cheaper and better. By the time America jumped on the quality bandwagon, there was a lot of ground to make up.

This whole quality revolution in America started at the beginning of my career in the late 1980s and continues to this day. Over those years, I have earned dozens of certifications in quality processes, techniques, rules, tools and procedures. I have spent countless hours working with teams of people dedicated to improving quality in order to cut costs and remain competitive. This has been a 25-year marathon, taken at a sprinter's pace.

For executives of long-standing companies, improving quality was the strategy of choice. If you improved quality or reduced costs by a percentage point or two each year, you were assured a bonus and maybe a promotion. Eking out these improvements each year became more difficult, as first the low-hanging, then the mid-hanging, then the high-hanging fruit was picked from the tree. For a long time most of us didn't have to be too creative in developing our business plan for the following year.

This has now changed. We have trained ourselves to expect perfection. Once you reach Six Sigma quality, I really won't tolerate any errors, ever. And that's how most of us operate these days. As a result, the path of differentiation for the last 50 years has come to an end. Nearly all of the rules and processes in nearly all organizations are designed to create the best possible outcomes and to do so all of the time. We strive for that perfection. We measure it, we obsess over it, and we pay our people based upon it. But as long as quality is present, customers no longer value it.

This necessarily requires a complete reorientation in most company's metrics, rules, organization and, worst of all, processes. If you get this right, it will be an extraordinarily painful transition. If you get this wrong, it likely won't matter what you do. Quality isn't what you need to focus on anymore; what you do when you necessarily screw up, is. This is a New Normal.

Ubiquity

New Normal #2: Ubiquity. What I want, where I want it, no matter how irrational this may be.

Like Quality, Ubiquity is the result of a half-century of laser-like focus on a business outcome. Organizations have been working on optimizing global logistics for a very long time. We've made enormous gains in the efficiency, speed and flexibility of the world's supply chains over the last several decades. From *Shopkins* to smartphones, from antacids to automobiles, you can get practically anything you want, practically anywhere you want it.

Because of this, we have managed to train ourselves to have completely ridiculous expectations for getting whatever we want, wherever we want it. Bananas in Iceland in January? No problem. Chinese loose leaf tea in Dubai? Of course. Fresh sushi a thousand miles from the nearest ocean? Naturally. Just-picked strawberries six months out of season? What's a season? If you spend just a little time thinking about any of these examples it should occur to you that each of these things should be considered practically impossible. And yet, we simply expect this sort of thing. You've probably played out at least one of these scenarios yourself without even thinking about it.

Figure 3.4: The 20-foot shipping container, key to the revolution in global logistics

The end result of the lean-Six-Sigma, hyper-containerized, multi-modal, drone-shipped, GPS-tracked, mega-warehoused, predictively-shipped world that we've spent decades to construct is this: ubiquity. I want what I want where I want it; and you had better deliver, or someone else will. And if I want a fair-trade, solar-powered, single-batch, ancient-grained, GMO-free, organically-grown, French-mountain-spring-watered, hand-churned-buttered croissant, fresh-baked in a wood-fired, hand-thrown Italian masonry oven, in Moose Jaw, Saskatchewan, Canada at two in the morning, someone's going to give it to me. And once that happens, I'm ruined for anything less.

Ubiquity is like training your kids to not be spoiled by giving them everything they want, in the hope that they'll be satisfied. Unfortunately, many humans don't work that way. Because we have created such an efficient, effective, comprehensive global logistics network, Ubiquity is now a New Normal.

Immediacy

New Normal #3: Immediacy. When you absolutely, positively, have to get it there, predictively!

Quite naturally, Immediacy is intimately tied to Ubiquity. It's not enough to get me what I want; I want it now! Immediacy is hyper-optimized global logistics, paired with our use of smartphones and apps. I described our addiction to the instant gratification in *Data Crush*. I call this condition *appification*, and almost all of us who use apps have become appified. Smartphones allow us to find, download and own the answer to almost any question or any need, instantly.

Nearly all of us who use smartphones have experienced this phenomenon. You have some sort of need. You do a search, and find one or two or 50 apps, each claiming to be the answer to your problem. You pick one, download and install it, then log in. If that app doesn't solve your problem, in almost no time with almost no effort, you instantly log off and look for another. The problem is, there is almost always another one out there.

 By 2015, smartphone users had downloaded more than 150 billion apps over the 10 years that there has been such a thing. Of those, about 98 per cent of all apps are downloaded, opened once, and never opened again. The other two per cent apparently meet our appified expectations, and we cannot and will not live without them. This should be sobering news to any company that is still thinking about building and deploying an app. Whatever you do, you have only a two per cent chance of getting it right, and a 98 per cent chance of screwing up comprehensively. In an appified world, Immediacy is king, and if you cannot meet my needs instantaneously I will leave you and never come back.

Immediacy is the driver of the huge interest in predictive analytics. Interest in predictive analytics is an inevitable result of our demand for immediacy; these days, just-in-time no longer is. When Federal Express (FedEx) started back in the late 1970s, most people believed that they'd never succeed; people wouldn't pay the huge premium for express shipping. Who in their right mind needed something to be delivered overnight, anyway!?! It's easy to be a naysayer in the face of innovation.

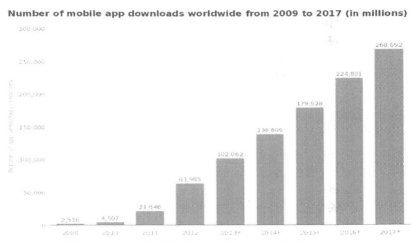

Number of mobile app downloads worldwide from 2009 to 2017 (in millions)

Figure 3.5: Global app downloads by 2015

By the 1980s, FedEx was growing rapidly, adopting the slogan, 'When it Absolutely, Positively, has to be There Overnight.' The more they grew the more they were able to grow, which increased both their efficiency and their customers' expectations of speed. Appification was born!

Flash forward to today, and FedEx's slogan should be, 'When it absolutely, positively should have been there already, predictively.' This is exactly where immediacy has taken us. To remain relevant to your customers, you had *better* be able to deliver at their speed of expectation, which has rapidly become negative; you should have delivered before I knew to place an order! And because we continue to squeeze more and more cost out of our value chain, maintaining infinite inventory on hand simply isn't an option. So, as demonstrated by the enormous increase in interest in predictive analytics, immediacy is a New Normal.

Disengagement

New Normal #4: Disengagement. Just do it. I don't care how.

It doesn't matter how many episodes of Mad Men you may have seen. No matter how many minutes of network television you may have watched this month, if any, it appears that the age of Mass Marketing is rapidly coming to its end. I find this to be a shame, really. I'll miss all of the catchy jingles we enjoyed during something that we used to call 'prime time.'

Of the Six New Normals, Disengagement is the greatest threat to established companies. Disengagement is a direct result of the previous three New Normals, and it works against any organization that has invested a lot of time and money in making the first three New Normals possible.

The world's leading companies have worked tirelessly to make everything we want or need perfect. They have figured out how to get them to us wherever we are and wherever they are. And they've worked to get it to us as quickly as possible, if not sooner. For all of their effort, how do we show our appreciation? How do we demonstrate that we value all of this investment in time, energy and treasure in order to meet our needs? We don't.

Disengagement means that customers no longer care about what it takes for organizations to give them what they want, they just want it. They only care about the result. Indeed, I use the term Results as a Service (RaaS) to describe this phenomenon, because that's exactly what consumers now expect. I don't want to build it, I don't want to buy it, I don't want to rent it, I just want a result, and I want it right now… or sooner.

I don't want to be bothered with pesky details like price, complexity, rules, regulations, logistics, licenses and so on. I'm too coddled in a world of quality, ubiquity and immediacy to be bothered with such details. Just get me to my desired result, magically, and I'll reward you with my business, at least until the next time. Then, again, I'll be totally disengaged from you, and you have to start all over again.

This directly contradicts about a century of marketing and advertising thinking. Companies invested in their brand in order to build loyalty and a perception of value in customers' minds. Unfortunately, it seems that most of us have been branded-out. Once everyone delivers quality, ubiquity and immediacy, none of these things matter anymore.

Price matters, but only in a world where consumers still accept the price that you ask. Those days are nearly dead, as anyone can go online and instantly find someone who will sell them what they want, only a bit cheaper. If, even five years ago, you told most people that they could walk into most major retailers and *tell them* what price you would pay for a product or service, they would likely have said that you were perhaps a bit confused. Now, it's *abnormal* to pay a retail price, and if you do you 'should know better.'

Disengagement starts to get really worrisome when you combine it with the rising tide of Jerks in the world. The tiny companies, sprouting up all over the world, have almost no overhead, no constraints, no oversight and most tellingly, nothing to lose. Capital-centric companies have armies of people who staff gigantic capital fortresses, operating in vast, Rube-Goldberg-like processes, all designed to maximize control of the capital required to deliver products and services to their customers. Looking at modern capital-centric companies, it's a wonder any of them manage to ever push a product out the door.

Jerks have none of this nonsense. Indeed, that's why you and I reward them with our business. We don't care how they get us what we want, as long as they do it better. It's massively unfair, and none of us really care, now do we?

What's interesting is that most of us actually *do* care about how companies give us what we want. It's just that none of the old measures matter anymore because companies have made the traditional measures of quality, speed and price irrelevant, even to the guys at NASA. If you are an existing player, your success in meeting my expectations means that I can now take what you've done completely for granted, and expect something else from you. And, everything that you did to meet my previous expectations largely works against you as you try to shift your delivery as quickly as I shift my demands.

No matter how agile you think you're making the 20,000 employees of your North American Market Agility Subsidiary, Incorporated, PLC, they'll never be able to assemble their Tiger Teams and Return on Investment spreadsheets as fast as you or I wander through the latest of our appified whims. For Jerks, disengagement is *the* opportunity to disintermediate existing organizations. Customers are forcing this change to happen.

Intimacy

New Normal #5: Help me feel like I belong.

Watching each of us meander through our day, deeply engaged in our 'Smartphone Stare,' constantly chatting and tweeting and texting and OMG'ing, you'd think that all of us would feel more connected and more a part of a global commune than ever before. You'd think that, but I'd argue that you'd be wrong. Despite all of our connectedness, most of us feel lonelier than ever before.

A recent study by the World Health Organization (WHO) has found that the number one health issue for the global population is not heart disease, cancer or HIV. It's not obesity, global warming, dolphin-fatal tuna or genetically-modified franken-carrots. It's not gluten, high fructose corn syrup or fluoridated water. According to WHO, the number one health issue affecting humanity today is mental health. If all eight billion of us spent an hour with a psychologist, one in five of us would be diagnosed with some mental defect. That's 1.6 billion unwell people out there, and I'm pretty sure that every one of them is on Facebook!

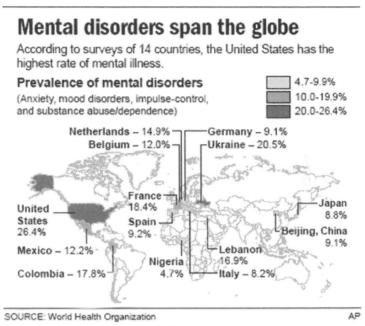

Mental disorders span the globe

According to surveys of 14 countries, the United States has the highest rate of mental illness.

Prevalence of mental disorders

(Anxiety, mood disorders, impulse-control, and substance abuse/dependence)

- 4.7-9.9%
- 10.0-19.9%
- 20.0-26.4%

Netherlands – 14.9%
Belgium – 12.0%
Germany – 9.1%
Ukraine – 20.5%
France 18.4%
United States 26.4%
Spain 9.2%
Japan 8.8%
Beijing, China 9.1%
Mexico – 12.2%
Lebanon 16.9%
Nigeria 4.7%
Colombia – 17.8%
Italy – 8.2%

SOURCE: World Health Organization   AP

Figure 3.6: Mental health is a growing global problem

It is true, we are constantly connected to one another, practically all of the time. We measure our self-worth by the number of friends we have on Facebook or followers we have on Twitter. We can drown our sorrows in a billion hours of fuzzy cat videos on YouTube, or act out our fantasies in any number of online virtual worlds. You'd think with all of this connectedness and stimulation, we'd all be happier than ever.

But I'd argue that this over-supply of stimulation and connectivity may be exactly what is making us crazy. All of these connections are incredibly superficial, and we hunger for something more. We post the best possible pictures of ourselves, in the coolest possible locations, with the widest smiles and the wittiest labels that we can think of, all in an effort to be understood. If most of us lived lives that were anything remotely like how we portray ourselves online,

we'd *all* be the most magnificent people around, and Kanye West
would be out of a job.
Like it or not, we are social creatures. We long to be part of a clan,
tribe, team or extended family. We want to be both understood and
accepted. And in a world where many of us have the lower levels of
our Maslow's hierarchy of needs delivered by drone, from Amazon
Prime, it's this unmet need for connection that drives us absolutely
crazy.

What does all of this mean to you? Well, as a consumer, you'll *love*
any experience or product that helps you feel understood and
connected. Organizations that figure you out, even just a little bit,
start to scratch at a constant itch, and it is addictive. If you are a
company, this means that you *must* find a way to know your
customers better. And I don't mean 'customers' in the aggregated,
18-to-24-year-old-college-educated-Hispanic-male-who-likes-
poodles-and-sushi sort of way. I mean you need to know each and
every one of your customers as a unique individual. Anything short
of this appears to be, and indeed is, disingenuous.

This sort of intimate understanding of customers used to be normal.
Before the Industrial Revolution, customers would go to their
neighbor who was a tailor, a blacksmith, a cobbler, a seamstress or a
butcher and these people would give their customers exactly what
each desired. These people didn't just know their customers, they
knew them—their hopes, dreams, foibles, preferences, and so on.
Shopping fulfilled a social need as well as a material one, and going
down to the market meant connecting with your neighbors and
friends.

In our modern world, most if not all of this connectedness has been
lost in the name of efficiency. In our efforts to meet customers'
expectation of the first three New Normals, we created in them the
fourth, Disconnectedness. Once companies did that, the one thing
that customers want back again, the thing that they desperately want
to find, and will pay a great deal to get, is connectedness. It may
sound odd that we now want from companies the very thing that we
previously rewarded them for giving up, in the name of our other

needs. It is odd, but remember that at least 20 per cent of us are a bit crazy.

This longing for connectedness, for belonging, for intimacy is now a New Normal in our world. Organizations that can tap into this will win us over in a heartbeat, especially when we are disconnected from what it takes to meet our lesser needs. This is fundamentally why this New Normal is as much of a golden opportunity for Jerks as it is an enormous challenge for traditional organizations, still trying to maximize returns on capital.

Purpose

New Normal #6: What am I doing here?

The final New Normal is purpose, or understanding our place in the universe. Despite all that we do, all that we consume and all that we think and believe, people are starved for purpose.

We all wonder:
   "Why are we here?"
   "Is this all that I am?"
   "Is this all that I will be?"

This is a natural outcome of living in a world where many things come to us with relative ease. Few of us are running from lions, tigers or bears on a regular basis. Obtaining food is much easier than just a century ago. Globally, our health has never been better. We live longer, and most of us have seen substantial improvements in our quality of life over the last hundred years. I don't mean to minimize the plight of the billions of impoverished people still struggling to make it through every single day, but on average we're doing better than we ever have before.

Once our basic needs are met, we tend to yearn for something more. Intimacy is one of those higher-order needs, and it is how we connect with others. Purpose is how we connect with ourselves, and with the universe. When we sit in a quiet place (when we can still find one) and have a conversation with ourselves in our minds, we are trying to connect with our sense of purpose. Each of us has that inner voice with whom we converse far more than with anyone else. When we are searching for a sense of purpose, we are trying to connect with that inner voice, and have it tell us, "You're OK."

This is pretty deep stuff, and as you read this you may be thinking this is a lot of new-age mumbo-jumbo. Believe me, I used to think that too. I have a ton of formal education in science, technology and the law, and I come from a background where things are what they are, and evidence speaks for itself. Only five or six years ago, if you told me that connecting with people's inner need for purpose was the key to future business success I'd almost certainly think you were a twenty-per-center, and you needed a little couch time with a therapist.

As a scientist and engineer I learned long ago that it's not the known and knowable that's going to get you. Rather, it's the stuff you didn't analyze, measure or quantify that will mess up your best laid plans, spreadsheets and quarterly reports. As businesses get better at measuring nearly everything, whatever is left over will be the source of whatever unpredictability is left. Once we fully understand everything that makes sense to us, the only questions left to ask are of those things that no longer make sense. The more data we create, and the better our analytics, the more influential the unmeasured and unknown will become.

Once I've moved from Six Sigma quality to Nine Sigma quality, something other than quality will determine my success. Things like intimacy and purpose will become the sole difference between you and your competitor, and the stakes will keep getting higher.

What evidence do I have of this? Look all around you. The answer may lie in a simple cup of joe. When it was first discovered, coffee was a luxury item, reserved for the few who could afford it. Then, through industrialization, coffee began to stimulate the masses. By World War II coffee was practically a weapon, as American soldiers won battle after battle on a wave of caffeinated highs.

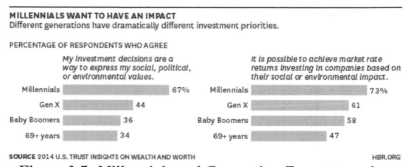

MILLENNIALS WANT TO HAVE AN IMPACT
Different generations have dramatically different investment priorities.

PERCENTAGE OF RESPONDENTS WHO AGREE

My investment decisions are a way to express my social, political, or environmental values.		It is possible to achieve market rate returns investing in companies based on their social or environmental impact.	
Millennials	67%	Millennials	73%
Gen X	44	Gen X	61
Baby Boomers	36	Baby Boomers	58
69+ years	34	69+ years	47

SOURCE 2014 U.S. TRUST INSIGHTS ON WEALTH AND WORTH   HBR.ORG

Figure 3.7: Millennials and Generation Z want to make a difference

Today, if you go out to buy a cup of coffee it seems there are two extremes. On one end, you can buy a 44-ounce super-big-gulp of Morning Buzz at your local convenient store for $1.99. At the other end of the scale is a 12-ounce 'tall' cup of fair-trade, sole-source, solar-powered, non-fat, low-sodium, gluten-free essence of Arabia, for the bargain price of $9.99.

Clearly, the former is the efficiency and effectiveness play of the last 200 years, turned up to a setting of '12.' The latter is the purpose and intimacy play, sneaking in and taking over. Why do I say that? The reason people are willing to pay five times as much for even less morning pick-me-up is because all of those labels make them feel like they're contributing to the universe. Sure, I pay double to get the all-organic coffee beans from an independent farmer in Kenya, but I'm helping that guy feed his family. That makes me feel better about myself.

That simple distinction, feeding my need for purpose, can make one commodity worth many times as much to me as another. Suddenly, commodities aren't so fungible anymore, and we are desperate to buy the ones that make us feel better about ourselves. Purpose, the last of the New Normals, will be a key determinant of who is successful and who falters over the coming decade. Companies that have dedicated themselves to commoditization and efficiency will still survive; after all, we still have basic needs to fulfill. But the organizations that figure out how to tap into our desperate need for purpose will earn from us our most precious possessions: our time, our attention, our loyalty and our disposable income.

As If We've Always Been This Way

I hope the list of Six New Normals resonates with your own life experiences. If they sound familiar to you, it's likely because you are already thinking, acting and living this way. These have evolved over time as the result of thousands of incremental changes over the last couple of centuries. These New Normals feel, well, *normal,* as if we've always thought, felt and acted this way. It may seem like this is the case, and that is why the New Normals are so disruptive. These New Normals undermine most of the strategies companies have pursued for decades. They undermine the value of the efficient use of capital, which has logically been a key tenet of capitalism.

If you combine these six trends with the global shift from capital-centricity to information-centricity, the resulting disruption becomes enormous. It is now accepted that efficient use of capital doesn't matter to most of us; that game has played itself out. Instead, there is a new game to be played, where information is used to meet my irrational expectations effortlessly, predictively and easily. That same information allows you to understand my needs and desires intimately, and to help me find my sense of purpose in the universe.

Jerks not only understand that this transition is under way, they are actively feeding on our expectations of it. Unfettered by all of the effort that got us to this point, Jerks are able to use these New Normals to outcompete those that made these six things normal to us. That is entirely unfair, and nobody cares.

Chapter Summary:

1. The dramatic success of capitalism over the last 200 years has largely undermined the principles that society has been working towards.
2. Because of the success of capitalism, continued growth will be determined by a new set of rules and expectations.

3. These Six New Normals are Quality, Ubiquity, Immediacy, Disengagement, Intimacy and Purpose.
4. Recognizing these Six New Normals, and orienting your strategies and tactics to them, will be critical to future success.

Chapter Four: Power and The Four Trinities

"Power concedes nothing without a demand. It never did and it never will."- Frederick Douglass

"We need new versions of history to allow for our current prejudices."- Bill Watterson as Calvin in 'Calvin and Hobbes'

Welcome to Chapter 4. I hope you made it through the New Normals unscathed, or perhaps you skipped over them. I hope it was the former and not the latter. The reason is this: like the shift from Capital to Information, the shift to New Normals changes everything. Both of these societal shifts are happening at deep structural levels, so we need to question some of our basic assumptions about how the world works.

This is heady, disquieting stuff. I tell people all of the time, "If this doesn't make you a little bit uncomfortable, then you're getting it wrong." Questioning your core beliefs about the world is not easy. Our brains have been programmed for millennia to assess the world around us, form an understanding of how things work, and then *hold on* to that belief or perception as our way of making sense of the world. This is the survival skill we call learning, and it's pretty useful to us.

Every once in a while we are exposed to something new that forces us to change our core beliefs so that we are better able to cope. Our brains don't do this very often, and they are less prone to accepting change the older we get, but still we keep some degree of mental plasticity as we age. Our challenge today is that these changes are not coming at us in dribs and drabs; rather, they are flooding us in a torrent of constant change. That is why you may feel like you're riding a surfboard in a tsunami, while wearing roller skates. It's a lot of change to accept all at once.

Can't We Just All Get Along?

Cooperation is a concept deeply rooted in the human psyche. For millennia, humans have lived and for the most part prospered together using our collective skills, knowledge and strengths to help ensure survival. We aren't the only species to realize that there's strength in numbers. From bees and ants, to wolves, lions, sheep, buffalo, and even penguins, many animals do better by doing together.

Through cooperation, individuals are able to achieve more than they can on their own. Whether it's surrounding and overpowering prey (lions and wolves), defense against predators (the herd prey of lions and wolves), protection against the elements (penguins), or maintenance of communal knowledge (migrating geese and elephants) cooperation gives a wide range of animals a leg up on their solitary competition.

The success of humans as a species was not a foregone conclusion. We are much lighter, weaker and slower than most apex predators such as lions, tigers, bears or great white sharks. Our senses aren't nearly as well attuned as those animals that might hunt us or those which we might hunt. Individually, humans are a pretty sad sight from a Darwinian point of view.

However, at some point in our past we began to work together and this, along with our burgeoning intelligence and our use of tools and technology, allowed us to eventually dominate our planet. While there is always variation within any population, most of us have a pretty strong sense of community and cooperation, if only because mavericks, rogues and misanthropes rapidly found themselves to be lion hors d'oeuvres.

Follow the Leader

Cooperation is great, but as with all things in life you don't get something for nothing. For animals to cooperate effectively someone

58

has to be in charge. That is after all the basis of cooperation. One individual makes decisions for the whole, and the whole can then act as one. The problem with this transaction is this: someone has to lose a degree of control in order for someone else to gain some control. For there to be a leader of a pack, someone else has to agree to be led.

This then is the politics of social beings. For individuals to gain from cooperation, someone has to give power to another so that the benefits of cooperation can accrue. Some with a more liberal interpretation of cooperation might suggest that people 'take turns at leading.' But, anyone who has ever taken a class in statistics knows that such a course of action almost always leads to worse results than individual action. No, to get better than average performance, those of less than average ability must yield to those with better than average ability. Otherwise, you end up with the United States Congress.

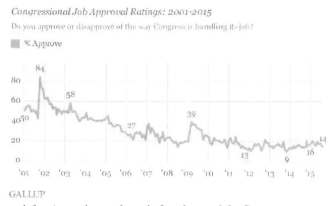

Figure 4.1: Americans' satisfaction with Congress over time

For a population to benefit from cooperation, power must be transferred from those with lesser abilities to those with greater abilities so that, collectively, the group produces better outcomes. And since giving up power to another is a highly personal, highly intimate, and highly risky affair, we humans put a lot of effort and focus into trying to get it right. When we choose to give power to another person, and to follow them, we literally put our lives in their hands. So, making good decisions on who to give our power to is critical to our own survival.

The Trinities of Power

I've been developing a model of this transaction of social power for a while now, and it recently gelled into what I call the Trinities of Power. When we enter into a cooperative social contract, the contract needs three things in order to be effective: a means of distribution, a means of application, and a means of control. The means of distribution is the mechanism used to collect a group's power, give it to a leader, and allow for the leader to subsequently put it to use. The means of application is how the power is used to obtain the result that the collective desires. And finally there must be a means of controlling the group's power. This control is both how the power is applied, and what recourse the collective has in case someone reneges on the contract.

For power in a social contract to be transferred and effectively used, all three of these mechanisms must be defined, understood and agreed to by all parties. If any of these three elements are missing, or if any party to the social contract disagrees with a term, then the contract won't work. Because these three elements are interdependent, and each is required for social contracts to work, I call them the Trinity of Power.

Every time one of us agrees to cooperate with another there is a trinity at work in the agreement. If not, the agreement is just an illusion, or is doomed to fail for lack of structure. If I am going to agree to cooperate with and follow another, I want to know what they're taking from me, how they intend to use it, and what benefits and potential consequences I will face in making the deal. Once these are defined and agreed to, benefits may ensue.

The Four Trinities

While the elements of the Trinity of Power (distribution, application and control) have remained the same throughout human history, their basis has changed as our society and technology have advanced. As I worked up this model for how and why we cooperate, it seems that there were four eras of human history, each of which had a different trinity in operation. Let's look at each in turn, as society advanced through the ages.

The Tool Trinity

Evidence suggests that the earliest humans were nomadic hunter-gatherers. These groups moved about a relatively unpopulated world, and collected what they needed as they moved from place to place. As nomads, knowing when and where the clan should go was critically important. A berry patch or wild orchard would be in season only for a few days each year, so knowing what that date was, how far you were from the resource, and how long it would take to get there were all crucial to a clan's survival.

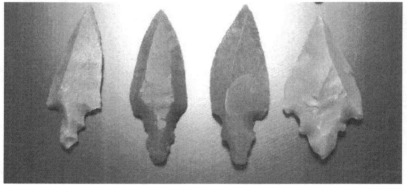

Figure 4.2: Knowledge of tools determined who lived and who died

Knowing where and when to go, and how to make tools that would help you once you got there, were critical to clan survival. If you had this kind of knowledge, others would willingly follow you in order to learn what you knew. Hence, the first basis of power in human culture was knowledge. If you had knowledge, you had power.

Early humans could only keep with them what they could carry, and so space and weight were at a premium. If you were going to carry something with you everywhere you went it had better be very useful. Many of these objects were early tools. They were implements that allowed these people to better harvest food and provide for themselves, and for many, these items were literally the difference between life and death.

Naturally enough, this power base was supported by a trinity and I call this first trinity the Tool Trinity. The use of tools gave humans an early leg-up over other animals, and knowledge of how to make and use tools ensured that you were the Warren Buffet or Bill Gates of this era.

The Tool Trinity consisted of the following three elements:

        Distribution: Memories
        Application: Story Telling
        Control: Teaching

In the Tool Trinity, power in the form of knowledge was passed from person to person through their memories. Whether it was how to make an arrowhead or how to get to the next watering hole, memory served as the basis of having and using knowledge. There were early forms of writing in this era, but this was so rudimentary that it was basically memory with better retention.
The way that this knowledge was applied was through story telling. Someone with knowledge would share it with others through stories, either about how a stone could cut wood, or how to find the cave in the next valley. Access to knowledge was controlled by teaching. If I taught you how to make a fish hook, you had knowledge and power; if I didn't teach you, you had none. The Tool Trinity determined which clans thrived and which died, and who in each clan was chosen to be shaman. In this era, knowledge truly *was* power.

The Dirt Trinity

Over time, clans discovered that not all land was created equal. Some locations were clearly better for survival, and it paid to stay put every once in a while. This understanding of local advantage, when combined with animal husbandry and agriculture, soon meant that *where* you were was pretty important. This began the age of land control and land ownership, echoes of which still govern our world today. Indeed, each Trinity remains with us over time, just diminished in importance as new sources of power are discovered.

Over thousands of years land became more and more central to one's power in the world. If you controlled land you were powerful. If you controlled good land, you were even *more* powerful. This led to the age of kings and queens, dukes and duchesses, barons and baronesses. The landed gentry were those who held control of land, and hence they had power over those who needed access to land in order to make a living.

Figure 4.3: Egyptian hieroglyphics. Farming made land valuable

I call the Trinity used to govern land the Dirt Trinity. The elements of the Dirt Trinity are:

Distribution: Heredity
Application: Edict
Control: Violence

Land was distributed through heredity. If your parents had land, you would too, upon their passing (at least if you were the first-born male). As noted by actor Mel Brooks in his optimistically-titled movie *History of the World, Part 1*, "It's good to be the king."

Figure 4.4: Actor Mel Brooks as King Louis XVI

Royals applied their power through the use of edicts, or pronunciations. If a king wanted to use his power he said, "Make it so." Subordinates complied. If people didn't submit to the king's power, the method of control used on them was violence. You were either thrown off the king's land, or you were simply killed. Life was tough for non-royals under the Dirt Trinity. The Dirt Trinity reigned supreme over human society for millennia, and remains of it can still be seen inside of any number of tabloids still available in grocery store checkout stands the world-over.

The Analog Trinity

The Industrial Revolution spelled the entry of a new source of power: capital. Land was still important, but capital took over for land as the dominant determinant of wealth and power in the world. For the 200 years that we have been a capital-centric society, our means for managing capital as our source of power formed what I call the Analog trinity. The Analog Trinity is defined by:

Distribution: Bureaucracy
Application: Processes
Control: Rules

Every company that has been successful since the Industrial Revolution has figured out how to employ these factors to effectively use capital to create more wealth and power. Since we still live in the tail end of the Capital Era, let's take a bit more time in developing each of these three pillars of the Analog Trinity.

Bureaucracy: How Capital is Distributed

We know bureaucracy from standing in line at the Department of Motor Vehicles, or filling out a form at the hospital. When we submit a form in triplicate or wait for our manager to approve our request for a box of pencils, we are all interacting with bureaucracy.

Bureaucracies grew up in the Industrial Era because capital needed to be managed, and books were the only way to effectively do so. For most of the Industrial Revolution, keeping books literally meant 'keeping books.' Organizations would record every transaction that impacted the use of capital in an actual, physical book...or more correctly, tens of thousands of them.

Figure 4.5: Ellis Island, New York. Waiting in line: An American tradition for more than 200 years

The only way to keep track of all of those physical books was through the efforts of a whole army of individuals. Low-level people would each maintain detailed records regarding a small part of a company's capital. The results of their bookkeeping were handed upward to a person who summarized their results into yet another book. These summaries were passed up to yet another layer of management, who summarized the summaries, and so on.

Companies that existed before the creation of the computer required deep hierarchies of bureaucracy in order to function. A single person could handle only so many transactions per day, and so large companies needed large numbers of people, both to manage the individual transactions and to do the roll-ups required to provide an overview of all of the organization's capital.

Without these massive bureaucracies, companies simply could not keep track of all of the stuff that they bought, sold and owned; that is, their capital. And, since capital ownership was what wealth was all about, knowing what you had and where you had it was critical to your success. Though we may complain about bureaucracies, before computers arrived they were the best approach that we had for managing and creating wealth.

Process: How Capital is Applied

Bureaucracies are large, spread out (physically) and distributed (responsibility). Still, their outputs had to harmonize and come together in a way that allowed senior executives to have an accurate view of the capital for which they were responsible. If dozens or hundreds of departments all had to report their results upwards to management, they all needed to do it the same way, or there would be chaos.

This need for synchronicity, commonality and consistency led to defined processes, which were the method for managing capital during the age of capital. Defined business processes were the only way that the outputs of hundreds or thousands of accountants could possibly be consolidated into a single view of a business. So, companies spent enormous amounts of money defining how capital was collected, spent, transformed and consumed, all in the name of making sure the organization kept making more of it.

Most of us have experience with capital-centric processes. If you
have ever bought a car or a house, you have gone through such
capital-management processes. If you have applied for a loan, set up
a stock portfolio, or tried to get a license to do something, you've
been exposed to all of this. As you filled out whichever forms were
necessary, you provided details that the bureaucracy used use to
determine if what you wanted to do was an appropriate use of
capital.

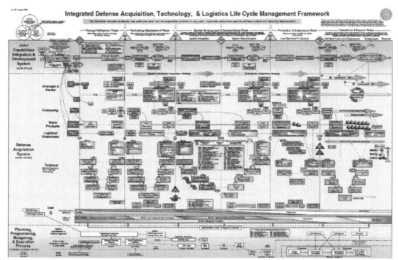

Figure 4.6: U.S. Department of Defense procurement process

Many of us in the business-process business spent our entire careers
trying to figure out how to do this faster and more efficiently, as a
means of improving our control over capital. We reduced cycle
times, streamlined approvals, automated the collection of
information and so on, but always with the assumption that the
process itself was absolutely necessary. This is why processes are
part of this Trinity. We couldn't imagine working without them.

Rules: How Capital is Controlled

Finally, capital-centric organizations needed rules, so that their
bureaucracies could actually use processes in a predictable and
effective manner. Business rules drive nearly all aspects of how
capital-centric organizations operate. They are the if/then statements

in our business processes. They are the gate keepers and key masters in our bureaucracies which ensure that our capital is being managed wisely. If processes allowed all of the members of a bureaucracy to contribute to the organization in a harmonious way, rules ensured that they indeed did so.

Figure 4.7: One complete copy of the Affordable Care Act, or 'Obamacare'

Capitalist society loves, and I mean LOVES rules. Our governments create more and more bureaus whose sole purpose is to create and enforce more and more rules. In response, businesses are forced to create more and more roles and departments to ensure that these rules are followed. Over time, these rules have accumulated, and these bureaucracies have grown to the point that they exist largely to exist. The primary purpose of these structures is to ensure their own survival, regardless of their drag on our society and economy.

Inefficient, but Faster

This Analog Trinity has been the basis of organizational structure for 200 years. It enabled a capital-centric society to take hold, grow and eventually take over. Certainly it had its shortcomings, but realistically, within the technology constraints of the time, the Analog Trinity served us well. It was only after the computer entered the workplace in the 1960s and 1970s that we started to see room for improvement.

Automation was designed with the goal to do the same things we've always done, only faster. Large-scale computer systems were designed to replicate exactly what was done in the Analog world. I spent countless hours trying to document, precisely, how my employer used the Trinity to manage capital, so that it could be replicated in the software in the computer. Because computers were much better than people at doing tasks like bookkeeping, and they performed those same tasks at much larger scale, a lot of improvement was gained initially by automating the Analog Trinity.

However, by speeding up our ways of doing things the same old way, we realized that this speed was itself disruptive. Before we had computers, it was a monumental task to 'roll up' a company's books every quarter (which is why we still have quarterly reports, by the way). Once we automated the process, we could do it over a weekend. Before computers were widely used, managers would be considered highly productive if they generated one final-draft memo per day. Before computers, a three-martini lunch was not only possible, it was often thought of as necessary fortitude in order to get a whole memo out by the end of the day!

Computational Conundrum

By the 1990s, most companies had deployed their first generation of business process automation software. As they did so, it quickly became apparent that many aspects of the Analog Trinity did not translate well into the digital world. Bureaucracies could be easily replicated in database hierarchies, but the politics and relationships that defined those bureaucracies could not. Business processes could be defined and written into software code, but all of the externalities that made the processes actually work were often lost in translation. And, all of the business rules that controlled the ebb and flow of data through the organization could be defined in these information systems, but nowhere was it feasible to capture every possible exception, nuance and work-around to the rules that were required for the business to be effective.

I worked on many of these projects back in that era, and the challenges we faced in trying to digitize the Analog Trinity can be summed up in one simple phrase: Business Process Reengineering (BPR). BPR was a *huge* topic of discussion in the 1990s. Indeed, my first attempt at writing a business book was from this timeframe, as we all struggled with how to automate a set of business tools and principles that were never meant to be automated.

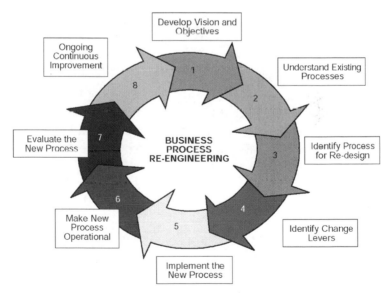

Figure 4.8: Business Process Engineering, 1990s business fad

BPR was a nightmare for everyone involved. For business people, it meant unlearning everything that you had ever learned, rejecting things for which you used to be measured and rewarded, and operating at speeds that you never previously believed possible. For technical people, you had to try to replicate the organizations' conditional, Analog, "well that depends" sort of thinking as a collection of definitive, yes-or-no logic – because that's all that the computers could understand. And management had to be convinced that all of this expenditure on weird new technologies would actually help them manage capital more effectively.

The BPR era was lucrative for many software and consulting companies that were brave enough to try to address these problems. Many of us learned a great deal in trying to digitize the Analog Trinity, more often from our failures than our successes. This attempted transition from the Analog Trinity to a Digital Trinity was unavoidably painful, because information and capital aren't the same thing, and they want to be created, consumed and managed in different ways.

It's true that information technology helped us to better manage capital at the end of the last century. Many gains were made, and many investments in automating capital management paid off during those 25 years. However, many of us who were working on digitizing the Analog Trinity completely missed the point of information technology. Information technology wasn't valuable because it would help us to better manage capital. Rather, information technology was valuable because it gave us something entirely new to manage.

Welcoming the Digital Trinity

The combination of PCs, business software and the Internet fundamentally changed how businesses operated, or so we thought. What once took weeks now took hours. What used to require a fact-finding field trip to a factory could now be seen instantly on a desktop, hundreds of miles away at headquarters. The connected PC allowed us to automate the Analog Trinity in a way that greatly improved our productivity and our ability to manage capital. The general growth in productivity in the 1980s and 1990s was a direct result.

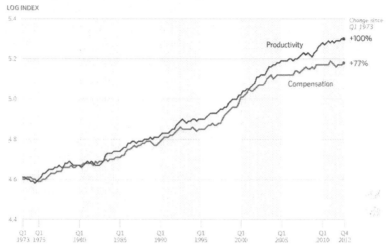

Figure 4.9: U.S. productivity over time

However, our access to and familiarity with PCs and the Internet did something else to us: it introduced us to a whole new carrier of economic value – information. By the 2000s enough of us were spending sufficient leisure time on the Internet that we started to value this thing called information in new ways. Suddenly, people could know things that they never knew before, and they could find things that they could never find before. Also, people could create things that they never created before, and often found an audience for these information products, which continued to feed this whole process.

From Bronze to Browsers to Billions

At some point in human history, some person decided to use fire for something other than cooking meat and staying warm. They melted some greenish rocks, which turned into an orange-ish metal: copper. Then, someone mixed this with a little molten tin, creating bronze, and a new era in human history was born. Many were happy to continue with their cooking and heating, while others saw in the new technology of fire a whole new way of living.

At the turn of the 21st century many of us were still struggling to digitize the Analog Trinity. The whole Y2K fiasco sort of showed us how far off the mark we were in trying to make things better instead of worse. But by and large our efforts led to many improvements in how our society managed capital. At the same time some brave souls started to see that this approach completely missed the point of information technology.

People like Steve Jobs (at least in the 3.0 version of himself), Jeff Bezos, Mark Zuckerberg, Sergey Brin and others began to see that information itself had value, independent of its association with capital. This was a huge insight, and the people who saw it first are among the wealthiest people in the world today. What these people realized is that digitizing capital was sort of like putting wheels on a donkey. The donkey might go faster, but it really wasn't meant to do that, it really didn't like participating, and there were more effective ways of using the wheels.

These early captains of Information recognized that a different Trinity was essential to manage information, and they implemented a new Digital Trinity with zeal. The Digital Trinity comprises:

> Distribution: Mobility
> Application: Social Media
> Control:　　Analytics

The Digital Trinity managed information in the same ways that the Analog Trinity allowed us to manage capital. The new medium demanded new mechanisms. The old ways of doing things were square pegs for round holes. Those people stopped trying to automate the past, and instead embraced the future, created new wealth from new sources, in new ways. Here's how.

Mobility: How Information is Distributed

Mobility is essential to the Digital Trinity, because we want to produce, consume and manage information all of the time. Indeed, context, or our place in space and time, is perhaps the most valuable part of the information that we all use. Mobility started with the cell phone; that old device that used to be the size of your head, and actually used your skull as an antenna. As we became more used to the idea of mobile talking, we became exposed to the idea of wireless internetworking, or WiFi, and things were never the same.

Mobility not only *allowed* us to access information anywhere, it made us *want* to access information anywhere. Think of how you use your smartphone today. When you wonder about something (what does a certain word mean, what team won the 1963 World Series, what's the atomic weight of Polonium in all of its forms, and so on), you just pull out your phone and look it up. Google now answers billions of such questions every day. What did we do with all of those questions before there was a Google? That's an excellent question. Some say the current generation of 20-somethings is the dumbest ever. I'd say the volume of questions that are now asked and answered, rather than asked and shrugged off, would suggest otherwise.

Year	Annual Number of Google Searches	Average Searches Per Day
2013	2,161,530,000,000	5,922,000,000
2012	1,873,910,000,000	5,134,000,000
2011	1,722,071,000,000	4,717,000,000
2010	1,324,670,000,000	3,627,000,000
2009	953,700,000,000	2,610,000,000
2008	637,200,000,000	1,745,000,000
2007	438,000,000,000	1,200,000,000
2000	22,000,000,000	60,000,000
1998	3,600,000 *Googles official first year	9,800

Figure 4.10: Google search statistics

Mobility also allowed us to constantly participate in the information economy. Before 2000, people would go to work, then spend some leisure time, and then spend some time asleep. Now, these distinctions are completely blurred. In a 2014 survey of people under the age of 30 in the United States, more than 80 per cent reported sleeping with their smartphone by their side. I'm guilty too, and I wish that I wasn't. Our perpetual connectivity to the information economy compels us to perpetually participate, whether as a producer, a consumer or a manager of information. This connectivity serves the same purpose as bureaucracies did in the capital economy. Our connectivity keeps things moving, it keeps creating raw material, and it keeps generating finished goods in the world of information.

Social Media: How Information is Applied

Social media is the next element of the Digital Trinity. While mobility provides the mechanism for connecting and contributing to the information economy, social media represent how we do so. I use the term social media far more broadly than just Facebook, Twitter and Instagram. In my definition I refer to information's enhancement through social contribution. Our communications on the Internet are the raw material of the information economy. What we say and do with those communications are the value-added processes that turn raw material into finished goods of higher value.

The way that we create value in information is through our collective contribution to it. It's not enough that you or I create a post on Facebook. That's just raw material, and as most of us know it has minimal value. My post starts to actually become valuable when others add to it, through their comments, reposts or retweets, emojis and so on. People have been contributing content to the Internet for almost 30 years. But the power of the Information Economy really came to light as soon as we allowed each other to contribute to each other's content, and create new value as a result.

Analytics: How Information is Controlled

Finally, analytics represents the mechanism for controlling how Information gains, retains, and multiplies in value. We use advanced analytics to search for, identify and put to use new insights, in order to create more new information. In an ocean of apparently meaningless noise that is the contemporary Internet, analytics allows us to find the information that either has value or *could* have value, and then do something useful with it.

This is why so much attention is paid to Big Data, Predictive Analytics, Machine Learning, Artificial Intelligence and so on.

Through analytics, it is possible to mine the vast wasteland of fuzzy cat photos, fake dating profiles and once-in-a-lifetime offers from a disenfranchised Nigerian prince in order to find and create wealth through this new medium of information. Companies who get analytics right stand to pretty much inherit the Earth. Those who do not will likely maintain gigantic stockpiles of data, and yet they won't realize that all of that data is purely a capital cost *until you do something with it*. Having data without analyzing it is like carrying around gold-bearing rocks without ever smelting the gold out. It's heavy, it's a drag, and it's worse than worthless. Only through analysis of the data that we all generate can real value be identified and leveraged in an Information economy. Just like business rules ensured that organizations maximize the value of capital, data analytics ensures that they maximize the value of information.

Chapter Summary:

1. Cooperation between individuals requires a social contract. In that contract, someone gains power and someone gives power, in order to create better outcomes for all.
2. Power is the currency of social contracts, and the source of power in human society has changed over time, as a result of social and technological advancements.
3. Power in society is managed through three mechanisms: Distribution, Application and Control. These three mechanisms form the Trinity of Power.
4. Over time, there have been four different sources of power in human society, and hence four different Trinities of Power. The four sources of power have been Knowledge, Land, Capital and Information. The four Trinities are the Tool, Dirt, Analog and Digital Trinities.
5. No Trinity fades away completely when another one arises, but the dominance of each does change over time. We are currently living in the end of the Capital Era, and the new Information Era is bringing forth the new Digital Trinity as the basis for managing wealth and power.

SECTION II: The 'Dirty Dozen' of Being a Jerk

In the 1967 movie *The Dirty Dozen*, actor Lee Marvin played a rebellious major in the American Army in World War II. His leaders recognized his rebellious nature, and used it to assign him an impossible task far behind enemy lines. Marvin's character knew that his only chance of completing his mission was to break every rule and to defy conventional wisdom. He recruited 12 soldiers, each convicted of capital felonies, to execute his impossible plan. In the end this Dirty Dozen achieved their mission and did what no one else believed could be done.

And so it is with Jerks. Jerks purposefully reject the view of the Analogs they seek to replace, and play an entirely different game. They don't ignore the Analog Trinity, they actually use Analogs' adherence to this trinity to defeat Analogs at their own game. Jerks circumvent Analogs, and use the Digital trinity to seek out and create Information wealth.

It turns out there is a formula for causing this disruption. There is a recipe for advancing the Digital Trinity at the expense of Analogs and their Trinity. These twelve principles, or 'Dirty Dozen of Being a Jerk' define how Jerks do what they do, how and why they succeed, and why Analogs have such difficulty in defending against them.

The 'Dirty Dozen of Being a Jerk' are:
1. Use Other People's Capital
2. Replace Capital with Information
3. Focus on Context Not Content
4. Eliminate Friction
5. Create Value Webs Not Value Chains
6. Invert Economies of Scale and Scope
7. Sell With and Through, Not To
8. Print Your Own Money
9. Flout the Rules
10. Hightail It
11. Do Then Learn

12. Look Forward

In the following section, we will explore each of these principles and explain how and why they cause disruption.

Chapter Five: Jerks Use Other People's Capital

"Money is not wealth. Money is a claim on wealth."- David Korten

"A man is usually more careful of his money than he is of his principles."- Ralph Waldo Emerson

Rule One is simple and powerful: Jerks don't focus on the creation, management and investment of capital. Instead, they focus on the creation, management and investment of information. I'm not suggesting that these companies don't need or use capital; far from it. But Jerks are conceived, born, grow and will mature as data-centric, rather than capital-centric organizations. The distinction may seem subtle, but it is not. Traditional companies still follow the Analog Trinity, so they use data to better manage their capital. Jerks follow the Digital Trinity, and so use capital to better manage their data. Jerks use capital dollars to accumulate data, which they then analyze, manage, hoard, sell, mine and ultimately trade or sell, in order to create wealth.

How is this different from existing companies? Unlike traditional companies, Jerks have recognized that the power shift described in Section One is upon us. It is inevitable. They have aligned themselves with this new reality and in so doing they are positioning themselves to dominate the business they have chosen. Jerks concentrate on the Digital Trinity, rather than the Analog Trinity, and leverage the Six New Normals to turn information into wealth and power. Analog companies are capital-centric in all aspects of what they do. Their processes, their reports, their rules, even the titles for their executives are all focused upon capital. If they refer to a 'controller' they are referring to someone who controls capital. If they are discussing one of their approval processes, that process is almost certainly one that controls the movement or expenditure of capital. And if they are reviewing some report characterizing their business performance, the metrics in hand very likely discuss capital performance, rather than anything else. These organizations simply cannot fathom a world that *doesn't* organize around capital; such a thing doesn't even register with them.

Jerks see the world differently. They see value in access (Mobility), interest (Social Media) and trends (Analytics). Traditional inputs of production, value and productivity are just background, filler, ambiance.

This may seem too simplistic, but let's go through some examples to demonstrate how this is working.

How do Jerks Create Wealth?

Examples of these new, information-oriented companies abound. Many of the names you already know, such as Uber, Airbnb, Doctor On Demand, Lyft, Turo, Simple Bank, FarmLogs or Convoy. Others are just starting or perhaps are only an idea in someone's mind. But, if you follow any mainstream source of media, it seems these organizations are constantly in the news. I discuss the topics in this book with executives every week. Just before each meeting I grab a major newspaper or magazine, browse a news app, or watch 15 minutes of news programming. Invariably, I will find a report about some Jerk doing something new and innovative, and causing disruption.

This perpetual coverage of Jerks isn't an accident because, according to the Digital Trinity, simply being talked about increases an organization's worth. Many executives of traditional businesses are annoyed by the fact that Jerks get so much coverage, without recognizing that this *is* their strategy. Being talked about in social media, wherever the audiences are, and creating data to analyze are the whole purpose of these companies. They aren't driving for this media coverage because they're bragging, they're doing it because it gives them power in an information-centric world.

Analog companies try to maximize returns on their capital by optimizing their processes, rules and bureaucracies. Jerks maximize wealth by reaching people wherever they are, getting noticed and talked about, and then figuring out how to maximize those conversations. Analog companies spend money on marketing and advertising in order to sell more products and services. Jerks drive conversations among their customers because it's the conversation that has value, not the result of the conversation.

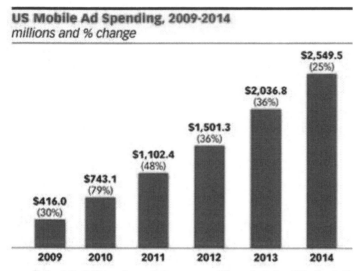

Figure 5.1: Mobile advertising spending in the United States

If you've spent your career in the capital-centric, Analog world, this all probably sounds like nonsense. Advertising isn't a profit center, it's a cost center. Marketing isn't a sale, it's how you get to a sale. We have loosely defined some relationship between advertising and capital generation, but simply getting people to talk about your product or service has no value. It's just a means to getting to a sale where value is created.

In the Analog world, this is totally right. In the Digital world where Jerks live, this thinking is totally wrong.

The Exceptions that Prove the Rule

To emphasize the point, look at the great cross-over companies created by Elon Musk: SpaceX and Tesla Motors. Both of these businesses are hugely capital-intensive. Indeed, automobiles and rockets put the 'heavy' in heavy industries. These companies seem to be Analog Trinity all the way, and Elon is constantly cast as the renegade who dares to challenge the good ol' boys of the Capital era at their own game. The existing companies that dominate these two industries continually foretell the eventual failure of SpaceX and Tesla, as these industries realign themselves to beat this new upstart.

Will they? Elon gets this whole Digital Trinity and Six New Normals thing, but he also seems to get that the transition will take a while. Clearly, he's a motivated and impatient guy, and so rather than waiting for the transition to happen, he's forcing it upon us. He's effectively playing in both worlds with both world views, and he's doing it remarkably well. I for one would not bet against him.

Tesla Stock Price Since June 2010 IPO

Figure 5.2: Stock price of Tesla Motors

Elon took his initial, not-unsubstantial, capital wealth and used it to build a possible competitor to the old-school players in the automotive and space industries. Both of these industries are deeply entrenched in the Capital mindset. When it comes to the Analog Trinity they are all-in. To play against them toe-to-toe, you needed to actually replicate much of their same capital investment, which was a very tall order for anyone.

Elon had just enough capital to make it look like he was wasting a fortune. He has been quoted as saying, "the best way to make a million in the space industry was to start with a billion." In launching both companies, Elon very nearly bankrupted himself because the barriers to entry had been set so high by the entrenched players.

But here's where the crossover from Analog to Digital began to change the rules. After a while, SpaceX and Tesla didn't look like fool's errands, they began to look cool. Both companies began to do what the existing players believed to be impossible: create an electric car that didn't suck; create a cheap, reliable rocket that was reusable. Elon began to do things that those who were still completely bought into the Analog Trinity believed to be impossible; because their bureaucracies, processes and rules told them that those things were impossible, and that made it true.

	Tesla	GM	Ford
Enterprise Value	$28 B	$81 B	$152 B
Revenue (TTM)	$3.8 B	$152 B	$145 B
GM	26%	12%	14%
EBITDA (TTM)	-$184 M	$13.5 B	$13.2 B
# Employees	10161	216000	187000
EV/Revenue	7.38 x	0.53 x	1.05 x
Revenue/Employee	$ 373,979	$ 703,704	$ 775,401

Figure 5.3: Revenue multiple for Car Companies, January, 2016

Soon, Tesla and SpaceX began to beat the odds and yield impossible results. Rather than silence the doubters, this made them protest even louder. And this is where the Digital Trinity started to take over. The more the naysayers talked about Tesla and SpaceX, the more *everyone* talked about them. This increase in buzz became not only self-reinforcing, it became self-accelerating. Soon, everybody was talking about these companies because everyone was talking about these companies.

Then a funny thing happened. Both companies started to become more valuable. Shortly after both companies seemed to hit rock bottom, they turned a corner and saw their popularity and valuation skyrocket. Soon, all of the buzz about SpaceX and Tesla grew so large, so fast, that both of these traditional, big-iron, heavy-industry, capital-intensive, four-per-cent-annual-return-on-investment companies were receiving valuations against revenue that looked more like an Internet startup instead of a tired old company.

This annoyed the existing Analog players to no end, as it seemed not only unfair, it seemed irrational. The valuations that these two companies received seemed to defy all of the rules and logic set by the Analog Trinity. The valuations looked more like Digital Trinity valuations, because they were. And both companies' valuations continue to climb as both companies defy the rules, preconceptions and constraints of their competitors. Neither company is playing by those old, Analog rules, they are playing by the new Digital rules, according to the Six New Normals.

Capital Isn't Dead, It's Just Irrelevant

There is an open secret to all of this. There is a reason that Jerks are able to create value out of thin air in a world still dominated by capital and not yet dominated by information; someone else already provides the capital. None of what I'm saying is meant to suggest that people still don't want or need things - far from it. But, when I know that *what* I want is readily available, it's the *how*, *when*, *where* and most of all *why* that I value most. As long as there are existing companies bringing capital to the game, Jerks are able to skip over that need, and fulfill all of the unmet needs that customers still have.

We talk about this all of the time, and it's almost a running joke. Jerks don't make sense in the physical, Analog world. Uber is often described as the world's largest taxi company, which owns no taxis. Airbnb is the world's largest hotelier, yet it owns no hotels. Netflix is the world's largest movie house, yet it owns no theaters. In each of these examples a Jerk has simply figured out that as long as *someone* provides the capital, customers value everything else.

As we discussed with the Six New Normals, capital is noticed only when it is absent. As long as it's there, we no longer care about it. I care about getting a ride to my destination, not who provides the taxi. I care about getting my illness diagnosed, not how well-decorated the doctor's office is. I don't care how comfortable the seats are in the theatre, because they'll never compare to the couch in my own home. All of our efforts to better utilize capital worked, but it seems they worked too well.

This is the result of 200 years of trying to optimally manage capital, and ensure that customers had what they needed and wanted. Analog companies were so successful at this that they've made themselves necessary, but largely irrelevant.

Other People's Money

So, the model for being a Jerk requires that someone else provide the capital before they can cash in. They can provide all of the coverage and commentary for the tennis match, as long as someone else provides the court, rackets and balls. As long as access to capital-intensive products and services is assured, Jerks are positioned to capture all of the perceived value from their use. This is how they monetize information, according to the Digital Trinity.

Some Jerks don't wait for the capital to come along, they provide it themselves. Elon Musk had to provide his own rockets to disrupt the space industry, because no existing player was going to sell a $100-million rocket through an app. Tesla had to *first* prove that an electric car could go 250 miles on a single charge before anyone would line up to pay $100,000 for one. But, where there are players who provide the capital that consumers crave, Jerks can readily disintermediate suppliers from their customers and take control of entire value chains.

FarmLogs doesn't sell farmers the fertilizer that they put on their crops. A 150-year-old, capital-intensive, vertically-integrated, publicly-traded, multibillion-dollar corporation does that. What FarmLogs does is tell you the best time and place to use that fertilizer to grow your crops as effectively as possible.

Uber doesn't finance, buy, manage, maintain or fuel taxis, they just make sure that you get picked up as quickly and conveniently as possible from someone who does.

Doctor On Demand does just what its name suggests; it gives you a doctor on demand. No matter where you are or when you are, you get a doctor's consultation within 60 seconds. You don't have to bring your ailment to your doctor, instead they bring a doctor to your ailment.

Airbnb doesn't own properties, *you* do. Airbnb simply makes it incredibly easy for those who own property to loan it to those who don't, at least for a time. If you leave your home to go on a week's vacation, your home is a financial loss for you while you're away (discounting appreciation, which will be ever more elusive in a world with negative interest rates). Airbnb helps you turn that temporary loss into a temporary gain, allowing all the parties involved to benefit.

Who Is Next?

A big part of the message of Part Two of Jerk is this: There's a formula for causing Jerk. The approach to causing Jerk in an existing industry is not only possible, it's inevitable. Making capital irrelevant is a precondition to all of this, since we are still in a period of transition. But, as long as capital is being provided by *somebody*, the opportunity to Jerk is there.

From this it should be easy to see where Jerk will come next. Look for industries where capital is king, there is relatively little innovation, information exists but is not being put to use, and people have come to expect a poor experience in accessing the benefits of that capital. If all of these conditions exist, and the companies that currently dominate the industry are aligned with the Analog Trinity, then Jerk is inevitable. Somehow, someone will figure out some way to apply the Digital Trinity and the Six New Normals to that business, and they'll make the existing players irrelevant, even while they still own and manage the underlying capital.

Chapter Summary:

1. Jerks recognize that information is rapidly becoming the basis of wealth and power in the world.
2. Therefore, Jerks emphasize the collection, use and growth of data rather than capital.
3. Jerks need capital, but only as a means to another end.

Chapter Six: Jerks Replace Capital with Information

"The universe is not required to be in perfect harmony with human ambition."- Carl Sagan

"The strength to change what I can, the inability to accept what I can't, and the incapacity to tell the difference."- Bill Watterson as Calvin in 'Calvin and Hobbes'

Rule Two: Jerks focus on information rather than capital. Once accessing capital is no longer an issue, Jerks largely ignore capital as an asset. Obviously this is a sweeping statement, and it is not entirely true because we still live in a largely capital world, at least for now. But philosophically Jerks pretty much ignore capital as a measure of success, and instead find value and worth in what information they have at their disposal.

Jerks aren't focused upon the creation, management and investment of capital. Rather, they are focused upon the creation, management and investment of information. I'm not suggesting that these companies don't need or use capital; far from it. But Jerks are conceived, born, grow and will mature as data-centric, rather than capital-centric organizations.

Once Jerks have accessed other people's capital and have launched their business, they do not expend nearly the same amount of time, energy and attention on capital. For them it is merely a means to an end. What they do focus on is doing more and better things with more and better information.

I get that if I left this argument at this point, you'd probably say that I was a crackpot. You might be thinking that this rule is complete nonsense. It's one thing to say that Jerks profit off of other people's capital; we see this every day with Uber, Airbnb, Waze and so on. But it's something entirely different to say that they don't even care about capital. That has to be hogwash ... doesn't it? Please bear with me for a few more paragraphs and let me put some wood behind this arrow.

Metrics Don't Lie

All companies with any kind of track record have metrics that tell them how well they are performing. Indeed, these metrics *are* their track record. You can tell a lot about what an organization stands for, believes in and cares about when you look at the metrics that they track and discuss. Analog companies track balance sheets, cash flow, liabilities, assets and so on. Jerks keep track of page views, GPS coordinates, sentiment, click paths and 'likes.' They focus all of their time, attention and resources on obtaining, understanding and using more information, and they care about capital only as much as it assists in this effort.

If you are an Analog veteran you're likely thinking to yourself, "Wait a minute, my organization tracks all kinds of things other than capital!" Sure you do. Analog companies track all kinds of qualitative, less tangible things like quality, customer satisfaction, cycle times, call hold times, carbon emissions and so on. I agree that these are things that superficially look like they are not capital-focused.

However, almost every time I've seen one of these 'soft' Key Performance Indicators (KPIs) reported by an organization, I've also seen that organization rush to justify the metric by relating it back to some capital impact. Every. Single. Time. Analog companies might bother to measure qualitative things, but they never, ever leave them dangling as such. How could they, they're all about capital. Indeed, most Analog organizations sound almost apologetic for caring about something other than capital, and they feel compelled to tie every non-capital-centric metric *back* to one that *is* capital-centric.

For example, look at companies reporting their 'green-ness.' These days, everybody cares about being 'green,' mostly because everybody cares about being 'green.' (That's a Digital Trinity concept, by the way.) Sure, our environment is under enormous stress from human activities, and all of us probably *should* care about that. (In the 1990s I was an engineer working on NASA's TERRA satellite, one of the spacecraft that allowed us to actually measure the global environment and measure our impact on the planet. The science is sound.) Because environmentalism is now popular, companies have recognized a benefit (in capital) from showing that they too care about the environment.

Figure 6.1: NASA's TERRA Satellite, used to study the Earth's climate

But take some time to check out how companies report on how they're reducing their carbon footprint, or recycling their waste, or rescuing orphaned panda cubs, and then look at all of the wording they wrap *around* those pronouncements. These Analog companies feel compelled to immediately talk about how their environmental efforts benefit their bottom line. They can't *not* do so; they don't know how. These companies will talk about cutting their carbon emissions, which earned them carbon credits, which change their tax position or in some way improves their capital position. Ta-da! Right there is their reflexive apology for appearing to care about something other than capital, and the reminder that it really is about capital after all.

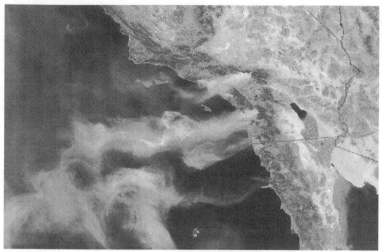

Figure 6.2: TERRA tracks wildfires in California

Different Metrics, Different Motivations

Jerks don't behave this way. Jerks also measure all kinds of things. They have to; it's the third leg of the Digital Trinity. But, what they measure and how they value those measurements are completely different from their Analog ancestors. When Jerks talk about measuring customer satisfaction they mean to measure *actual* satisfaction. Qualitatively and quantitatively, was their customer happy? This metric has inherent value to them, and they feel no need to immediately tie it back to dollars and cents.

Need proof of this? When was the last time that you gave some app or website a rating? You know what I mean: one star or two stars or five stars, from your smartphone, immediately after you experienced some sort of interaction (all of these things are critical, and are coming up later). Regardless of the score that you provided, you felt a certain degree of satisfaction in doing so, didn't you? Whether you slammed someone for giving you a poor experience or raved about some way in which you received great service, you felt better after giving a rating.

Bingo! That was quantifiable value to you, the customer. It didn't even really matter what score you gave, good or bad. In that instant (Mobility) your participation in providing a score that others could see (Social Media) gave others something of value (Analytics) and you benefitted, too. From an information-centric view, value was just created *before* I even measured or analyzed the data. Mere participation was enough to change the equation.

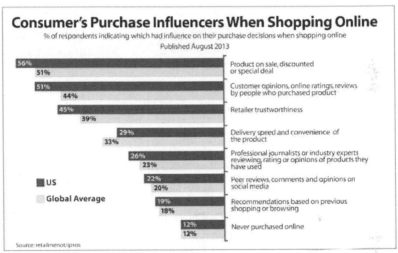

Figure 6.3: What influences online shoppers

For Jerks, this is just the beginning. Once your score was posted, you contributed to a metric about something qualitative and information-based. Maybe you gave four stars for speed of service, or perhaps you gave three stars for ease of use. Whatever. At no point in the creation of these metrics did you say anything about how effectively capital was converted. Maybe you were asked about price, but you were asked about how you *felt* about the price, not about the price itself. The difference may be subtle, but it is enormous in its implications.

Correlation: The New Compounding Interest

To transition from the Analog world to the Digital world, it helps to think of information correlation as the equivalent to compounding interest. To grow the value of your capital, you somehow figure out how to get a positive interest rate – some kind of growth in the value of your capital. If you can keep this growth going, the interest begins to build upon itself, or compounds. A 10 per cent interest rate, compounded annually, leads to a doubling of your capital in a little less than eight years. In the early 21st century, this is a *great* return on capital.

Similarly, in the Information economy, finding correlations in otherwise uncorrelated data adds value to that data. And the more data you collect, the more correlated the data becomes and the more its value grows. This is sort of ethereal, I know. But this is a real effect, because *you* make it so. This is exactly how Jerks use information and the Digital Trinity to create wealth.

I'm sure that it's time for some more wood for this arrow. Let me explain.

Jerks collect *massive* quantities of this semi- or un-correlated data. It is their currency. They love this stuff for exactly the reason that Analog companies do not: it's uncorrelated. To an Analog company, this sort of uncorrelated stuff is usually considered to be annoying because it can't be tied back to what they value: capital. I've lost track of the number of times I've heard business people dismiss this sort of data as 'irrelevant,' 'useless,' 'fluff,' or 'noise.' If they can't put a dollar sign against it, it can't possibly be useful, right?

Of course it can. We see this every day. When we shop online, those stars or points or 'likes' mean a great deal to us. They often make or break our decisions. Often, they mean more to us than the product or service we're actually trying to buy! Don't believe me? Fine. If, while buying something online, you filtered the search results based upon the number of stars the item had, you proved my point. The information about what you were trying to buy was more important than the thing itself.

This is what makes Jerks different. They hunger for uncorrelated data because they know that there is opportunity in correlating it to something. They pick metrics that define, harvest and exchange information, after transforming it from uncorrelated to correlated.

This *is* their value proposition! And the more of this kind of information they can gather, the better their correlations and the more valuable their results become to you and me.

Again, look at your own behavior. If something on amazon.com has 4.6 stars, but only five ratings, it's suspect. If a similar item has 3.7 stars, but 7,000 ratings, that's a much more reliable score. If you wanted something with a score over four, you might still hesitate with the first item, because its score is still somewhat uncorrelated. With the latter item, if a score of 3.5 is good enough, you'll go ahead and buy with confidence. Five ratings might be an accident or coincidence. Seven thousand ratings represent a correlation that you value and you're willing to count on.

And that's the point.

Handing Off the Keys to the Kingdom

So, beyond putting other people's capital to work, Jerks also collect uncorrelated data *about* other people's capital, and then work to correlate it to something. In this way, they not only get free access to other people's capital, they create vast amounts of information wealth by taking the data too. They don't just injure the capital-centric Analog companies, they kick a bit of dirt on them when they're done!

Think of the Jerks that we all talk about. Because we are talking about them, we are helping them to create information wealth with the Digital Trinity. These guys are taking Analog companies to the cleaners. Uber doesn't just make money off taxi companies, they collect all of the uncorrelated data about each ride, and use it to make correlations about the driver, the car, the passenger, the route, the city's traffic, pollution, the weather and all kinds of other pieces of information. The people who actually *own* the taxis could just as easily capture all of this same information, they just choose not to. Why? In their way of thinking, it doesn't translate into cash.

How about Airbnb? They rent out someone else's property, they take a cut of the money that changes hands (they need *some* cash to pay expenses), and then they take *all* of the information related to the renter, the lessor, the property, the neighborhood, the climate, the ambiance in the place, the local humidity, the quality of the air conditioning, and so on. They take all of this uncorrelated data, correlate it, and then 'sell' it back to the next customer who is looking for a place to rent.

Room to Grow

Airbnb is showing solid growth to investors as it seeks to raise funds.

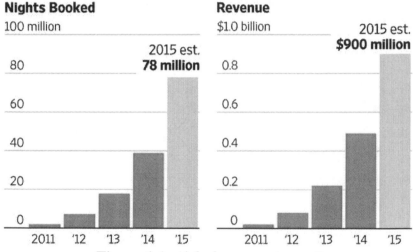

Figure 6.4: Airbnb revenue growth

Still not enough? Try any of the Internet 1.0 companies that are effective at bridging the gap between our Analog and Digital worlds. Amazon? You already know how they do it, and they excel at it. Wall Street constantly whines that Amazon never makes a profit, that they're over-valued, and that their investment strategy doesn't make sense. In a capital world, Wall Street is exactly right. In an Information world, the people who hang on to Amazon stock for more than 91.25 days at a time are exactly right.

Facebook is right there, too. Facebook cracks me up. This is a company that doesn't actually *do* anything. I'm being facetious here, but really, what do they *do*? In an Analog world Facebook makes no sense whatsoever. And for over a decade this is exactly what most capital investors have said. Facebook doesn't produce anything, their users do. Facebook doesn't do anything, their users do. Facebook doesn't provide anything, their users do. In a capital world, except as a marketing vehicle, Facebook is completely irrational.

And yet in late 2015 Facebook surpassed General Electric in market capitalization, exceeding $260 billion. How is that possible? Easy, if you understand the value of information correlation. Take a billion or two people, have them spend a few billion hours each day creating uncorrelated data and have *them* correlate it for you, then effectively resell the correlation to the highest bidder - which is currently mostly advertisers, but only thus far.

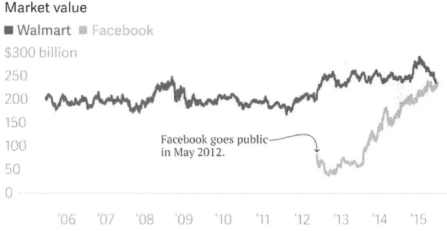

Figure 6.5: Market Capitalization, Facebook and Walmart

All I can say is this. If, after these examples, you don't see the value of collecting and correlating data, of measuring and analyzing qualitative metrics for their own sake, and in trying to collect your own uncorrelated data, instead of handing it off to some Jerk, you just might be Analog.
If this is true, I wish you luck in trying to find and maintain opportunities that provide meaningful compounding interest rates for

your capital. This train is leaving the station, potentially for good, and I understand that the conductor yelling 'all aboard' has 4.7 stars!

Chapter Summary:

1. In an information-centric world, creating value from information must be every organization's dominant goal.
2. Information value is created when uncorrelated data is correlated, leading to new insights and new results.
3. Uncorrelated data can be correlated by identifying and adding context.
4. Correlating uncorrelated data, by adding context, is the compounding interest of the information age.
5. Companies such as Facebook, Google, Amazon, Uber, Simple Bank and other Jerks are primarily context engines.

Note: When I wrote this chapter, I was struck by the notion that the correlation of otherwise uncorrelated data might explain why companies such as Uber, Apple, Facebook, Google and Amazon receive the valuations that they do. By traditional, Analog measures, their market valuations do not make sense. Jerks such as Uber and Airbnb derive their valuations almost exclusively from the value of correlation that they create in information. Companies that bridge the gap between Analogs and Digitals, such as Amazon or Google, derive their valuations from both sides of the gap, capital and information wealth.

However, if there really is value in using context to create previously unknown correlations in otherwise uncorrelated data, then the valuations of these companies makes total sense, only with a different governing equation. The basis of this equation is this:

Uncorrelated Data + Context

=

Correlated Data

=

Information Wealth

Of course the actual math is far more complicated than this, but I am working on that. I believe that this equation is knowable, and as soon as I had this insight, I began working on figuring out what this governing equation may be. If the valuations of these information-centered companies is rational, then it is knowable with the right equation. If their valuation, in terms of information value, is knowable then it should also be predictable. If this is also true, then the misalignment of corporate capital valuations and their information valuations could be collapsed, with potentially dramatic implications to the world of investing.

Chapter Seven: Jerks Monetize Context Not Content

"Space and time not only affect, but are also affected by, everything that happens in the universe."- Stephen Hawking

"Better three hours too soon than a minute too late."- William Shakespeare

My thesis is that controlling information is essential to business success. There is ample evidence of this, as we can see that information-oriented companies such as Google, Facebook, Amazon, Microsoft and Apple have become some of the world's most capital-rich companies.

So what remains for Jerks? If these information companies have already used the Internet to become dominant corporate entities, how can Jerks find room for their own explosive growth? The answer is in *what* information is being targeted.

When Content Was King

The companies listed above, and their peers who succeeded through the Internet 1.0 revolution, did so by monetizing content. The early Internet was a content engine. People went online to find information, rather than go to the library, ask a friend, or draft a letter to Dear Abby. It was much easier to just fire up your PC, plug in your modem, dial into America Online and ask the Internet. As more and more people went online, their demand for content grew in volume and diversity. The need for content was born, and the race to dominate content was on.

When you look at the giants who came out of the content land-grab, they're all companies that each of us now use practically every day. Google became the dominant search engine. Amazon became the content retailer, our favorite place to find content on just about anything we wanted to buy. Apple used iTunes to grab the content high ground and took control of music, movies, TV shows and other high-cost, high-return content. In doing so, it crushed the once-dominant entertainment industry. Facebook took the low ground, and fed people's basest need to entertain, and to be entertained by toilet humor and politics (if there's a difference).

As the world went online in the 1990s and 2000s, these companies became giants of capital by feeding society's ever-growing hunger for content. Because they were so successful, one wonders how anyone could possibly compete with these behemoths. How could a Jerk replace Google, Apple or Facebook? The answer is: they can't, as long as they try to play the content game. To win in a market that is already dominated by others, you have to play a new game, by new rules, preferably in a new stadium. And that's exactly what Jerks are doing.

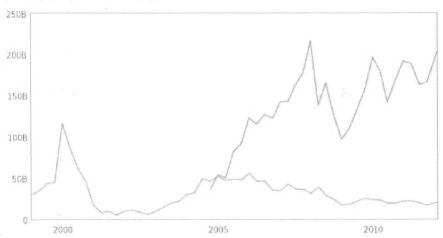

Figure 7.1: Yahoo versus Google, market capitalization

The next group of companies that will join, or may even replace, these content barons are those who focus on context, rather than content.

From Baltic Avenue to Boardwalk

As any Monopoly player will tell you, not all property is created equal. The board game's various properties are largely alike, but have widely varying prices and values. Baltic Avenue is worth $60, while Boardwalk is worth $400. This is a reasonable reflection of reality, as anyone who has strolled between neighborhoods in any major city can readily attest. While both may be located in New York City, there's a big difference in value between a loft in Soho and a tenement out in Flushing Meadows. Not all land is equal, and that's been true for 5,000 years.

Similarly, not all capital is equal. If I offered to trade you my ounce of gold for your ounce of silver, you'd probably be pretty happy with the trade, albeit highly suspicious. You'd likely not trade your new BMW for my 20-year-old Oldsmobile (an Industrial Revolution stalwart that died a while back), and you'd likely not trade your shares of Apple stock for my shares of Radio Shack. In each era society's assets have a normal distribution of value.

The Value Continuum of Information

The same holds true for information. The least valuable may simply be thought of as 'data.' Data are just the facts, ma'am. Data are numbers, figures, journal entries and such. It's the stuff that would be stored in the accounting books of the Industrial Revolution by Analog companies. (These books are different from those that Amazon sells. I wouldn't include Amazon's books as data, because they transmit more than just facts; they carry concepts. However, books that an accountant keeps are emphatically data repositories).

One step above data is content. Content is data (facts) that also carry concepts, knowledge or ideas. This is a higher order of complication and value, and represents a clear step up from mere data. Story books are content, and so are most of the sites found on the early Internet. Much of what is posted on social media these days might also be considered to be content; but only just. Content is clearly more valuable than data, because it delivers more to the consumer than just facts.

The King is Dead, Long Live the King

So, what trumps content for information value? Meet context, the new king. Context is information about the state of affairs in the universe. It is information that describes how things change, flow, evolve or adapt. Content talks about the state of affairs, too. But it does so only at one point in space and time. Content is static in how it describes the universe. Context is different. Context reveals the *dynamics* of the universe, or how things change moment by moment.

Let me give an example. Imagine that you post a picture of yourself on Facebook. That picture represents content about what you were doing at that moment. If I return to that picture a day, week or month later, it will still be the same picture, the same content. It is what it is, and that's all that it is. Now, a year later, take that picture, wrap it with some *context*, and repost it. Facebook now shows you that picture with a headline telling you, "Here's what you were up to a year ago." That picture, with context, is now an anniversary present; the anniversary of whatever was going on at the time of the picture. You may or may not have been doing something special when you took the picture, but mentioning the anniversary of that event has enhanced the content with remembrance.

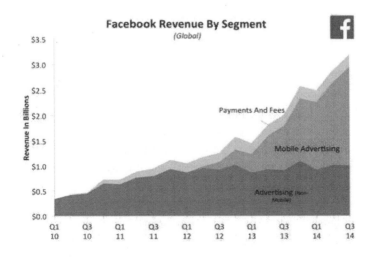

Figure 7.2: Facebook revenue trends

This example may seem trite, but don't underestimate the power of context. When you get context right, it is powerful, heady stuff. That is why Facebook recently deployed this feature. Facebook has recognized that content is being eclipsed by context, and they want a seat at the context table.

Context and a Little Yellow Taxi

Further examples abound. Uber is a Jerk, because they applied context to the game of getting around. For more than 100 years, taxi companies enjoyed highly regulated, protected status. To legally operate a taxi you needed to buy a license, be bondable, and register with the state. You needed to accede to the controls of a government bureaucracy. You also needed to have a fair amount of capital on hand, as you needed to buy the taxi, maintain it, feed it gas, and so on. All of this structure was intended to ensure the safety of passengers, and superficially, this was the case.

But, make no mistake, a lot of this regulation of the taxi industry was political. It was about controlling who had access to the livery industry, and who could participate in the game of getting people from point A to point B. Over time, the taxi industry was controlled by a relatively small number of companies, each of which was necessarily capital-rich. The regulations created high barriers to entry for anyone thinking of getting into the taxi game, which is exactly what Analog companies count on.

Along came a Jerk named Uber, and suddenly this whole well-oiled machine was turned on its head. Uber didn't own or operate taxis. Heck, they really didn't own *anything* based on capital. What they did do is create an app that captured two things; the context of potential taxi riders, and the context of unused taxis. They took these two bits of information, and they put the two together. Effectively, Uber is merely a context engine that constantly compares the changes in two sets of context, and seeks to find their optimal intersection.

This is a subtle concept, but it is fundamental. Context is information about something's position in space and time; your context in the universe. Context changes over time, and this represents useful information. Your condition at one moment in time might change in the next, and this can be very useful information when it is put to use. Uber keeps track of where potential taxi riders are, at every instant, and also keeps track of every available vehicle in close proximity to each potential rider, also at every instant. They are a context engine, keeping track of the ever-changing context of their customers and suppliers.

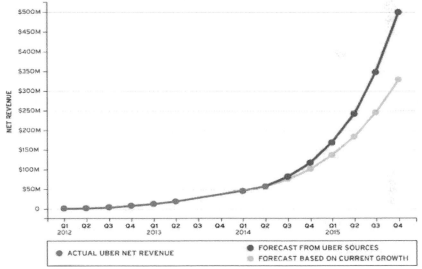

Figure 7.3: Uber revenue, reported and projected

When you let Uber know you need a ride, they instantly capture your context at that moment, i.e., your *when* and your *where*. Then they scan for available cars whose context is most similar to yours (meaning that they're close to you), and then they electronically put the two of you together. Once the matches are made, Uber sends the car to your location, usually very quickly, and a value transaction ensues. You get on your way to your destination, with your context ever-changing as you go.

Contextification: The Next Information Revolution

I discussed this process of leveraging context information in my first book, *Data Crush,* and I predicted that it would be a game changer. This *contextification* takes information to a new, higher level of value for us all, and it greatly enhances all aspects of the transactions we perform.

The new wave of successful companies, the new wave of Jerks, are using context to massively disrupt existing industries which have not yet contextified themselves. Uber applies context to private vehicles, Airbnb applies it to land, Turo applies it to private cars left by travelers at airports, BigRentz applies it to underutilized construction equipment. Contextifying existing businesses is *exactly* what Jerks are doing, because it is the next step up in the information value chain. And, it is massively disruptive to those who haven't done this themselves.

Context: It's Not Your Grandma's Data

Context information is incredibly valuable because it is incredibly intimate. It captures how, why and where we live our lives. Knowing that you just bought a birthday cake is valuable. Knowing that you bought it for your mother, rather than yourself, is dramatically *more* valuable. Context is also incredibly valuable because it is fleeting. What is valuable in one context, in one place in space and time, may be of no value a moment later, or a meter to the left or right. Consider again the Uber example. Knowing that I need a taxi *right here, right now* is extremely valuable information, until I'm picked up. The very next second, that information is worthless, at least to me.

The challenge of leveraging context is that your perception, understanding and use of context must be at least as fast as the rate that context changes, if not faster. For Analog companies, this is an almost incomprehensible task. For Jerks, it's just what they do. They don't need committees, tiger teams, Return on Investment analyses, review boards, or approval processes to find and act on context. They just do it. Indeed, these old, Analog Trinity tools and mechanisms necessarily *can't* operate at the speed of changing context, because capital likes to move slowly; not as slowly as land, but pretty close to it.

Jerks use the extremely slow information metabolism of Analog companies to completely take advantage of their Analog capital. Jerks can even leverage context to take advantage of the information metabolism of content companies, a metabolism far faster than that of capital companies but still much slower than context metabolism. Content kings like Apple, Amazon, Google and Facebook are working diligently to speed up their information metabolism so that they can also put context to work.

Drones, Amazon Dash, Google Glass and Apple Pay and Apple Watch are evidence of their efforts. These content companies have metabolisms much closer to content than Analog companies, so they have a much better chance of success. Analog companies are massively challenged to bridge this gap, but fortunately most of them have tiger teams and committees working diligently on the problem, at an offsite meeting somewhere in the Caribbean.

Waste Heat

As mentioned, the value of context data is fleeting. It comes and goes at the rate of context change, which according to Einstein can be as fast as the speed of light. Indeed, Einstein was right that nothing in the physical world can go faster, except maybe context. I argued that context has no value once it changes, and this is largely correct. But there's an exception to every rule. Context has a very limited shelf life. You have only so long to see it, understand it and act upon it, and if you don't, the opportunity is gone. If it takes you more than a second or two to recognize that that car coming at you may not come to a stop, that information suddenly loses its usefulness, at least until your court date comes along.

This brings up an interesting point. While nearly all of the value of context is lost once it changes, there remains some residual value, after the fact. From calmly walking down the road to being flattened by an errant driver, the change in your context happened pretty quickly. Knowing you were about to be hit would have been momentarily useful to you, but then suddenly it became irrelevant: until sometime later, when the circumstances around changing context become valuable as evidence.

Figure 7.4: Predictive analytics market forecast ($ billions)

In mechanical engineering we talk about a concept called waste heat. Waste heat is energy left over after much of it is used to produce work. We heat up water to make steam, in order to spin a turbine to produce electricity. The superheated steam passes through the turbine, and its heat energy is turned into mechanical energy. The best designs try to take *all* of the added heat out of the steam and convert *all* of it into electricity, but the first two laws of thermodynamics tell us that we can never convert 100 per cent. There's always a little heat left over after the conversion takes place.

Smart utility companies use this left over heat, this waste heat, to do other useful things like heating homes, so there's some residual value there after all. The same goes for context information. When

Uber sent me a pickup, my need to be picked up, or my context, no longer matters. The *second* taxi to show up received no value from my context, and I received no value from them. The transaction is over, and the conversion of context-to-value is over. Or is it?
The context about my need for a ride may be valueless one second after I was picked up, but there's some waste heat still left in that information. My old, expired context may still have *some* value to the vehicle that made the pickup, and even to the car that arrived one second late. But *only if* someone bothers to analyze that data, turn it into information and then into knowledge, like where to better pre-position cars in the future, or who to track online in order to send them a predictive coupon for their next ride. The waste heat of context can be harvested and put to use, through the processes of analytics – the third element of the Digital Trinity.

This explains the tremendous interest in predictive analytics, prescriptive analytics, and what I've termed persuasive analytics. (The industry uses prescriptive analytics to describe what they see coming after predictive analytics, but for me that's far too passive for what we will see.)
Organizations are highly focused on predictive, prescriptive and persuasive analytics, because they are looking for value in their data. But looking for value in old data and old content is played out; that song has been sung and we've all moved along from there, or at least the content kings and Jerks have.

No, the real value in these analytics is trying to harvest the waste heat in old context data. Doing so allows you to better predict your customers' future contexts, so that you are more likely to meet them there. In this way, and *only* in this way, can you surpass the universe's inherent speed limit: the speed of light. Predictive analytics is so compelling because, when done correctly, it is the only way we mere mortals will ever travel faster than the speed of light – the speed of context.

Content is dead ... Context is now king, as are the Jerks who rule it!

Chapter Summary:

1. The focus of the first 30 years of the Internet has been the creation and distribution of content. This created content giants such as Amazon, Google, Microsoft, Twitter and Facebook.
2. The next revolution in the Internet will be the creation and use of context. Context is information that describes other information, and defines its place in space and time.
3. The next wave of leading companies will be those that collect, analyze, apply and monetize context.
4. Jerks such as Uber, Simple Bank, Airbnb and Waze are context engines, rather than content engines.

Chapter Eight: Jerks Eliminate Friction

"In skating over thin ice our safety is in our speed."- Ralph Waldo Emerson

"I'd rather learn from one bird how to sing than teach ten thousand stars how not to dance."- E.E. Cummings

In the previous chapter we discussed how, to create value, context is the new sheriff in town. We also discussed how the value of context is fleeting. It can disappear in an instant. In this way, context is like rainfall in a desert. It's the thing that you value most, but it evaporates in an instant, leaving you high and dry. To extract value from context you need to see it, understand it, and act on it as fast as it comes and goes. If you don't you will never be able to harness it properly, and you'll likely frustrate yourself, your organization and your customers as you fumble about trying to catch up.

As a result, being a Jerk is all about speed, and if there's one thing that speed hates, it's friction. Friction saps the energy out of whatever it touches. It creates heat instead of movement. With enough friction, you can permanently bind two objects (google 'friction stir welding' if you're intrigued by this), or destroy it outright (regrettably, the cause of the loss of the Space Shuttle Columbia in 2003). To be a Jerk, you need to do anything and everything you can to eliminate friction in every transaction with your products, organization and customers. Do that, and you just might be able to keep up with context as its value pops from place to place and time to time.

Connecting in the Early Analog Era

Analog companies don't understand this, and with good reason: The Analog Trinity is focused on protecting and growing capital. Consider this Trinity's elements: Bureaucracy, Processes and Rules.

These are all mechanisms of communication, and so it should be apparent that communication is the key to controlling capital. Throughout the Industrial Revolution and Capitalist Era, improving one's control and acquisition of capital meant improving control of communications. In order to keep up-to-date books on what I own, I need to be fed a constant stream of timely information.

When the Industrial Revolution first began, information was very limited and it moved very slowly. At the time, a horse was a really fast means of communication. To travel 20 kilometers (or 12 miles) in a day meant you were really burning rubber, or rather, hay. If you wanted to send a letter to your family on the other side of the Atlantic, it would take a month to get there and their reply would take at least another month. In those days information was hand-written into ledgers and books, and those books would be balanced by the use of correspondence that took weeks or months to reach their destinations.

In the early Capitalist Era, being a branch manager meant exactly what it sounded like: you managed a branch on a tree of capitalism. That branch was hanging off a limb that was connected to the trunk of your organization. You were expected to use any number of leaves (capital) and water pumped up from its roots (raw material) along with sunlight and oxygen (production inputs) to create what the tree needed to grow (more capital). The goal was for the tree to better connect its roots and its leaves, in order to improve its chances of survival.

With the advance of the Industrial Revolution, our ability to communicate accelerated. As the United States acquired (or conquered, if you prefer) California, there was a dramatic need to communicate between the capitalists in the East and the gold miners, merchants and the others who preyed upon them in the new West. The bankers back in New York, Boston and Philadelphia (and London, Paris and Amsterdam, for that matter) needed to keep their books about their capital up to date, and this meant that they needed a steady stream of information on the status of their California investments. This need for speed led to two innovations that are famous to this day: the clipper ship and the Pony Express.

Clipper Ships: The 19th Century's FedEx

Clipper ships were the Federal Express of their day. They were sailing vessels dialed up to 120 percent. In their time they were the Concorde, the Space Shuttle, and the Starship Enterprise all rolled up into one; the pinnacle of what humans could achieve with wood and sail. Clipper ships were long, slim, rakish sailing vessels that carried an acre or more of sails, all optimized for one purpose: speed. Typically, they were twice as fast as traditional ships and for more than 100 years their speed was legendary. One such ship, the Flying Cloud, held the record for the fastest transit between New York and San Francisco around South America. It took her 89 days and eight hours to complete the journey back in 1854. A record that stood for more than a century.

Figure 8.1: Clipper ships, 19th Century time machines

You never get something for nothing, and Clippers sacrificed efficiency and utility in the name of speed. Clippers carried little cargo compared to less speedy vessels of the time. Also, because they carried so much sail, they required much larger crews, further reducing their cost efficiency. Nonetheless, clippers were in high demand. Why? Because clippers weren't just ships, they were time machines to those who used them. They were the souped-up, lightning-powered, 1.21 jigawatt DeLoreans of their day, able to cut weeks or even months off the time required to communicate with, and maintain control of, people's capital.

As with FedEx, early capitalists used a clipper when it absolutely, positively had to get there … before the end of the year. Using a clipper was much more expensive than traditional naval transport, but for many capitalists the added cost was worth it. Bankers in America's East needed to keep tabs on their investments in the American West. European bankers needed to keep tabs on their investments in their colonies, spread all over the globe. Given the constraints of their contemporary technology and the Analog Trinity, paying for clipper service was well worth the expense. But, it was awfully hard to pull together a quarterly report when it took four quarters to send out and receive your request for status. At a time when an interoffice memo took a year to make the rounds, you tended to invest a lot more in its drafting. And you needed a representative, the dreaded Regional Vice President, on the other end of the communication to assess, implement, and report back.

So, clippers were time machines used to shorten the time required to control the flow of capital, as proven by the ships' manifests of the day. The dominant cargoes carried by clippers were: a) people (managers and users of capital); b) tea, coffee, tobacco and opium (goods with high capital value); c) silver and gold bullion (real capital); and d) the mail (information). This is pretty close to the desires of our present day: sex, drugs, money and rock n' roll. Clippers carried people, capital and information as capitalists, separated by thousands of miles in space and months in time, struggled to stay in control.

The Pony Express: The 19th Century's UPS

Catalyzed by the same need for faster control, the Pony Express began in 1859 as an additional means of speeding up communications between the East and the new West of the United States. The Express consisted of a chain of more than 100 way stations connecting Missouri and Sacramento, through which letters and other goods were carried. Rather than using stagecoaches (the over-the-road shipping containers of their day), the Express used individual riders mounted on single horses. The stations were spaced such that a horse could just reach the next station at a full run, without falling over dead from exhaustion. The riders would carry their cargo on their persons, and would run each horse to the next station, where the cargo would be transferred to a fresh rider and horse.

Figure 8.2: Pony Express route map

Naturally, riders could carry very little cargo, and the cost per ounce was relatively enormous. But the Express guaranteed coast-to-coast communication in 10 days, truly the disruptive time machine of its era. The Pony Express was so massively disruptive, it removed *so much* friction from the process of communicating under the Analog Trinity, that we still talk about it with awe and respect today. This is remarkable, because the Express was actually a commercial failure. It was shut down only 19 months after it began, eclipsed by an even more effective time machine, the telegraph.

Relentless Acceleration of the Analog

In the century following the brief appearance of the Pony Express, tremendous wealth and energy was expended on trying to speed up communications, i.e., to reduce friction in the economy and get things moving along smartly. Railroads were at least as valuable for communication as for transportation and logistics. The telegraph both caused a revolution and literally prevented one. President Lincoln provided direct oversight and command of the Union Army in the American Civil War through a steady stream of telegraphs to his generals. The telegraph in turn was eclipsed by the telephone and again the nature of our communications, and our ability to optimally control capital, accelerated dramatically.

Figure 8.3: President Lincoln used telegraphs to control his forces in the American Civil War

By World War II, the radio completely changed battlefield strategies and tactics. Generals could issue orders directly to lowly lieutenants or sergeants in real time, circumventing layers of bureaucracy and centuries of tradition. Similarly, executives could call their subordinates a few floors below, or a few states away, and get immediate responses to their questions. Imagine! Fifty years earlier, that same capitalist would have had to wait more than a year for a response. Suddenly, people were annoyed if they had to wait 10 seconds for someone to answer the new-fangled talkie-box sitting on their desk (their telephone). It's no accident that capitalism's explosive growth in the 20th century coincided with the vast increase in the speed of our communications. The latter was a prerequisite for the former.

Acceleration via Automation

As I have shown, the invention and deployment of information technology further sped up the Analog Trinity. Suddenly we had tools that could calculate, summarize and communicate facts thousands or even millions of times faster than humans, and we could communicate those facts at the speed of light. This was an enormous advance for Analog companies, as they found that they had the tools to improve their communications (and hence their control of their capital) by several orders of magnitude. In the 1950s and 1960s computers were huge, slow, and expensive. Nevertheless, a room-sized computer with less computing power than a modern refrigerator still managed to vastly out-perform a few thousand accountants busily keeping books by hand.

Figure 8.4: an IBM 360 mainframe computer from the 1960s

These improvements in the speed and efficiency with which capital could be controlled, exposed a new issue for organizations: misalignment. The new communications technologies enabled vastly faster control of capital, yet the mechanisms of control had not advanced at the same speed. Organizations found that the old Analog Trinity of Bureaucracy, Processes and Rules which had served them so well in the sails-and-stallions era couldn't possibly keep up with the capabilities brought on by the silicon-and-spreadsheets era of the computer. In a time when communications were exceedingly slow, you needed the Analog Trinity to maintain control of your capital. Once our ability to communicate reached the speed of light, these old communication structures couldn't keep up. They prevented ongoing acceleration because of organizational friction.

It's Getting Hot in Here

As stated earlier in this chapter, when friction acts against something in motion, some of that motion is converted into heat. For people following the structures of the Analog Trinity, heat is exactly what they felt as these digital technologies were deployed around them.

Telecommunications and computers allowed information to flow instantly between people rather than in days, weeks or even months. Now they were expected to respond to incoming information at a speed unthinkable to them just a decade or two before. As business people had PCs on their desktops, many of them rebelled at the inhuman pace of expectations that automation was placing upon them. By the 1980s Analog business people were starting to feel a digital burn and suddenly the heat was on, as pointed out by the Eagles' musician Glenn Frye in his famous song *'The Heat is On'* from that era.

With automation, Analog practices such as meetings, reviews, approval processes, business rules, sign-offs, authorizations and so on not only looked out of place, they began to create massive friction. Every step in our Analog processes and every edict made by our Analog rules were designed to prevent the misuse of far-away capital. Without direct and timely oversight, people needed to be constrained in what they could do. This was the purpose of the Analog Trinity: control and predictability.

As soon as direct and timely oversight was enabled through information technology, those same mechanisms went from providing control to generating friction. And the better we became in monitoring ourselves, the more obvious the loss of speed and value became, due to these frictional losses.

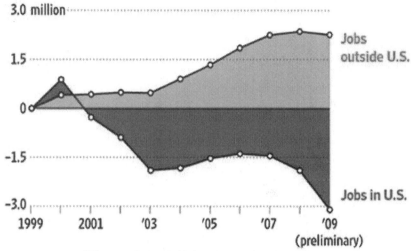

U.S.-based multinational companies added jobs overseas during the 2000s and cut them at home. Cumulative change since 1999

Figure 8.5: Offshoring of U.S. jobs

Our efforts to deal with this mismatch in speed were discussed in Section One, so we won't revisit them here. It's sufficient to say that here, at the start of the Information Era, Analog Trinity constructs like committees, authorizing signatures, approval processes and policy manuals look like the friction-causing relics that they are. These Analog throwbacks now slow down communications and cause friction. They turn information into waste heat, in the form of expended capital, lost time and the destruction of the value inherent in context.

Digital Super Lube

Jerks avoid these sources of friction like the plagues they are. Jerks hold meetings like other people hold dead skunks, with revulsion. Jerks are as likely to convene a tiger team to reengineer a business process as they are to lick a live sparkplug. Jerks review policy manuals with the same relish that other people contemplate a weeping sore. Jerks recognize that any delay in responding to contextual information is a loss of treasure. What slows down their ability to respond to context creates friction and destroys wealth.

Jerks avoid the Analog Trinity because they recognize the friction inherent in this centuries-old structure. Instead, they use the Digital Trinity to hunt down and kill sources of friction, in order to approach and, where possible, exceed the speed of context.

Chapter Summary:

1. Capitalism uses the Analog Trinity to control capital. Jerks use the Digital Trinity to set information free.
2. Information wants to move as fast as possible, up to and even surpassing the speed of light (through predictive analytics).
3. Jerks do whatever they possibly can to remove barriers to speed in their Analog Trinity, in order to work to Digital Trinity speeds.

Chapter Nine: Jerks Replace Chains with Webs

"We live in a society exquisitely dependent on science and technology, in which hardly anyone knows anything about science and technology."- Carl Sagan

"To be free is not merely to cast off one's chains, but to live in a way that respects and enhances the freedom of others."- Nelson Mandela

Jerks don't pay much attention to the rules everyone else follows. It's not that they're rude. They just live in a different world view. This philosophy extends to things that Analogs have taken as 'laws' for a century or more, and which they dutifully follow to a 'T.' Among the rules and laws ignored by Jerks is the notion of value or supply chains.

Jerks recognize that chains are good to hold things down and keep them in place. Chains are restraints, shackles, impediments, accumulated over time like those dragged about by Jacob Marley in Dickens' tale, *A Christmas Carol*. Jerks realize that no matter how streamlined, efficient, automated and 'lean' you make your chain, its ultimate point is to hold *you* down and control *you*.

So when they need to get something done, Jerks build, nurture and leverage value webs, or nets, rather than chains. Webs and nets are about harvesting, not binding. You use webs and nets to capture and collect things that are free, rather than to control things that are not. Jerks aren't interested in tying information down, or trapping it for some later purpose. Rather, they recognize that information is something to be harvested, like fish from an ocean or fruit from an orchard, and that webs or nets are far more effective.

Taylorism: A Victory for Capital, a Defeat for Humanity?

All capital-centric organizations follow the same path of value creation. They take in raw materials, they process it in some way to increase its value, and then they distribute it to their customers who pay a premium for the cost of conversion and delivery. Products that go through very little conversion are called commodities. For commodities, the value to the customer is mostly in delivery. The commodity itself is largely unchanged.

Figure 9.1: Jacob Marley, supply chain expert

Other items require a great deal of conversion before they meet a customer's need. These items are called 'finished goods' and command a premium for the cost of conversion. The highest form of conversion is from commodities into services, where practically all of the customers' demands are met in intangible ways despite lots of input of raw materials, labor and capital.

This process is called the Supply Chain. The chain analogy is appropriate, because of dear old Henry Ford and his quaint-jock sidekick, Frederick Winslow Taylor. In the late 1800s the world was still getting accustomed to capital-centricity, and Henry and Freddy had a problem. They needed the most effective way to combine the inputs of raw material, capital and labor.

This wasn't a trivial matter in the late 1800s. Massed capital was creating heretofore unavailable technologies, like steel, electricity, rubber, oil, and synthetic chemicals. It was also a time marked by a great migration of labor, mostly from the Old World to the New

World. Immigrants escaped the decaying remains of the Old as the gentry struggled to hold on to their legacy of land-based power, governed by the Dirt Trinity (Heredity, Edicts and Violence). Capitalists were keen to put this pool of unskilled labor to work.

Figure 9.2: Frederick Winslow Taylor, father of the time and motion study

Taylor was an economist who wanted to understand how to most efficiently combine this unskilled labor with new technologies and new sources of raw materials. He used time and motion studies to analyze every movement made by workers as they worked. Taylor sought to eliminate wasted time, effort and cost.

Taylor's work led to the invention of the assembly line, where workers stayed in one place and goods moved past them. This was the opposite of the previous practice of workshop-based production, where the goods stayed put and workers swarmed over them. Workshops were great for skilled craftsmen, looking to make items of fine quality that required exacting knowledge and skill. They were terrible, however, for making huge volumes of mass produced trinkets, using tools that were worth more than an unskilled laborer's monthly wages.

Some felt that Taylor's work was dehumanizing. That was the point.
He performed his studies with the knowledgeable yet indifferent eye
of a goat herder or cattleman, viewing the workers as another form
of livestock. Variables such as skill, knowledge, intuition and
problem solving, so valuable in a workshop-oriented economy, were
to be eliminated because they were variable. Taylor was big on the
notion of keeping everyone on the same page, even if that page was
merely average. Capitalists like profits, but they like predictability
even more. This is the way it is in the Analog Trinity.

Freddy's work created the foundation of both industrialization and
unionization. The former intended to maximize return on capital,
while the latter was an unintended response to the appalling working
conditions that resulted. Through the end of the 19th century, labor
and capital battled passionately, viciously and often violently as
capitalists adopted the new religion of Taylorism.

Around this time the automobile was born. When most people of the
era first saw an automobile, they were horrified, mystified and
mesmerized, likely in equal parts. Early vehicles were built using the
workshop model, because people were still trying to figure out the
basic mechanics of the thing, and that required craftspeople of high
skill. As a result, early automobiles were the playthings of the rich
who enjoyed driving about at several times the speed of common
folks' horse-drawn carriages (there's that pesky value-of-speed thing
again).

Henry Ford came along near the turn of the 20th century with the
disruptive notion that every person should own and enjoy these new-
fangled transports, including his own employees. Many people know
Henry Ford as an innovator in applying Taylor's production-line
methods to the previously workshop-oriented auto industry. It seems
far fewer people know of Ford's dedication to making the lives of
his workers better by paying them well above standard wages, giving
them medical care, cafeterias and daycare. Capitalists also own
media channels; they tend to emphasize aspects of history that
promote their own thinking, and discount the things that don't.

Ford, the Model 'T,' and the Invention of the Supply Chain

Ford put his contrarian plan to work, and it proved to be wildly successful. His first mass produced car fit consumers to a 'T,' and they were priced so that almost everyone could afford one. A key to this low price was production efficiency, unlocked through Taylorism and the assembly line. But for assembly lines to work, they had to be fed a steady diet of material, giving birth to the supply chain.

Figure 9.3: Henry Ford's Model 'T', available in any color as long as it was black

A goal of the supply chain was to ensure that production inputs operated at 100 per cent utilization. The line had to keep moving, and to maximize output, the workers could not stop working. Ford soon found that it was far cheaper to maintain a little extra supply of parts rather than shut down his production line in their absence. So Ford set out to ensure a reliable stream of raw materials.

Economies of Scale and of Scope: 'Laws' of Capitalism

Initially, this was achieved through massive vertical integration of his supply chain. Ford gobbled up the means to make all of the things he used to make his cars, including rubber tree plantations, iron ore deposits and transport ships. He collected these assets (this capital) under one roof and hired an army of bookkeepers and accountants to keep track of it all. Soon, Ford had created a classic, post-Industrial-Revolution, capital-centric corporation, The Ford Motor Company. It was enormous, profitable and powerful, and it prayed at the altar of the Analog Trinity.

Like other massive corporations, the Ford Motor Company sought to exploit economies of scale and scope. Producing more from a given capital investment meant a greater return on that investment, i.e., capturing economies of scale. The more you control all of the inputs required by your operations, the more you can leverage similar inputs (labor, bookkeeping or electricity, for instance) across all of those inputs. This gives each an advantage of shared scale, leading to what's known as economies of scope. These concepts are so central to capitalist thinking that many people believe that these are economic 'laws.' This is the kind of stuff I was taught in college and graduate school at the end of the 20th century.

Information: Once Again, the 'Bug' in the Ointment

While it started out as a war between different economic, political and social systems, World War II ended as a war of manufacturing and logistics. In many ways the Axis powers of Germany, Italy and Japan out-fought and out-thought the Allies. But fortunately for society, the Allies out-produced and out-shipped the Axis, thanks to a century of capitalistic growth. In fighting and winning World War II, western companies had optimized the production of war-making materials and the logistics required to get them to the fight. America and her allies had perfected the first synchronized, output-maximizing, globally integrated supply chain, in order to save their way of life.

As this production and logistics juggernaut retooled for the relative peace of the Cold War (a term so oxymoronic to us today that it's practically politically incorrect), information technology again reared its head. Once again, all elements of the Analog Trinity rely upon the transfer of information. Computers kept much better and faster track of production inputs and of products as they were demanded. From these humble post-war beginnings grew an enormous industry that was soon called Supply Chain Management (SCM).

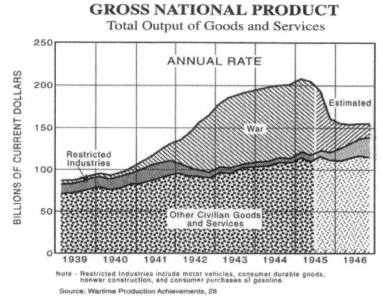

Figure 9.4: American GDP growth during World War II

Whip Me, Beat Me, Make Me Buy SCM Software

Throughout the 1980s and 1990s, the SCM industry took off as engineers looked to combine Taylor's principles of supply chain optimization with emerging information technologies. I was just starting my career then, and I was swept up in the hype and hysteria that better management of supply chain information would set capital free. The reality is that it tied our organizations to the ground.

I worked on SCM technology projects through the late 20th century. For some, SCM is more of a religion than a technology solution. I, like perhaps millions of other professionals, have been trained, certified, and indoctrinated in the thinking behind supply chains. I was inculcated with the teachings, principles, canons and edicts of Taylorism. I was saturated with its dogma. For almost two decades I used all manner of tools, software, equations, and models to figure out how to better optimize supply chains, i.e., how to better track and utilize capital so it could self-replicate.

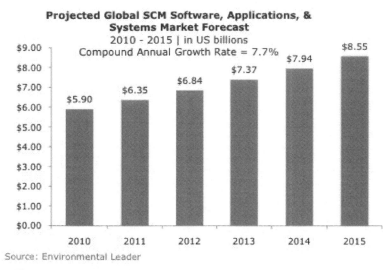

Figure 9.5: Supply Chain Management software market

There's a reasonable amount of sadomasochism involved in designing an effective supply chain; hence the chain analogy is apropos. Nonetheless, SCM systems digitized the Analog Trinity. The chains leading to and from organizations could be better understood, managed and optimized. As the technology improved, more and more people in the supply chain became obsolete. Taylorism in production began to take over the minds of the workers, as well as their bodies.

Shangri La for Capitalists?

In the 1990s the SCM revolution converged with three other global trends, creating a perfect storm of change in how companies optimized their capital. The first of these was globalization, or the freeing up of inexpensive labor in previously closed markets of the Far and Middle East. The second was the lowly shipping container, which contributed vastly to the shrinkage of our modern world. The third was the fiber optic, invented by the technology company

Corning Incorporated, where my father worked in IT for 33 years. These three innovations facilitated the adoption of SCM by Analog companies, which they believed was essential to their survival.

At the end of World War II, Asia was in turmoil. China was being torn apart in civil war. India was struggling with both gaining its independence from its old land-centric masters from Great Britain and the internal stresses of its diverse population. The Middle East and Southeast Asia were also coping with liberation from imperial rule. Korea would be fractured along the 38th parallel. And Russia continued its old imperial ways, wrapped in a cloak of Soviet communism. The result is that the economies and societies of the world's largest land mass were in chaos. This helped America ascend as an economic power.

By the end of the Cold War, Asia was more stable. First China, and then India, opened their factory doors, if not their markets, allowing a third of the world's population to join the global workforce. But their wages were low because there were so many potential workers and so few jobs. The 'Law of Supply and Demand' prevailed. Many Western Analog companies lusted after these vast and untapped pools of labor. Globalization presented an unprecedented opportunity to slash costs and improve returns on capital. If only these cheap workers weren't so damned far away.

The World in a Box

To make these cheap but far-away workers useful, organizations had to figure out how to get stuff to and back from them at low cost. Shipping underwent some innovation during World War II, as getting butter, bullets and boots to the right place at the right time is what won the war. Innovation exploded in the post-war logistics industry, and the biggest game-changer was the simple shipping container.

Before containers, products were shipped in all sorts of shapes, sizes and weights. When a ship pulled into port, dock workers never really knew what to expect. A hodgepodge of cargoes would be hauled off the ship, often by hand and by back, like animals spilling from Noah's Ark. This non-standardization was the biggest barrier to moving things around quickly and easily. The Twenty-foot-long Equivalent Unit (TEU) standardized shipping container solved the problem.

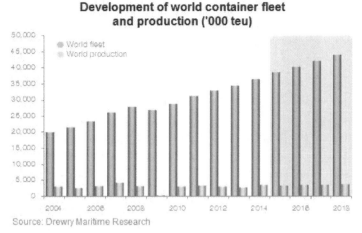

Figure 9.6: Global container shipping infrastructure in TEUs

Once shippers converged on the TEU standard for managing cargo, the industry aligned to this standard. Ports were rebuilt around it, ships were built according to it, trucks and railroads redeployed to adhere to it, and so on. The entire logistics industry suddenly became standardized, efficient and predictable – just what the Analog Trinity ordered!

It took a few decades for full transition to the TEU, as a great deal of capital had to be replaced, redesigned or redeployed. But the move to TEUs slashed the cost of shipping. With TEUs, if it fits, it ships, cheaper and faster than ever before.

TEUs were the Analog Trinity in a box, delivered at precisely the same time as labor markets were opening up in Asia.

Hanging (Up) By a Thread

The last innovation required for globalized supply chains was communications. It was great that cheap labor was available around the globe, and that its output could easily be shipped anywhere. But, capital-centric organizations still needed to keep track and control the whole process. That's what the Analog Trinity required. Global communications hadn't advanced much beyond the telephone and radio of the early 20th century, as anyone trying to make a trans-ocean phone call could attest. In college, my then-girlfriend spent a semester abroad in Europe, and I spent tens of hours every week scooping ice cream at Ben & Jerry's in order to pay for mere minutes of phone time with her on the other side of the Atlantic.

For globalization to work, communications needed a breakthrough. And fortunately, one showed up just in time, in the form of the fiber optic. Fiber optics are long, thin and optically perfect strands of glass. When a laser is shot into the end of the fiber, it bounces back and forth within the fiber and down its length. If the glass is sufficiently perfect, what goes in at one end, such as an email or digitized phone conversation, comes out reasonably unscathed at the other, even over thousands of miles. These beams of light could carry far more information than a big copper wire, which was the 19th century's answer to trans-ocean communications.

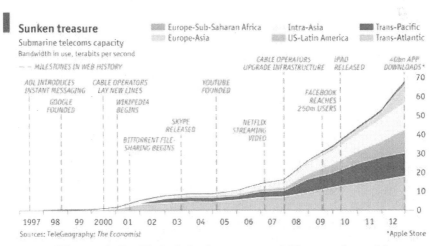

Figure 9.7: Global deployments of fiber optic cable

Corning Incorporated, the century-old glass manufacturer, stumbled upon the fiber optic, almost by accident. Although they work with glass, Corning is really an engineering and science company; they value knowledge and innovation. When their scientists came upon the fiber optic, they unleashed the ability to communicate globally at scale. This happened at the same time the Internet was exploding, shipping containers had been figured out, and labor markets had opened up in Asia. An Outsourcing Trinity had coalesced, consisting of Cheap Labor, TEUs and Fiber Optics, making globalization not only possible, but inevitable.

In Through the Out Door

So began, in the mid-1990s, the outsourcing craze in America. The cost of making and transporting stuff from overseas fell dramatically, at the same time as our ability to control it all accelerated to the speed of light. Outsourcing began as a wave, grew to a swell, then turned into a reverse tsunami, as jobs flowed from America's shores like an enormous riptide. The craze turned into a panic, as American companies collected their jobs and launched them overseas like a Cold War first strike on an enemy. By the mid-2000s the thinking had become that if your production inputs weren't coming from off-shore you were pretty much washed up on the beach.

Lean: The Logistics Singularity

SCM thinking evolved during this process. It moved from statistical process control (SPC) and bill of material management (BOMMs) to continuous process improvement (CPI), Six-Sigma and just-in-time (JIT) logistics. A chain is no stronger than its weakest link, so managers and engineers worked tirelessly to make their chains as strong, stable, and unbreakable as possible. The goal was to lock down the inputs and outputs of production, using the Analog Trinity, in order to maximize the use of capital.

Over time, our chains were made so strong, so reliable and so predictable that we actually were able to eliminate many of their links, and all of their slack. Capitalists flocked to the so-called 'lean' revolution. By the late 1900s our capital was firmly held down by these slack-less, immensely strong, heavily monitored chains, held taut by the constant screw of SCM information, traveling at the speed of light.

Figure 9.8: Global supply command centers look like early NASA mission control

This is largely where Analog companies reside today, with globally optimized value chains delivering raw materials just-in-time to the cheapest workers available in the world. Their outputs are packed into TEUs, and then shipped all over the world, under the watchful eye of a digitized, fiber-optically connected Sauron we call Supply Chain Management. This structure, this Middle Earth of production, this kingdom of control is the final optimization of the inputs and outputs of production defined by Taylor, Ford and other capitalists that resulted from the Industrial Revolution. It is indeed a singularity, the point of perfection that cannot be eclipsed, or so many people currently believe.

Breaking Your Chains

While supply chains are great for an Analog, capital-centric world, they are exactly wrong for the digital, information-centric world we are advancing into. Because I place so much value on context, I'm thankful that the powers that be chose to call our present approach value chains, instead of something else. For, as we transition away from Capital and towards Information, these pathways of capital control will surely hold us in Digital bondage.

Information wants to be free. It needs to be free. When information is constrained, protected or locked down, people cannot access it, consume it and add to it. The processes of consuming, leveraging and correlating data, the basis of creating value in the information age, cannot take place when information is locked down, constrained, chained. Information wants to wander about unfettered, so that it can grow and multiply, like salmon spawn returning to the sea. In the digital sea of the Internet, information grows fat from moving around through social media, creating new ideas, new knowledge and new context as it goes.

On the Internet, there are billions of people helping to fatten up this data. They are sowing the seeds of information, so that companies can reap the rewards of context. They are tending the orchards of Facebook, Twitter, YouTube and Waze, so that the harvest can be made, come autumn.

After some time at sea, information is now rich in value, and ready to be harvested. The fields are ripe with context and the orchards are loaded with fruit, awaiting correlation. This is the time to catch it all in a net, or a web. This is the moment where information, rich in context, must be scooped up in large batches and processed for use (analytics). You need to cast your nets far and wide, capturing as much as you can. You must spread your webs under these trees, capturing all of their context-ripened fruit.

Jerks understand this new perspective, and they follow it to a 'T'. Chains don't capture this harvest; they're linear, inflexible and heavy. You need nets to catch the value of information, which is the source of wealth in the world to come. Jerks use webs and nets, and they cast them wide across the Internet. They use the billions of members of the Internet community as fellow harvesters, and reward them for their assistance in the harvest. Jerks use the Digital Trinity to harvest the free, rather than control the enchained, and this, fundamentally, is how they will come to dominate wealth in the Digital Era.

Chapter Summary:

1. The notion of supply chains has been fundamental to the use of the Analog Trinity under capitalism.
2. Supply chains are designed to ensure that every step in process is used with optimal efficiency.
3. This focus on efficiency and returns on capital investment directly led to and drove globalization of the workforce, trade and communications.
4. Regardless of how much they are optimized, chains are necessarily linear and occur serially.
5. Jerks organize around value nets instead of value chains. Value nets are flexible, dynamic and allow for multiple contributors to act in unison and harvest value, rather than hold it down.

Chapter Ten: Jerks Invert Economies of Scale and Scope

"Nothing recedes like progress."- E.E. Cummings

"Whenever you find yourself on the side of the majority, it is time to pause and reflect."- Mark Twain

If you're a capitalist by training or birth, Chapter 9 may have irritated you. Before proceeding it may be time for a couple of stiff drinks. Check your front door, they may have just arrived, predictively, by drone, compliments of Amazon and your Kindle app!

As I mentioned earlier, Jerks don't follow the 'laws' of economies of scale and scope. Indeed, they hardly acknowledge their existence. They follow a new set of rules constrained and defined by the Digital Trinity instead of the Analog Trinity. In the Digital Trinity, scale and scope do occur. But they're in the background. They're the prerequisites for the Digital Trinity to even exist. As such, scale and scope become almost meaningless. Like gravity, we know they are there, we know they are still important, but we've adapted to them and we pay them no mind.

It's one thing to say that information may someday replace capital, but to some, questioning the 'laws' of economies of scale and scope may seem heretical. Sorry, but I am just getting started.

As I learned as a boy scout, sometimes it's a lot of fun to toss gasoline on a well-fed bonfire. So, here it goes; not only do Jerks not follow the so-called laws of economies of scale and scope, they strive to do the exact opposite, at least locally. How can this possibly be? How can Jerks create what customers want and need without the 'advantages' of size, mass, weight, breadth, girth, overhead, workflows, committees, paperwork, e-signatures, policy manuals, compliance departments, budgets, reports, supply chains, bills of lading, manifests and … you see where this is going, so let's not waste a moment getting there.

Losing for Trying

Economies of scale and scope are falling away as meaningless, even detrimental, because of the first four of the Six New Normals of our world. For review, these are Quality, Ubiquity, Immediacy and Disengagement. What these say is that as long as *someone's* capital delivers what I want, where I want, when I want, perfectly, I no longer care about it. This dismissive attitude about the 200-year-long human struggle to triumph over capital can be pretty annoying, if not insulting.

For generations, business people, scientists, engineers, tradespeople, policymakers and factory workers around the globe have toiled to create our modern, safe, convenient and, ultimately, livable world. From these same people we often hear the immortal, universal generational lament, "People have it so easy these days!" There is some truth to this, as each generation builds upon the successes and failures of its predecessors. "I wish I could walk to school, uphill both ways, in the snow, like grandpa did," said no teenager. Ever!

Figure 10.1: 19ᵗʰ Century school room

For 200 years we have been optimizing our use of the Analog Trinity, approaching perfection in quality, ubiquity and immediacy. Unfortunately, our efforts have been so effective, and our results so successful, that we generated widespread disengagement as a result. Our victories in delivering predictively selected, drone-transported, priced-just-right thingamabobs straight to your door elicit nothing more than a shrug, an LOL, and a "So what?" from disengaged customers. It's enough to make Ebenezer Scrooge yell, "Bah! Humbug!" as he adds to his impending chains.

Capitalists have won an enormous victory for themselves and our society, and they have lost us all as a result.

How could this have happened? How could we all have come so far, only to find out that the score didn't count, and we all get a trophy for participation instead? The answer lies with a quirky, 'mentally unstable' American psychologist who dared to believe that people could be motivated by more than the Dirt Trinity and Analog Trinity gave them credit for.

Maslow's Hierarchy of Needs

Figure 10.2: Abraham Maslow

Abraham Maslow was born in Brooklyn, New York, in 1908, a few blocks away from where my grandparents lived around the same time. He grew up at a time where being a child of Russian Jewish immigrants, unskilled and fresh off the boat, wasn't likely to get you voted as king of the prom. Throughout his childhood, Maslow suffered greatly from the prejudice, scorn and ignorance of others. At the end of the Victorian era a person's psychological and emotional 'safe zone' usually extended only as far as his living room, and then only if Auntie Em wasn't paying a visit.

Given their humble origins, Maslow's parents instilled in him a love of education, and Abraham used books and learning as an escape from his surroundings. He studied psychology in college, at a time when Freud, Skinner and other pioneers in the field were convinced that we were all half a step away from beating each other's brains in. Maslow's view of the world rose above both his upbringing and the dogma of the day, and somehow he managed to see the good in all of us, struggling to come out.

Maslow's work was based upon his belief that humans have needs higher than other organisms. As animals, we still have basic needs that have to be met but, once those have been achieved, we strive for something more. Our consciousness, our awareness of ourselves and each other, lead to appetites that transcend our lungs and our stomachs; we have needs that eclipse the physical world. Maslow created what he called his Hierarchy of Needs to explain how our motivations are ranked.

Figure 10.3: Maslow's hierarchy of needs

Maslow's work formed a basis for understanding both our human need for advancement and our human tendency to take what we have for granted. Let's review the elements of this hierarchy and see if it sounds familiar.

Basic Needs: I Just Wanna Live

At the bottom of the hierarchy come physiological needs: air, water, food and shelter. These needs are the most basic that any living animal can relate to, at least if she hopes to survive from one minute to another.

Safety: Gimme Shelter

Next up the chain are safety needs, which relate to our ability to feel at ease with our environment. Once early humans had adequate access to food, they could sit around their campfires sharing stories about how scared they were by lightning, thunder and the neighboring clan. They started looking for safety and security, discovered that bears had a good racket in cornering the cave market, and they set about putting those bears out on the non-street. And so began life under the Dirt Trinity, and then the Ana ... I digress.

Intimacy: Can't We All Just Get Along?

When we feel secure in our world we again turn our attention to something higher. Next up is our sense of belonging, or of intimacy. Yes, you've heard me use this term before, and yes, it's one of the Six New Normals. This is no accident. Once we took control of Bearsville, we realized that we found ourselves in pretty close proximity to one another. When we were wandering all over the savanna, one-night stands, rude rebuffs and Neanderthal flame-fests were acceptable; the chances of consequences were remote.

Once we were stuck in close proximity with one another, getting along suddenly became important to us. We not only sought connection with one another for the sake of clan stability, we found that we actually liked feeling connected. Soon we craved it, and that connection, that intimacy, that seeking to understand and to be understood, became a higher-order desire in our lives. I've captured this need in the Six New Normals because we still hunger for belonging, intimacy and connectedness; at least that's what our use of Facebook, eHarmony and Tinder seems to indicate.

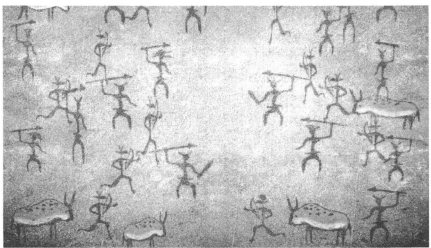

Figure 10.4: Ancient cave art. Is the empty space in the middle a prehistoric 'safe zone?'

Esteem: I'm OK, You're OK

Above our need for connectedness comes our need for esteem. It's not enough to just be part of the clan, most of us want to have more 'likes' than our clan-mates. We want others to think well of us, from which we can start feeling good about ourselves. We need esteem first from others, and then it comes from within ourselves. Once we have enough followers on Twitter, we start to feel as if we actually deserve those followers, and we start to think we actually *are* 'the bomb'! If there's a better explanation for the apparent success of Facebook, Twitter, and Justin Bieber, I have yet to stumble upon it.

Self-Actualization: Is This All That I Am?

Once we get 4.5 stars from our friends, we find that we kind of like the attention, and we start to seek out ways of earning more. And, after we start believing our own profile on LinkedIn or Match.com, we strive to actually live up to our own hype; at least *some* of us do. Self-actualization is the satisfaction we gain by realizing that we are living up to our abilities. We are using our capacities to contribute to the universe, and we get the sense that our existence matters. We gain enormous satisfaction from being our best selves, if and when we get there. Like Intimacy, New Normal Number Six, Purpose, was courtesy of Maslow's great insights.

What May Be Beyond?

Late in his career, Maslow felt that each of us has another level of need, one still higher than achieving our personal best. Maslow, as with any good mentor, postulated that even greater satisfaction can be found in helping others to reach *their* personal bests. In this way, our goals, desires, hopes and dreams can transcend our physical selves, and continue in our eventual absence. If our genes are our legacy to the physical world, our efforts to help others self-actualize become our legacy to our society.

If this mumbo-jumbo sounds eerily like finding correlations in uncorrelated data, you may be as re-freaked-out by Chapter 6 as I am, as I write this.

One Trinity Ends and Another Begins

If you've never read any of Maslow's work, I strongly recommend that you do so. I'm not insisting that you buy into any of his discussion or rationale. Our society will evolve as we collectively see fit, no matter how many committees or analysts tell your shareholders otherwise. If there is one thing that the collective conscious of the Internet tells us, it is what is on all of our minds. In a world built upon the successful application of the Analog Trinity, many of us no longer worry about our own access to food, water and zones safe from ornery predators. (Unfortunately, many of us still do have these worries, as the future isn't evenly distributed. If you worry about these unfortunate people, you're suffering from a mild case of transcendence-hunger … thanks for proving my point!)

Figure 10.5: Americans walk to end hunger

Capitalism wasn't a spontaneous outgrowth of our social and economic evolution. It had to undergo its own birth. The Dirt Trinity had to succeed *before* the Analog Trinity could possibly have a chance to replace it. Capitalism could not have taken off if Imperialism hadn't first reached its natural apex. During the Industrial Revolution entire armies fought to keep the Dirt Trinity in place; they fought for what they believed to be the natural order of things. Revolutionary thinkers in revolutionary armies fought right back, believing as they did in a new world order. In their time, Washington, Jefferson, Lafayette and Cromwell were Jerks of the highest order.

Figure 10.6: Somalis walk to end hunger, too

As soon as capitalism delivered the goods with our lesser needs, we pretty much just moved on, trying to feed our other hungers. As it was with food, water and shelter, once our society's desperate need for McMuffins, Evian and condos was fulfilled, we began to search for something more. This doesn't mean that we don't value these things in their absence. Naturally we do. But, as with oxygen, as long as we have ready access, we forget about it.

Evidence of this transition is all around us. McMuffins are no longer adequate, unless they are gluten-free, cage-free, antibiotic-free, BVGH-free, pork-free, and prepared by recently liberated slave labor from some misbegotten dictatorship overthrown in a bloodless coup; in which case, we will pay double the price. Our water must be tapped from a retreating glacier in the foothills of the Alps, borne to us from there by the fastest transport available. Or, conversely, it must come from our own well, dug through the sub-basement of our eight-story brownstone walkup and filtered through cheesecloth, woven from the donated hair of local farmers, in order to minimize our global impact. Again, we'll pay double.

10.7: Millennial Trend: Everything free?

We trade in our over-priced, thrice-mortgaged, uninsulated, oil-heated condo for a refurbished, solar-powered, evaporation-cooled shipping container that's been transformed into 75 percent of a decent apartment; and we pay double for the privilege.

The behaviors we see all around us may not make sense to us, because we are seeing with capitalist's eyes. The American Revolution made absolutely no sense to the landed royalty of the era, because they saw it with imperial eyes. Same is same, only now we are the ones participating in the disruption. We are the ones surrounded by Jerks with new ideas. Like the rules of handing down power under the Dirt Trinity, everything is relative.

Putting Maslow to Work in the Digital Era

Jerks don't live in the first 99.999 per cent of the normal curve; they leave that to the capitalists. Instead, Jerks focus on the remainder. In that 0.001per cent of what's left sits the rounding error of our world-class, Six-Sigma, lean-supply-chain, big-data-analyzed, prescriptively monitored, real-time-tracked, fast-tracked-and-tiger-teamed efforts at optimizing our control and use of capital. In that tiny minority lies the sediment left after we have stripped-mined all of the data we have, following all of the processes and rules laid out by the Analog Trinity, as faithfully applied by our bureaucracies. In this castaway, this chaff of the Analog Trinity, lies the gold yet to be harvested through the Digital Trinity.

The Dis-Economies of Scale and Scope

Jerks invert economies of scale and scope by using the scale and scope already deployed in the world to create the mass customization that people have discussed for 20 years. By collecting, correlating and applying huge volumes of contextual information, Jerks are able to understand the unique, deep-seated, qualitative needs of each individual, and deliver exactly what each of their hearts desire, instantaneously. They focus upon our higher-order appetites, according to Maslow, and they feed them in exactly the way that each of us, individually, care to be fed.

This couldn't possibly work through Analog Trinity techniques, unless you're operating a church. Indeed, this connection should make you pause for a moment. But with others delivering to our physical needs through the effective application of capital, Jerks focus on catering to our psychological needs through the effective application of information. A meal feeds our bodies. Christmas brunch, last Iftar, Shabbat dinner or a Diwali curry feed our souls.

Jerks understand that the game has changed. They understand that society has moved on from our simpler wants and needs, and we now seek out something more. The victory of capitalism has sown its own downfall, and Jerks are now lining up to bring in the harvest of the information cast aside as worthless under the foremanship of the Analog Trinity. Like soul food to slaves, in what the master casts aside as worthless, others find the ingredients for something delicious, rich, different and fulfilling.

Mobility, Social Media and Analytics; comparing the Digital Trinity to soul food feels strangely appropriate because, just like well-made grits and greens, the more humanity you put into them, the more they feed the soul.

Chapter Summary:

1. As Maslow points out, basic human needs, once satisfied, merely lead to the need to satisfy ever higher needs. We're now into self-gratification, self-awareness, self-actualization and a whole lot of other narcissistic 'stuff'. The preponderance of 'selfies' proves the point.
2. Analog organizations successfully use economies of scale and scope in meeting customers' basic needs.
3. In the vast majority of products and services industries, near perfection (or what is perceived as close enough) has been achieved. The problem is that now that perfection is expected, and customers have other needs to be met.

4. Jerks satisfy customers' *specific* needs, in defiance of economies of scale and scope. In this way Jerks achieve greater customer engagement and satisfaction, and can charge significantly more for this great delivery of value.

Chapter Eleven: Jerks Sell With and Through, Not To

"Nothing will work unless you do."- Maya Angelou

"The world is full of willing people; some willing to work, the rest willing to let them."- Robert Frost

Chapter 9 contrasted value chains with value webs. Value chains are linear, heavy and constraining. Webs and nets tend to be flexible and lightweight. They contain, rather than constrain. Conceptually, this comparison extends to those being hunted and bound. In some circles we call them customers.

I use this language purposefully, because the words we use are reflections of our thinking. Analog companies 'seek out' their customers with 'targeted' advertisements intended to 'score' points with them, and 'convince' them to buy from us. When viewed through the language they use, most Analog companies sound more like mob assassins or confidence men than businesses. They view their customers as merely the final link in their value chains (or 'marks' for a bullet, take your pick). Being at the end of a chain generally indicates that you're being confined – like a dog, or a prisoner, or a trucker's wallet.

Oh sure, Analog companies shower customers with all kinds of promises, flattery and coupons, but at the end of most days customers are just another tick-mark in a spreadsheet. Regardless of what their rhetoric or their Facebook site says, for capital-centric companies, customers are the end of the line. Customers mean revenues, which mean the desired conversion and expansion of capital has been achieved and the chain is complete.

Jerks don't use chains. They use nets. This is an entirely different metaphor, and for good reason. Jerks know that their customers aren't just customers, they're suppliers too. For Jerks, customers are the people who create correlations. They are the source of compounding wealth in the Information Age, as discussed in Chapter

6. Without customers, Jerks don't have suppliers. And without suppliers, Jerks wouldn't have customers. Rather than sticking customers at the end of a chain, Jerks work with customers to create a net or web of value, which is then shared by all.
Jerks don't sell *to* anyone. They sell *with* and *through* their customers, who they see more as partners than prisoners. This sounds like a simple notion, but its impact is profound. Let's dig into this a little deeper to see how the approaches differ.

Figure 11.1: Common uses of chains

Selling to Customers: Life at the End of the Chain Gang

Analog companies do their thing by converting capital into something else of value, then selling that result to customers. Once the sale is made, the company recovers its capital costs and, if it's successful, a little something extra. Analog companies almost always make sure that each transaction results in a gain in capital, called profits. Indeed, they measure this metric to death. I have done hundreds, if not thousands, of business models (in Excel, of course) in my career, typically with the same goal in mind: Find unprofitable transactions and eliminate them.

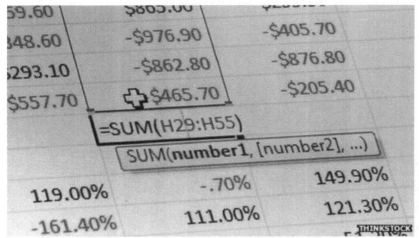

Figure 11.2: Most of the world runs on Excel spreadsheets. Are we better off?

This is linear thinking at its finest, and it is a longstanding tradition of capital-centric companies. Recall the discussion of good old Mr. Ford and his sidekick Mr. Taylor in Chapter 9? Recall the invention of the assembly line, and the decades of effort invested in making everything flow into that line? There's the source of your linear thinking. For more than a century we've trained ourselves to believe that this was the correct way to think.

In this thinking, every product that drops off the end of a production line must drop into the hands of a waiting customer, at a profit. If for any reason the next item to fall off the line doesn't have a customer waiting for it, it should not have been made in the first place. You should have stopped the production line before you started, and made sure that you didn't waste capital by putting things on the line that you didn't really need. Ah, linear thinking, logically flowing from and reinforcing the chains that bind us.

When Analog companies look at customers, they see end points to their Trinity. Their bureaucracies extend to the customer, but no further. Their processes lead to customers, then end. The Analog Trinity is about creating and then severing connections with customers, once the company has made its money.

Adding Dimensions Adds More Chains

Some companies have grown a bit more sophisticated than this, and they realize their customers just might buy something from them more than once. Aha! Repeat customers, the Holy Grail of value chains. With repeat customers, I don't just hook you up to the end of one of my chains, oh no, I can bind you down with two, three, even dozens of chains, Jacob-Marley-style! If the cost of getting an initial customer is very high (and generally it is) and the cost of getting a repeat customer is lower (generally it is), then repeat customers create greater profits and capitalists win (generally).

The beauty of repeat customers is that they take capitalists out of their one-dimensional world of linear chains, and they introduce a second dimension to the equation: time. If you buy from me once, that's good. If you buy from me every day, week or month, I now can use the dimension of time to see that I've made more money from you than I did the first time.

This is why Analog companies started to keep track of their customers. They did so only when they were extending credit to their customers, since this was a capital control necessitated by the Analog Trinity. Eventually, some enterprising young MBA graduate figured out that customers who used more credit to make more purchases somehow generated more profits, and the world of financial consulting was born.

Soon, companies tried to keep track of all kinds of information on their customers, their buying habits and their needs, so that they could create and keep repeat customers. It wasn't long before coupons, buyers' clubs and other mechanisms of retail bondage were conceived and deployed. Green Stamps, for those of you who have never heard of them, were the 'flash sales' and 'exploding coupons' of their day.

Jerking Before Jerking Was Acceptable

As computers took off, companies had the ability to collect more and more customer data, and smart companies did so with every chance they had. Radio Shack was one of the early innovators at this game, as anyone who shopped there back in the 1980s or 1990s would recall. Radio Shack was a huge believer in collecting customer data at the point of sale, and during the beginning of the computer era, every store had a desktop computer.

Their sales associates were trained to capture as much information as possible from every customer, in every transaction, because they believed that this information would be valuable somehow, someday. For shoppers, this was insanely annoying, but we tolerated it because the Shack was the only game in town if you needed parts to make your own flux capacitor, or whatever.

Unfortunately for them, Radio Shack acted like a Jerk before the world was ready. By 2015, Radio Shack became another victim of the Great Retail Polarization Neckdown, a process I described in *Data Crush*, and they were forced into bankruptcy. If you had visited Radio Shack in the few years before their closing, you probably felt pretty alone in there. I know I did! Their business model fell victim to several of the New Normals, as electronics tinkerers died off and were replaced instead with people who wanted drones that would self-assemble, as well as self-navigate.

Interestingly, as Radio Shack moved through the bankruptcy process in 2015, creditors looked to recover whatever they could of their capital. In a news release at the time, it was reported that the creditors were all fighting over the same thing. They weren't fighting over the land (their stores) or the capital (inventory, cash or goodwill). They were fighting over Radio Shack's decades of customer data, captured one transaction at a time, starting with old Commodore 64 laptop computers in the early 1980s.

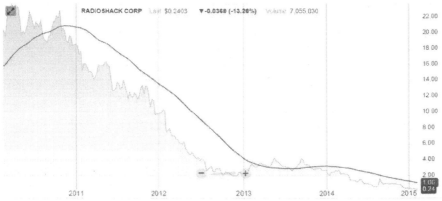

Figure 11.3: Radio Shack financial performance, at the end

The False Prophet of CRM

Adding the dimension of time to measuring customer profitability really took off in the late 1990s. Technology companies invented a new class of software, called Customer Relationship Management (CRM), which was designed to ensure that once customers were shackled to the end of a value chain, they stayed there. CRM software became a sort of mugshot catalog for the customer police. It allowed companies to identify their usual suspects, and from time to time, haul them into the hoosegow to shake them down, converting their cash into profits for the Analog company.

The vision behind CRM was that using all of the time-varying purchasing data about customers would allow capital-centric companies to find better ways of getting them to buy again. They would seek out and lock in profit-maximizing repeat business by ending more and more value chains with the same customer. Really advanced CRM systems captured customer data that began to look downright creepy to early companies. It was stuff like customers' birthdays, number of people in their household, whether they were married, and other crazy, non-value-chain-related information. It was Analog Trinity sacrilege, but some believed it would work.
By the early 2000s there were several major players in the CRM game. While billions of dollars were spent on these systems, there

was a dirty little secret that all Analog companies knew but wouldn't reveal. The stuff really didn't work. Sure, it could keep track of customers' birthdays or the last time each customer made a purchase. But CRM failed to generate any real, repeatable results, in terms of generating more capital returns. More and more Analog companies invested more and more capital in CRM systems to create more capital from each customer. Only, CRM generally did nothing of the sort. These companies collected a whole lot of data from their CRM systems, and little else.

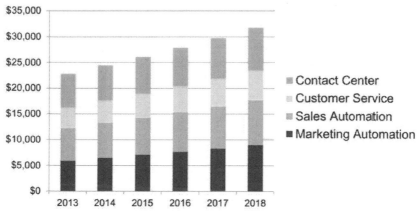

Figure 11.4: The market for Customer Relationship Management (CRM) software

The reason for the failure of CRM is fairly straightforward: it didn't change how customers were engaged. Sure, companies might know that a customer's birthday was coming up, so it was time to mail them a super-coupon, but CRM systems were simply digital repositories of Analog Trinity data. They looked only at the transactions taking place rather than the customer motivations that led to them. CRM only tracked the end points of their value chains, rather than analyzing everything that took place outside of the chain. Like nearly all enterprise information systems born from the pre-Digital-Trinity era, CRM was asking and answering questions about *what* each customer did, rather than *why* they did it. It's an eminently linear approach to the problem, and fundamentally flawed as a result.

Analog companies still invest gigantic amounts of capital in the build-out and maintenance of these linear, chain-monitoring, prison-population-maximizing tools. CRM has been dumped into the cloud, creating the $50-billion, cloud-hype-machine behemoth that is Salesforce.com. (I'm not bitter that Salesforce made good on the same business model of my last startup, which failed during the dotcom crash. Not at all). Salesforce.com made prisoner diagnostics much cheaper, and they also made it better, by allowing companies to track their prisoners' birthdays, favorite color, and breed of dog. Regardless of these stunning innovations in collecting customer insights, Salesforce.com, like all CRM systems, is fundamentally flawed because it still holds to the notion that customers are an endpoint in a chain. In this world, dominated by the Analog Trinity, customers are meant to be held in place and force-fed coupons, tchotchkes, and shallow 'happy birthday' promotions, in order to convert more of their cash into capital.

Building Webs, Casting Nets
Jerks don't build chains, they build webs. Jerks don't forge links, they weave nets. Jerks cast these webs or nets out into the Internet's information ocean and see what they catch. Rather than tying customers in chains, Jerks don't tie down their customers at all. Instead, Jerks invite their customers to help them make and then operate the nets, harvesting value from a sea they both created.

Jerks recognize that their customers are their partners, willing, able and better qualified to help produce correlations that others will value. Jerks recognize that the first step in this process is getting people to use their product or service, to kick off the net-building process. As discussed earlier, early Jerks did this by harnessing the data coming from Analog companies' businesses. Uber sopped up taxi information, Airbnb soaked up property rental information, and so on. These Jerks collected all of the same linear, transactional, structured information as the capital-centric companies did because it was still useful for context. But then, these companies did something different; they put their customers to work. Rather than viewing each customer as the end of a value chain, they saw the customer as the beginning of a node in a value net.

Jerks realize that each customer could be the source of new data about the transactions in which they participated. Customers could provide contextual information about each transaction. From this new data, Jerks find that they can ask an entirely new question of customers: "Why?" Sure, they still ask and answer "What" too, but asking and answering a customer's "Why?" is a game-changer. Two-dimensional transactional data collected by old-school CRM would tell companies *if* their customers will buy again. The multi-dimensional data that customers provide *to* Jerks tells them their customers *will* buy again.

As more and more customers engage with Jerks, they continue to add more and more value to the information at the Jerks' disposal. This is the process of correlation we discussed in Chapter 6. These correlations allow Jerks to continue to grow in understanding the hopes, dreams and motivations of their partner-customers, following the guidelines of the Six New Normals. These questions are remarkably non-linear, and so are their answers. But, only by understanding the unanswered questions in customers' minds can you find out what they value most, and then arrange to give it to them, pronto.

Uber recognized that their value proposition to customers wasn't just getting them to their destination. This is a forgone conclusion. Rather, Uber recognized that a customer's satisfaction in the value chain of getting a taxi came from things completely outside of the chain. Uber realized that good transportation meant that the driver was polite, freshly bathed, didn't talk on their mobile phone while driving and, generally, wasn't Danny DeVito or Robert De Niro. A good ride took place in a clean, safe, well-maintained vehicle, following the rules of the road, more or less. Finally, Uber realized that the Six New Normals mattered to riders, and so they're all appified. The perception of value coming from an Uber ride was maximized by picking the customer up as quickly as possible. A good ride started sooner than a bad ride. Wait time was critical. This was a piece of context data that no taxi company ever thought to measure, because it didn't involve the value chain. Indeed, most of them likely thought that this information was *unmeasurable*, conveniently for them.

Sixty billion dollars – plus – later, it would seem that Uber got it right. They use context data, outside of the value chain of the transactions that they serve, to give their customers what they want, as fast as possible. Then, they have their customers become their partners, by collecting ratings, rankings and feedback on the quality of the experience. Uber collects all of this non-linear, non-transaction, context-rich information and uses it to create correlations where before there were none. Uber is a correlation engine, feeding on context and customer contribution, in order to create new wealth, according to the framework laid out in Chapter 6.

It Takes a Village

To properly use a net, you need a great deal of support. In fishing-oriented human cultures, the entire society works together to take in the harvest. Collectively, they collect the raw material for the nets and help in weaving the materials to make the nets. They all work together, taking turns maintaining the nets and mending any breaks in the line. When fishing, the whole clan gathers the nets into boats and drag them out to sea. Then they all grab parts of the nets, deploy them together, and begin their collective harvest. The whole village participates in creating the nets, taking them into the sea and manning them to collect the catch for the common good of all.

Figure 11.5: Polynesians manning a fishing net

It takes a whole village operating the nets to ensure a bountiful harvest. When you cast a net you never know exactly what you're going to get. Fishing is an occupation of patience and chance. But, if you cast wisely and with knowledge and skill, you have the opportunity to choose whatever you like when the haul comes in, and everyone gains from their share of the harvest.

Breaking Chains, Weaving Nets

The Digital Trinity is about establishing and fostering relationships, which then create value to be harvested. There's tremendous motivation for customers to participate in a value web or net, rather than occupy the end of a chain. In the latter you get force-fed whatever is coming at you, but in the former you get to pick and choose what you like from the results of your collective efforts. Jerks understand that customers are partners, not prisoners. Jerks put customers to work, collaboratively, and then share with them the fruits of this collaboration, to the benefit of all. Well, everyone but the Analog companies, still trying to remember their login credentials for their CRM systems.

Chapter Summary:

1. Analog organizations have applied the Analog Trinity in creating value chains, optimized to create returns on capital. Customers are the last link in these value chains.
2. Jerks don't sell *to* their customers, they sell *with* and *through* their customers. Jerks form value nets, or webs, where they assemble value from a range of sources, and deliver this value to their customers interactively.
3. Examples of this include ratings on merchant sites like Amazon.com, online referrals, etc. Much of the value delivered comes from third parties.
4. Customer Relationship Management systems have historically allowed Analogs to track *what* customers want, but rarely track *why* they want it. Jerks focus on *why*.

Chapter Twelve: Jerks Print Their Own Money

"Money won't create success, the freedom to make it will."-
Nelson Mandela

"The lack of money is the root of all evil."- Mark Twain

Analog companies care about one thing: capital. Capital is the source of their wealth and power, and accumulating capital, in the form of money, is the overriding concern of capital-centric organizations. Of course this is so, because the Analog Trinity is completely aligned towards capital control. Money is the obsession of these organizations. It is their all-consuming concern and, in the end, it's the only thing that matters to them. So say their quarterly reports.

Jerks don't worry quite so much about money for a variety of reasons. Jerks don't need much of their own capital, because Analog companies provide it for them (Chapter 5). Jerks don't need a lot of money, because they get their customers to give them value for free (Chapter 6). Jerks also don't need money in honkin' big chunks, because it's much cheaper to weave a web than it is to forge the link in a chain (Chapter 9). Jerks deliver value in small, esoteric and non-physical ways, which are nonetheless hugely valuable to customers at a subconscious level (Chapter 10). They don't even really orient toward money, because money doesn't really count in the Digital Trinity, except as a means to an end.

All of these factors, in aggregate, support the notion that Jerks do not value money very highly – except when they are shopping for their new, corn-oil-lubricated, solar-powered, eco-friendly, self-driving, non-toxic, fake-leather-lined Ferrari. Hybrid.

No, Jerks don't value money for a lot of reasons, but there's one that stands out as particularly offensive to capitalists. Jerks know how to print their own money. Not counterfeit money, mind you, but real, live, dyed-in-the-paper money. That money has as much recognized value to you and to me as good old greenbacks or euros do in our still-capitalist world. How is this possible? Let's take a gander at the little process called gamification.

Figure 12.1: Jerk dream car

Hey Brother, Can You Make a Dime?

Through most of human history the gold standard was, indeed, a gold standard. This was for the simple fact that money was actually made out of gold (or silver or platinum or copper) in the form of coins. Anyone who has seen an old Disney film or a story about Robin Hood is familiar with this notion of 'money' as physical wealth; for much of the ages of Tools and of Dirt, people placed a lot of value on shiny little objects. Apple Incorporated is so glad that we never really outgrew this obsession!

This physical approach to wealth worked reasonably well, because land is not very portable. Also, the carrying of trinkets and tools as signs of wealth went way back to the Tool Trinity, so we were used to keeping valuable things in pouches tied around our waists. As long as most real wealth was tied up in land ownership, and the supply of precious metals was sufficient to keep up with economic growth, coinage worked great. But, in a world oriented towards physical currencies, when the supply of precious metals runs out, runaway inflation generally begins. This is one of those pesky relationships in economics that is put forth as a 'law.' Poppycock! Correlation does not guarantee causation.

Figure 12.2: Norse antiquities

Based on the 'laws' of supply and demand, running out of a ready supply of precious metals is a fairly bad thing. When wealth changed hands under the Dirt Trinity, it was easier to ship bullion than acreage. Gold and silver represented the dominant 'liquid assets' in a land-oriented society. But, as with machinery, if there isn't oil between the moving parts, things tend to grind to a halt. On many occasions during the Land Era, economies crashed for lack of enough fiscal lubricant.

A Buck Just Isn't What It Used to Be
One approach to this problem is to 'thin out the rations,' or to water down the content of precious metals in your coins and hope that nobody notices. If you mix 10 per cent bad stuff (say lead or tin) with 90 per cent good stuff (gold or silver), you suddenly appear to be richer than you were before. I say 'appear to be' richer with good reason: this only works if you're not caught. This new wealth isn't real, it's an illusion, a fraud. You only get actual wealth if and when you trade that loaded die to someone else, and they accept it in trade for the real thing. Once that occurs your fake wealth becomes real, and you pulled off a cute little heist. A better metaphor for stock markets, and Wall Street in particular, eludes me at the moment.

This went on for centuries, and people who were good at this trick were often referred to as 'alchemists,' or 'wizards.' These were people who were not only good at forging coins of lesser value (... in a forge. Yes, this is where the term 'forgery' comes from), but they could do it without getting caught. Such people were in extremely high demand because they could manufacture wealth out of nothing - sort of like the Facebook of their era. I hate to break it to you, but your friendly neighborhood Merlin or Dumbledore or Gandalf was more than likely a forger by trade. Hire a wizard, water down your treasure with 10 per cent crud, and presto! You're five percent richer than you used to be. (Five percent to the wizard; they don't work for free and they use dragons as their debt collectors.)

Figure 12.3: Ancient Roman coins varied greatly in purity

There is evidence of this cheating throughout human history, as a chemical analysis of coins from ancient Greece, Rome or Egypt shows a diminishing percentage of good stuff as the years rolled on. For example, Roman coins found throughout Europe have purities that vary widely through space and time; there's that pesky context thing again. The farther you were from Rome on a map, and the farther from its imperial peak in time, the less likely it was that there was actually precious metal in your money. Once again this is evidence that people in Scotland, Africa and the Middle East have been literally short-changed for millennia.

New World, New Silver, New Growth

By the Late Middle Ages, much of the world's ready supply of
precious metals had been tapped in the Old World. There were still
mines in operation, but the digging grew constantly harder, and the
technology of the time was hard-pressed to support the demand in a
growing economy. European economies grew a bit stagnant, and the
people there suffered something of a recession - for 500 years.
Fortunately, the enterprising Italian named Christopher Columbus
stumbled upon a 'New World' in 1492, and a new piggy bank was
thus smashed open.

Figure 12.4: Spanish pieces of eight, 16ᵗʰ Century liquid wealth

Both North and South America had enormous supplies of precious
metals on hand, waiting to be mined and minted. It's not that the
people already living there didn't value silver and gold; they did.
Gold's decorative value to these people is well displayed in the
many artifacts that still exist from pre-Columbian times. But to
Original Americans, silver and gold were only mildly valuable, and
weren't the portable wealth that they represented in the Old World.
Many of these societies were either still governed by the Tool
Trinity, or only just making the transition to the Dirt Trinity. The
concept of land ownership was only just beginning to take hold, and
their need for portable wealth was more closely aligned with things
of actual value, like tools, than things with abstract value, like coins.

When Europeans arrived in the Americas, they were drunk with dreams of silver and gold. And these things were there for the taking. In a matter of just a few decades the Spanish found the mother lodes they had dreamed of, and the stripping away of two continents' worth of riches began in earnest. This physical wealth was smelted into bullion and shipped to Europe aboard treasure ships, fat about the middle with Spanish pieces of eight.

This new physical wealth freed the moribund European economy to grow explosively. The Renaissance wasn't just an awakening of the Western mind, it was an enormous expansion of the Western wallet as well. The availability of this new-found liquid wealth fueled the Renaissance, and greased the engine of economic growth that laid the foundations of both the Industrial Revolution and the capitalism through which it was financed.

Paper: A More Portable Gold

Paper money seems to have originated in China in the seventh century AD. It was developed for the same reasons it eventually became popular in Europe: liquidity and portability of wealth. The Chinese economy prospered and grew for more than five centuries through the combination of technical innovation and financial lubrication. Unfortunately, leaders of the day fell into the alchemist's trap. Many forgers printed their own money and hoped that others accepted it at face value. The results, predictably enough, were massive inflation followed by economic collapse. This is the inevitable conclusion of every pyramid scheme in history. This collapse was so painful for the Chinese that they abandoned paper money in 1455 and did not return to it for hundreds of years - and then, only reluctantly.

Those crushed by false pyramids and collapsing bubbles have long memories.

Despite the warning signs from the Far East, Europeans flocked to paper money with vigor. Gold was a drag to carry around, literally, and by the 1700s the general population had figured out most of the alchemists' tricks. As with its early adoption in China, European and American cash was a direct representation of gold. A person holding cash could go to a bank or creditor, hand them a paper bill, and have it exchanged for an appropriate weight of gold bullion. This was and remains to be known as 'the Gold Standard' and directly connected paper money with what was perceived to be 'hard currency' or real wealth.

Figure 12.5: Chinese jiao zi, paper money from the Song Dynasty, from around 1,000 AD

The problem with the Gold Standard was the same problem found by Europe and Asia in the Middle Ages. There was only so much gold and silver to go around. Soon, the wealth of this easily obtained American booty had been absorbed by Europe and the new democracies of the New World. And once again society faced the terrifying pairing of inflation and economic retardation from a lack of portable wealth.

FIAT: Fix it Again, Treasury

In all fairness to the automobiles presently made by Fiat Chrysler (which I would volunteer are some of the best in the world, and many of which I deeply desire as an engineer and gear-head), not so long ago Fiat had a terrible reputation for quality, at least in America. The old quip was that FIAT stood for 'Fix It Again, Tony,' in deference to its poor quality and Romanesque heritage. Fiats were considered to be a terrible investment. They may have looked like other automobiles, and run like other automobiles, but not so long ago whatever you paid for a Fiat was a horrible exchange in value. The car seemed to have been manipulated to appear to be more than it really was, as if it had been watered down by some automotive alchemist to make it look like it was a fair value in exchange.

For economists and investors, the term 'fiat' means something else entirely. Fiat is the term used to describe money that isn't tied to something of real value. It doesn't follow the Gold Standard, or, for that matter, any other standard. Fiat money is that which, by decree of its manufacturer, has some declared value. As long as everyone (or at least someone) agrees to this stated value, the money is worth that much. Presto, changeo! The shortage of gold and silver is solved and the economy is sufficiently 'greased' that it can continue to grow.

Just like it did, for a time, in China, about a thousand years ago.

Figure 12.6: American $50 gold note from 1882 could be directly exchanged for gold

Artificially stretching out the value of a buck has been going on long before there was a meeting of the G6. Society has been doing this for centuries, as a means of manufacturing wealth, or at least the collective delusion of wealth, so that society appears to continue advancing, and the economy continues to at least seem to continue growing. Delusions of wealth can be fun, as anyone who has ever purchased a lottery ticket can attest.

Fiscal Policy at the End of the Capital Era

Today, all around us, we see signs that the Analog Trinity is reaching its apex. Everywhere there are signs that our generation of wealth through capitalism is not only slowing down, its deceleration itself may be decelerating. In the face of these trends, nation states, the issuers of fiat money, are desperately trying to figure out ways of ensuring that the Analog Trinity continues to be the path towards wealth and power, since these are the mechanisms that they control.

Figure 12.7: King George III mortgaged his lands in America in order to 'save them'

Nation states control capital through laws, regulations and bureaucracies, but more importantly they control capital with the printing press. In a stagnating world economy, where capital is losing its control of the world, people start acting a little crazy in defense of what they know. In a sort of anti-Jerk, central banks around the world are taking steps that, while adhering to the structures of the Analog Trinity, completely break with all of this Trinity's traditions, customs and norms.

The notion of central banks, and capitalists, paying negative interest on their capital is so far from what they believe to be correct thinking that it can only be an act of desperation. This may almost be like kings emptying their treasuries and mortgaging their land in order to send huge armies across vast oceans to force their will upon their subjects. Those subjects in turn were people who, rather cheekily, decided that maybe *they* should hold title to the king's land, even after he had mortgaged that same land in order to pay for its defense.

Those who do not understand history are doomed to repeat it.

Analog Experiments Point the Way

It took a while to get here, but trust me, the journey that you just took through time and space is about to be worth it. As we started this chapter I said that Jerks print their own money, and that it was real. It is important now to mention that the money that you and I use every day, the capital that our whole world runs on is not, itself, *real* in any real sense. The money that we think of as 'real wealth' is simply an illusion. Its value is based upon a collective belief that this wealth, this fiat money, has some inherent value to it, and that we can exchange it for something else that we value. As long as someone else will take our dollars, our euros, our yuan or our rupees in exchange for something that we want, their value is validated as 'real' - as long as you're not the last one standing without a chair when the music ends.

By this definition and explanation, it should be readily apparent that Jerks, or half-Jerks like Amazon, Google, Starbucks and others, have been printing their own money for some time now. While governments have their treasuries printing bills at breathtaking speed, these companies are creating their own fiat money too. You and I use this currency every single day, and the data shows that we love it, chase it, hoard it, and use it as if it were any other money.

This money, this fiat currency printed by corporations rather than nation states, is alternatively called points, stars, miles, nights-stayed, and so on. The various rewards that companies give to customers for their continued loyalty, transactions and attention are, in every meaningful respect, money in the eyes of their customers. Interestingly, I know of a co-worker who had his identity stolen about two years ago. The thieves didn't take his bank balances, they didn't take his credit card numbers and they didn't take his personal information. They stole his Hilton points.

They could trade these points for other things of value to them at an understood and agreed-to rate of exchange, in marketplaces where such transactions are made every day – naturally, on the Internet. If that doesn't sound like money, I'm at a loss for a better definition.

Figure 12.8: Points Loyalty Wallet turns points into money

Analog companies, as a natural extension of their desire to drive repeat business with their customers (Chapter 10), have created fiat currency that they use to keep their customers coming back for more. They are creating capital out of thin air, just like nation states do, and yet they don't really realize that they're doing it. Indeed, capturing the *potential* value of these as a capital asset or liability has only recently been recognized as part of the Generally Accepted Accounting Principles which is a marble pillar in the pantheon of the Analog Trinity.

Early Attempts at Treason: Gamification Challenges the Nation-State

If some Analog companies have figured out that they're sitting on a money machine, it seems to be something of an accident. This awakening to the notion that anyone, anywhere, can create money at any time, just by implementing some kind of point system, seems to be so simple and obvious after the fact that everyone should do it. Sure, it sounds that simple, but it isn't. Creating your own cash, and translating it into capital, runs completely counter to all of the norms and conventions set under the Analog Trinity.

Just like nation states struggle to break their own codes of conduct – agreed to and slavishly followed for centuries – many companies are afraid to do these sorts of point systems, because it 'just doesn't feel right.' As a result, you see a range of different approaches by traditional companies as they struggle with this notion of *gamification*, as I called it in *Data Crush*.

We humans love games. We love to keep score, we love to win or at least try to win, and we love coming out on top. This may sound remarkably like the lives of most people who try to climb the old corporate ladder, and there's at least a little bit of this psychology in all of us; a natural outgrowth of our Maslowian desire for security and comfort.

Analog companies who have embraced gamification, even tepidly, have generally gained great rewards from their efforts. Why wouldn't they? They're printing fiat currency, the same as the government, and in the end capitalism is all about keeping score – whether in thousands of books maintained by bookkeepers in office towers, or in some CRM system whirling away in some corporate computing cloud, smeared all over the Internet.

Quit Jerking Around with Cash

Jerks take this notion of gamification and they crank the throttle up to 'ludicrous' speed. Jerks don't contemplate the possibility of printing their own cash, they go in whole-hog. If you log into Airbnb, Doctor On Demand, Waze, Uber or even Facebook, you will see throughout those applications all manner of money-printing going on. With Uber, riders give drivers a score and drivers give riders a score. On Facebook people gather 'Likes,' and on Twitter they gather followers.

In each instance, some measure of value is being created all the time. Every person holding on to a part of the net is both giving and receiving packets of perceived value with every click that they make. Those packets may be exchanged for something else of value, either now or in time, with the price set by cooperative acquiescence of all participants.

If you were paying attention to the background paragraphs above, you might notice that this sounds eerily like what it takes to turn fiat money into 'real money'. But, Jerks do one better here. Because Jerks work according to the Digital Trinity, rather than the Analog, the fiat money that they produce with their points, stars, likes and so on, also creates actual real wealth, according to the processes we discussed in Chapter 6. Jerks get customers to create correlations out of uncorrelated data, giving them points and stars, and something they value in return, thereby paying their customers both in real value (Uber drops them off) and in fiat currency (frequent rider points).

Then, in addition to all of this, Jerks create actual wealth, in an information-centric world, by getting those same customers to create correlations where previously there were none. In a world where fake, fiat money is losing all of its gusto, Jerks not only take what's left of this old way of creating imaginary wealth, they also create what will be the future's real wealth, all without really caring much about capital, which to them is just about keeping score anyway. This is gamification by any other name.

Chapter Summary:

1. Capital is represented by money, such as dollars, euros, yuan, etc. This money is fiat currency. It has worth because society agrees that it has worth, and otherwise would simply be paper.
2. Systems of customer rewards such as points, stars, 'likes,' bucks and so on are also forms of fiat currency, and customers use them as such.
3. Using such loyalty rewards effectively allows organizations to print their own currency, and create real value out of nothing.
4. Jerks leverage this effect as much as possible.

Chapter Thirteen: Jerks Flout the Rules

"You are remembered for the rules you break."- Douglas MacArthur

"Why join the navy when you can be a pirate?"- Steve Jobs

If you are developing a sense of unease, or even taking offense as you work through these chapters, that's good. It means we're making progress.

One of the dominant advantages that Jerks have when they play to win is that they just don't follow the same rules as Analog companies. And I mean this literally. Analogs find this to be deeply offensive. Flouting the rules is a rejection of everything they have ever been taught to believe in. Analogs take rules very seriously because, after all, they are 'the Rules!'

Jerks couldn't care less about these rules. To them, rules are stupid. Rules are antiques, relics of an age that is quickly passing by. Rules are the Bayeux Tapestry, the Sphynx, the Coliseum, the Notre Dame of the Analog Era. They are the symbols of control and power from a bygone age. To Jerks, rules, laws, regulations and policies belong in a museum – curios and baubles from a time when such things were in style. Like a baseball struck by Babe Ruth, or a soccer ball caressed by Pele's noggin, they are nostalgia, but no more than that.

Jerks scoff when an umpire tries to throw them out of the game, or a referee gives them a yellow card. They don't care about these penalties because they weren't even playing the same game. No, these Jerks may be on the same field as Analogs but while Analogs are trying to play baseball or soccer by the rules, Jerks are out there playing 3D Modern-Combat-World-of-Warcraft-Jedi-Academy-Angry-Birds – full-contact and cage-match, too, just like they were taught as kids of the Digital Age.

Figure 13.1: An Analog playing golf with Jerks

Analogs' slavish adherence to the rules is both their greatest strength in a capital-centric world and their greatest weakness in an information-centric world. We will develop this thesis directly.

The 'Why' of the Rules

Recall that the Analog Trinity consists of Bureaucracy, Processes and Rules. Rules get fairly high standing in the world of capital, because in a world of physical and semi-physical wealth, people have to know their place. Analog companies have been taught that, in order to win at the game of Capital, you had to understand and play by these rules. Compliance has been baked into nearly every successful capitalist in the present world. I'm not saying that all capitalists *follow* all of the rules, far from it. But the rules of capitalism are there to establish a normal, consistent, predictable framework of controls over how, when, where and why wealth and power is distributed in our world.

Our present society is completely rules-oriented. We are dependent upon rules – or perhaps codependent is a better label. The rules for playing the capital game are found in our laws, our regulations, our traditions, our habits, and even our sense of decorum. As any police officer would point out at a traffic stop, not only is it important that you follow the rules, you had better be polite about it.

None of these structures was a foregone conclusion, mind you. There were entirely different 'norms' for living under the Tools and Dirt Trinities, and to win under those regimes of power you had to operate by those norms and customs. But, as we 'civilized' ourselves during the Industrial Revolution, we collectively created these new mechanisms of doling out and controlling power, which ensured both the destruction of the controls under imperialism and the rise of these new controls run by capitalists.

Rules: The Mechanics of Control

Recall from Chapter 8 the notion of control at a distance. As we globalized ourselves during the Industrial Revolution, those with wealth and power (increasingly capital-based) needed to control their capital over long distances in both space and time. Clipper ships and fast ponies helped, but to maintain control of capital in the early Analog Era you had to do it by proxy. Someone off in some far-flung land had to do your bidding in order to grow your capital. To make sure that they did it right, you had to establish rules that would control their conduct.

Rules are how Analogs create, maintain and most of all enforce their ownership of wealth and control of power. Our systems of laws and regulations are the embodiment of this collective belief in rules. Without such collective belief, these rules would be meaningless, even with attempts at enforcement. One need only spend a few minutes behind a radar gun next to a lightly traveled highway in America to see the effectiveness of rules that the population rejects. Rules apply because we accede to them. They have authority over us because we allow them to. After all, 'dems the rules'!

We don't do this because we are dolts, willing to give up our freedoms for little or no benefit. Far from it. Our society struggled for two centuries to figure out the rules that we currently live by, and there is no shortage of heroes who literally gave their lives to secure for us the set of rules and laws that now protect us. Without them we'd be in chaos and the world could not operate with the efficiency, effectiveness, and returns on capital that we enjoy today.

Figure 13.2: Jerks want to travel at the speed of light

Rules aren't all bad. In our capital-centric world we rely on them every day. Rules provide stability and predictability. They allow us to move through life with a sense of order and safety. This is incredibly important to us, only slightly less important than air, food and water, as Maslow pointed out. Rules also make our safety portable: when we move around the world we can take our traditions and manners with us and get pretty much the same results wherever we go.

This is partly why global travel isn't as 'exotic' as it once was. Today, wherever you travel in the world, the rules have developed such that they are pretty consistent wherever you go. It was necessary to synchronize the global catalog of rules for global trade to really take off. We still struggle with this, but tremendous strides have been made in achieving this synchronicity, at least as it pertains to capital.

Society has also been trying to synchronize how we globally manage information too. Have we achieved rules for global information synchronicity? Not so much.

Indeed, we can get ourselves into real trouble if and when we come across a set of rules that are different from what we are used to. I found this out, to my frequent dismay, while living in Saudi Arabia back in the 1990s. What is considered 'normal' in the U.S. is considered heretical in other places such as Saudi Arabia, Iraq, North Korea, and so on. I lived in Saudi Arabia for a while, and making cultural mistakes there, like being a single male and walking into a KFC restaurant through the door reserved for women, isn't just a faux pas, it's life-threatening!

If you want some insight into the causes of the high levels of social conflict in the world of the early 21st century, a good place to start looking is in the inconsistencies between the accepted rules of the stakeholders.

Figure 13.3: A KFC in Saudi Arabia. One of the scariest moments of my life

Jerks get all of this history stuff, but it all seems far too binding for them. Sure, where we have been and how we got to 'here' may be important, but Jerks don't really care about the path. They care about the destination. More on this in Chapters 15 and 16. If this feels similar to teenage rebellion, that's no accident, because it is.

Teens are notoriously skilled at ignoring the advice of their elders because they haven't yet learned to respect the past. They do not yet value the lessons learned by their parents when the parents were young. No, teens simply tell themselves that these crazy rules of their parents are wrong-headed, constraining, and 'like so yesterday, like.' So they ignore or even actively flout their parents' rules, in order to live their lives 'their way.'

In time, most teens come around to the same realizations as their parents did, assuming they survive the journey. After a while our children learn to live by 'the rules' as did the generations that preceded them. Or at least we fervently hope so.

Analog companies view Jerks in the same light as parents view their teens. Sure, they're rebellious now, but sooner or later Jerks will learn to accept the rules, and all will be right with the world.

Fat Chance, Daddy-o

Jerks aren't being rebellious, they're being observant. Jerks see the transition under way from Analog to Digital, and they are choosing to follow it. That they are doing so without the assistance of LSD, tie-dyed shirts and peace signs is utterly baffling to the present powers that be, but the times, they are a changing.' Jerks aren't contrarian to authority, they just see a different truth to follow than their parents did.

Apps of Fury

Can Jerks prevail in this migration from the Analog Trinity to the Digital Trinity? Can Analytics prevail over rules? Much turns on the eventual answer to this question. Perhaps some visuals will assist in making a forecast.

Envision a sumo wrestling match. On one side of the ring is a sumo wrestler, 427 pounds of rice-fed hugeness, piled six feet high, ready to smash bellies with his opponent. On the other side stands a Jerk: the martial arts legend Bruce Lee, five-foot-seven and 130 pounds of lithe muscle, piss and vinegar. By appearances the wrestler has all of the advantages: size, weight, strength, inertia, mass, all in hypo-carbohydrated, pre-diabetic abundance. Tiny little Bruce doesn't stand a chance!

Figure 13.4: Bruce Lee with his iNunchucks

The Sumo stomps around, casting salt about the ring to cleanse and purify it as ceremony and decorum dictate. Bruce replies by simply flexing his pectorals, a slight twinkle in his eye and grin in one corner of his mouth. The opponents bow to one another, an uncomfortable melding of contempt and respect, then take their places at opposite sides of the ring.

The sumo hikes up his *mawashi* about his waist, assumes the traditional four-point stance, and prepares to propel his full mass at his deft-but-diminutive opponent. The sumo thunders towards Bruce with all of his might, certain of victory. As this great wall of flesh descends upon him, Bruce merely shifts to the side, far faster than the sumo can perceive, let alone adjust to. The wrestler's inertia carries him well past Bruce and out of the ring – sprawled out on the edge of the *dohyō,* dazed and perplexed, his undefeatable bulk now simply *Shini-tai,* or dead body.

Bruce strides up to him, slowly extracting a modest pair of nunchucks with each step. In a flash he applies some brief but focused attention to the wrestler's temple, removing him from the tournament. Game over. Bruce then turns about, ready to address the next wrestler.

Jerks are to Analog companies as Bruce Lee is to a sumo wrestler. Both are masters of the arts to which they are dedicated. Each follows the norms of those arts, and benefits from their investments in those beliefs. For the sumo, success lies in bulk, mass, size, formality, and adherence to a stringent set of rules that define what is allowed and what is not. Bruce is a bit different. For him success lies in speed, agility, focused strength and, most of all, improvisation. These are two worlds, two sets of norms and beliefs, and two entirely different outcomes. Each world view produces predictable results within itself. It's when they cross paths that the dragon enters the ring, and unexpectedly kicks some enormous butt.

The Digital Trinity: The Way of the Dragon

While the Analog Trinity encourages mass, bulk, size, structure and so on as the means to create capital wealth, the Digital Trinity rewards speed, agility and adaptability. By the standards of the Information Era, mobility trumps bureaucracy every time. Ponder this the next time some clerk asks you to fill out a form in triplicate, and then attach a note from your mommy… and return in 45 days for an answer.

When dealing with information, social media is far more flexible, responsive and productive than any pre-defined, ISO9000'ed, monitored, measured, Six-Sigma'ed business process ever mapped out in Microsoft PowerPoint. Millions of users contributing context and correlation to information, in real time, are far more productive than the best efforts of the best-trained workers in the most optimized and hyper-measured business process. Social media is the nunchucks of the Digital Trinity.

Figure 13.5: The triplicate form, manna from Analog Heaven

Jerks use the new structures of the Digital Trinity to completely outmaneuver Analogs. They see rules for what they are: a means of maintaining the status quo, a means of producing control-at-a-distance like a New York City policy manual sitting on a desk in a gold-rush bank house in San Francisco. Jerks couldn't care less about rules or governing processes populated by bureaucracies, because these are elements of controlling capital, not information. Indeed, these mechanisms are perfectly horrible for effectively managing information, because they are purposefully designed to slow information down, through friction, from the speed of light to the speed of capital.

Send in the Bureaucrats

There is abundant evidence of Jerks flouting the rules all around us. Whether you research Uber, Airbnb, Tesla, SpaceX, Doctor On Demand, FanDuel or any of the dozens of other Jerks out there, the control structures of the Analog Trinity have been whipped up into a frenzy over these Jerks' disrespect for authority. All of these organizations are under intense legal and regulatory attack because, to the existing systems of control, Jerks are viruses – they are a disease causing dis-ease within and between the pillars of the Analog Trinity, and they must be stopped! A quick Google search on any of these companies will quickly show page after page of results detailing the regulatory, legal and even moral attacks suffered by Jerks as they go about their business. For the most part Jerks are OK with not being liked by Analogs. It validates them as Jerks, you see.

Naturally, Analog companies respond to the threat of Jerks by using their tried and true methods that are straight out of the Analog Trinity. Analogs deploy an arsenal of lawyers, auditors and regulators who launch fusillades of court orders, depositions, injunctions and such. They toss them about like sacred salt tossed about a sumo ring, in the hope that they can purify the game that *must be played by certain rules*. But to their dismay these Analog companies find that the Jerks can see their attacks coming, and they simply slip to the side, outmaneuvering assaults with the speed and agility unimaginable to an enormous sumo.

Laws: Now You See 'Em, Now You Don't

Jerks use the rules, judo-style, to get what they want. Because Jerks live in this temporal gap between the Ages of Capital and Information, they have to work both ways, at least for a time. Fortunately for them, the metabolism of the Digital Trinity is so much higher than that of the Analog Trinity, that Jerks are remarkably good at, well, Jerking the Analogs around. If Analogs can update their websites or apps in a year, Jerks can do it in a month. With every quarterly report that an Analog creates detailing its loss of market share, Jerks have taken another percentage point of customers, predictively. When Analogs get an injunction in under a week, Jerks appeal in a day. When Analogs issue a news release condemning the acts of some Jerk, the same day that darn Jerk posts the retort of millions of fans, within minutes. No matter how fast that sumo wrestler tries to move, Bruce Lee responds with fists of lightning.

Figure 13.6: Analog corporate attorneys, filing an appeal

The differences between how Analogs and Jerks acknowledge and deal with rules are stark, and foretell a future where social and economic governance looks entirely foreign. When FanDuel, the online gaming-or-gambling Jerk, hit the stage during the 2015 season of American football, the stage was set for a battle between the Old and the New. What happened over the course of those few weeks in October and November of that year was a vision of what governance will look like in an information age managed by the Digital Trinity. FanDuel basically automated the game of fantasy football, where fans pretended to be owners of make-believe football players based on real players and real player performance. FanDuel not only automated this extremely popular pastime, they monetized it. Using the steps I have described in this book, FanDuel Jerked the gaming industry and became an overnight success, much to the chagrin of many powers-that-be.

By the midpoint of the football season that year, those powers decided to act. This was lightning-fast for a process-enslaved, rules-constrained bureaucracy, but then again they knew that their entire way of life was at stake. Through various structures of the Analog Trinity, FanDuel was hit with all sorts of legal and regulatory actions intended to stop their evil Digital ways. Foremost among the complaints against FanDuel was that they are a gambling organization, not a skill-based game. For Analogs, playing games is all well and good, but gambling? That's a business that we want to closely control, largely because it's so ridiculously profitable.

By November 2015, FanDuel had been hit with multiple cease-and-desist orders from various courts of law (think of courts as the tool boxes of the Analog Trinity), and these Jerks were expected to comply. What was their initial response? Thanks, but no. FanDuel wasn't terribly fond of the notion of ceasing or desisting, given the millions of dollars they were earning every week from their website and app.

Figure 13.7: Fans of FanDuel protest New York Attorney General Schneiderman

This response was not taken kindly by the courts; it was practically rude of them not to comply! When the courts came back and told FanDuel that 'cease and desist' was not a suggestion, FanDuel bobbed and weaved like they were Bruce Lee himself, only in leggings and Under Armor T-shirts. What these Jerks did was incredibly disruptive. They used the Digital Trinity of Mobility, Social Media and Analytics to mobilize their customers and fans to contact these courts and instruments of Analog control and to force them to stand down.

In this remarkable turn of events, FanDuel arranged for people to protest, petition and then panic the powers that be, by using their app to drive attention to their predicament. This was sheer brilliance on their part and, inasmuch as their goal was to stay in business through the end of the football season and collect lots of money and lots of data over that time, it worked like a charm. No doubt those charms are shaped like nunchucks.

FanDuel is a Jerk that used the structures of the Digital Trinity to implement what I call *legislation by plebiscite,* where society at large decides what it does and does not like, or does or does not support, in real time, on a case-by-case basis, at up to the speed of light.

My uncle is a federal judge who is soon to retire. As I've spoken to him about both the speed and the mechanisms of change that are upon him, he said his retirement cannot come a moment too soon. It'll be a very different world, with very different norms, and the transition from one to another will be both terrifying and exhilarating, like a loop-the-loop rollercoaster at his favorite theme park. But, this is a story for another time and another book. It's working title is *Rupture*.

Chapter Summary:

1. Rules are the means of controlling power in the Analog Trinity. Analog organizations create, manage and enforce rules as their means of controlling capital.
2. Whether rules, laws, regulations or traditions and norms, Analogs respect these means of control because they are fundamental to success in the Analog Trinity.
3. Jerks follow a completely different Trinity, and rules are largely meaningless to them. Jerks view rules as artificial constraints that add little value, and may even be irrational.
4. Jerks bend or break rules whenever doing so leads to better outcomes for customers, and generates more information wealth.

Chapter Fourteen: Jerks Hightail It

"What you are comes to you."- Ralph Waldo Emerson

"The secret to good self-esteem is to lower your expectations to the point where they're already met."- Bill Watterson as Calvin in 'Calvin and Hobbes'

There is a slightly irreverent tone in my writing and the points that I'm making. I'm somewhat sorry if this bothers you, but I do it for two reasons. First, I hope that it helps some of these ideas stick in your mind. For survival, we are wired to remember those who offend or cross us, so I'm trying to tap into a little of this old Tool Trinity residue, deep in your cerebral cortex. Second, I'm just wired a little funny (some might say 'wrong') and I choose to be true to myself. I don't really mean to offend your sensibilities, or anyone else's. I just seem to have a knack for saying what I'm thinking, and the vast majority of people seem to appreciate this approach for its novelty. PC, I ain't!

You will understand the need for this detour as we proceed through Chapter 14. Here, we are about to tread on dangerous, controversial ground. Some people will be okay with this. Most will be a bit uncomfortable. But some will find this chapter offensive and it will anger them. There will be a range of responses to this topic, following a normal distribution, if you like. Interestingly, this distribution of responses actually reinforces, even proves, the point of this chapter, in a satisfying yet disturbing way.

So, take a deep breath, open your eyes, and let's jump in.

A Brief Introduction to Statistics

Jerks Hightail it. What does this mean? Well, what it means is this: The physical universe is an analog place, rather than a digital one (I'm referring to actual nature here, not human social or economic Trinities). Since it's analog, pretty much every population of anything in the universe follows some form of normal distribution.

In this distribution, for each characteristic of the population, the majority of its members are 'average.' They tend to share the same value for the characteristic in question.

But, in every normal distribution there are members who, for the characteristic in question, are a little bit away from normal. Some are a bit less than the average, others a bit more. The farther away from average you go, either up or down, the fewer the number of outliers. This distribution can be mathematically modeled, and generally creates the camel's hump curve that is commonly called the normal distribution, or bell curve.

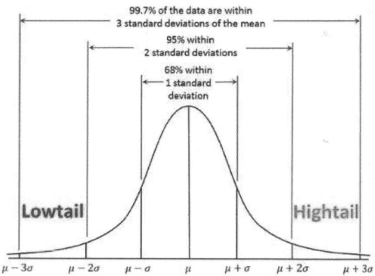

Figure 14.1: The normal distribution curve, with the average, hightail and lowtail

There are good reasons that normal distributions are normal: uncertainty, variation, and good old chaos. Variety creates subtle variations which, over time, allow for adaptability and even evolution. If some natural variation in a population benefits an individual over his differently endowed peers, he may have some advantage in the universe. Over time, the accumulation of small, incremental improvements and the elimination of small impediments or defects can lead to all kinds of good things. Taken together, these two effects can lead to improvements throughout a population and this is the basis of most of our economic wealth over the last 200 years. It's notable that, if either effect is not moderated by the other, these advances and retreats in a population can be too extreme and weirdness can result. The runaway addition of 'improvements' without a counterbalancing cull of baggage is about the best explanation I can come up with for Microsoft's Windows 8. That, or someone in Redmond, Washington has a twisted sense of humor. In the end, God, evolution and Microsoft users all love variety, but only in small doses.

Correlation and Causation

So, normal distributions are normal, and represent a useful way for mathematicians, statisticians and Jerks to understand the characteristics of a population. Guess what? You and I are part of a population! In fact, each of us is part of a zillion populations. It just depends on which characteristic you want to measure. When measuring one characteristic of a population, it's often easy to draw correlations: situation B seems to co-occur with situation C, and so on. These correlations help us to better understand the universe, and allow us to more accurately understand the past and predict the future. Our universe is overflowing with uncorrelated data about population characteristics just waiting to be correlated.

The problem is that sometimes statisticians, mathematicians and yes, Jerks, can read too much into their correlations. Sometimes, what is merely a correlation (*this corresponds with that*), is misinterpreted to be causation, or *this causes that*. This is a major error in the field of statistics. Many a modeler has fallen victim to the siren song of causation's discovery.

Pronouncing causation in populations of simple objects or events is possible because the number of variables is relatively small, and usually one characteristic dominates the other possibilities. If your child has a tummy ache and you go into the kitchen and find that the cookie jar is tipped over, emptied, and surrounded by crumbs, there's a decent chance that botulism is not the cause of their aches.

But, when looking at the characteristics of complex objects operating in complex systems, declaring causation is not only unwise, it can be deadly.

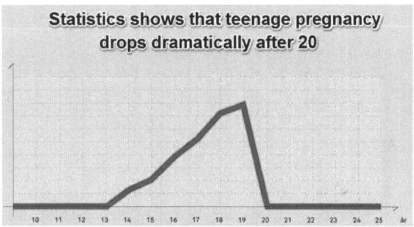

Figure 14.2: Poor understanding of statistics can be a dangerous thing

The Gangs of New York

The dynamics of populations have been studied for centuries, particularly with the dawn of the Industrial Revolution. Building upon the principles of the scientific method, rediscovered by Westerners in the Renaissance, capitalists digested the meager amounts of data then available, to attempt to better apply the Analog Trinity. As Taylor and Ford were quick to realize, workers were a population too, and they had a wide range of properties available for correlation. The preponderance of Taylor's work was designed to measure and evaluate those properties that most influenced a person's productivity – with the goal of maximizing the output of capital mind you.

Unfortunately, in the late 1800s while Taylor was doing his thing, society was still coming to grips with the mass disruption caused by the end of the Land Trinity and the growing influence of the Analog Trinity. One of the consequences of the collapse of Imperialism was a mass migration of people around the globe. This was a correlation, rather than a causal relationship! In this remixing of the global human population, a few different social trends merged together at precisely the wrong time. People from far-flung lands and cultures suddenly found themselves in close proximity to each other, and thus began the explosive urbanization of cities such as New York, London, Boston, Chicago and San Francisco.

Most of these people from different races, creeds and colors moved for specific reasons. They wanted to escape horrible living conditions in their homelands and find better lives elsewhere. When they showed up in foreign cities they were quick to look for work as a matter of survival. Once again, supply-and-demand played its hand, the amount of cheap labor in most urban markets soared, and wages dropped as a result.

Figure 14.3: Riots in the Streets of New York City, 1863

This trend collided with the rapid growth in production efficiency and output created by capitalization of the economy, the automation of a range of jobs, and yes, Taylor and Ford's infamous assembly line. All of these conspired to greatly reduce the need for labor, right about the time that cities had an overabundance of labor. For migrant aliens looking for work in the growing cities of the new world, this collision didn't lead to just a bad day, it led to a bad half-century.

The thinking and work of industrialists like Ford, economists like Taylor and psychiatrists like Freud all conspired to create and promote a truly radical notion for the 19th century: not all people are the same. The world of the 1800s was extremely religious, and the notions that all men were created equal was widely held to be true. Women were rather less than equal, and would remain so for another century... and counting. The captains of the Analog world began promoting the idea that not only were people different, these differences were both readily discernable and measureable.

The latter item wasn't an issue. Metrics are our friends. The former notion, that meaningful differences could be easily discernable simply by *looking* at someone, was substantially more troubling. Because migration, class conflict, and competition for jobs coincided with the arrival of this notion that you could determine someone's worth by simply looking at them, some very bad things started to happen in our world. People started to believe in *isms*, causing more than a century of bitter conflict and suffering.

Ringing Your Bell

Around the beginning of the 20th century the simple scientific acts of measuring a characteristic of a population, determining its average and mean, and defining a normal distribution, began to be perverted. Suddenly, people ripe with fear of unemployment and xenophobia felt that they had a means to mathematically justify their fear and their hatred of others. As Maslow showed us, we value personal safety just slightly less than we value water, food and air. Fear of outside threats comes right from our brain stems, which can short circuit our more rational brain functions.

People used data and statistics, fear and loathing, to try to mathematically justify their *isms*: Nazism, Communism, Racism, Idiotism, Sexism and so on. Proponents of the bell curve believed that through simple testing and measurement it was possible to classify people as smart or not, useful or not, talented or not, and so on.

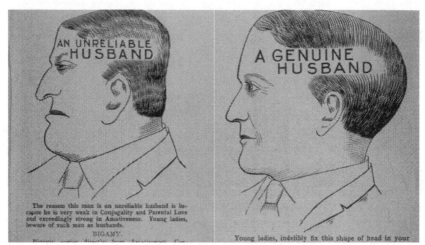

Figure 14.4: Phrenology: state-of-the-art advice for single women, 1890

Where this idea became truly offensive is when it was used to place people in overly broad categories and then overly judge them as a result. Once correlated, supporters of any number of these twisted *isms* began to declare that they had discovered causation rather than just ridiculously over-simplified correlations. They missed (or more likely ignored) that the extraordinary complexity of the subject at hand (humans) meant that even their correlations were highly suspect. This twisted application of mathematics and statistics led to a range of horrors throughout the era of our two World Wars and the rest of the 20th century.

Blame the Driver, Not the Car

Because of this misapplication of the science, the bell curve became notorious. It was vilified by social liberals as a means of holding the less fortunate in bondage. While the manner in which the science was perverted to meet these evil ends deserves our revulsion, the approaches used in creating the bell curve aren't the boogie man they have been made out to be.

Population statistics are not some embodiment of evil or a threat to our humanity - far from it. It's just math, applied to a characteristic of a population, in order to develop a statistical understanding of the members of that population. As we move into the Information Era, governed by the Digital Trinity, it is critical for all of us to remember this: statistics aren't racist, or sexist, or any -ists – but statisticians on occasion may be.

The approaches that were used to such ill effect in the Capitalist Era are exactly the same approaches that will define life in the Information Era, only this time there will be two major differences. First, our world will be run according to the new structures of the Digital Trinity. Second, this time around there will be dramatically more data to work with.

Analytics: The New Ruler in the Digital World

Jerks use analytics the same way capitalists use rules. In their respective Trinities, these mechanisms are used to drive decisions and to determine how wealth is created and distributed. When Jerks seek guidance on how to best create wealth through information, they use analytics, rather than rules, to determine their answers. For Jerks, applying population statistics to the data that we create on our mobile devices when we are using social media is the means by which they create value.

Jerks don't use the Digital Trinity to oppress us, although that danger is certainly there. Jerks use their Trinity to monitor and assess us all of the time because that is what we expect of them. Jerks are always measuring and evaluating us, because we insist on it. Most of us have a sense that this is going on all around us. Every time we get a great coupon for just what we want, at just the right time and just the right place, some Jerk has just judged us by our posts on social media, a digital *faux pas* we're all supposed to avoid. Polite or not, this sort of thing is exactly what we demand of Jerks, according to the expectations of our Six New Normals.

When Starbucks predicts that you're going to stop by in the next 15 minutes, and you will likely order a tall chai tea latte instead of a venti mocha Frappuccino, they are putting you in a box. They are forming prejudices about you. They are putting a label on you with every calculation. The math, the models and the approaches are all the same. The opportunity to subvert and oppress from all of this knowledge looms large, if we stop long enough to consider the implications.

From Blockbuster's Terms and Conditions: "Blockbuster may at any time, and at its sole discretion, modify these Terms and Conditions of Use, including without limitation the Privacy Policy, with or without notice. ... If you do not agree to any modification of these Terms and Conditions of Use, you must immediately stop using this Site."

Figure 14.5: Your continued use is your ongoing consent ...

It's the difference in their application that is critical. Jerks use these tools and techniques to improve their customers' lives, rather than end them. They use population statistics to delight, rather than oppress. They use Analytics, the governance mechanism of the Digital Trinity, to create better outcomes from the resources at hand, just like rules did in the Analog world.

Whither Privacy?

With our legacy of the misapplication of population statistics fresh in our minds, you'd think that we might be a little worried that we are reentering a world of mathematical discrimination on an industrialized scale. Based upon recent events, you'd be right. In 2014 and again in 2015, courts of the European Union and China made several decisions regarding their citizens' personal data.

In 2014 the EU ruled against Google in a case of a person's 'Right to Be Forgotten.' In essence this ruling allowed for any EU citizen to have an inaccurate, undesired or even merely unflattering link about them deleted by search engines upon demand. Then in 2015 the EU ruled that the Safe Harbor agreement between the EU and the United States was null and void. Here, the EU ended a decade-long rule that allowed for the free movement of information between these players, in order to further protect the misuse of private information of EU citizens. The horrors of a century of warfare, fed by quantified fear and hatred, seem fresh in the minds of Europeans and Asians alike. Rightfully so, given where they have been and where we collectively are heading.

Fears fueled by the notion that our every move, decision and click is being tracked by Analog institutions (such as nation-states and capital-centric corporations) as well as seemingly benign Jerks, are not misplaced. We know this because of Edward Snowden. We all face what I call the Privacy Paradox. We want our privacy but we want awesome coupons, too. We want to be safe from terrorists, but also safe from our own government. We want to be famous on social media, but anonymous when we buy unmentionables delivered by drones. These are not easy issues to resolve, and how we will do so is not yet clear. But one thing that I am sure of is this: collectively we will have to resolve these issues soon, and a bunch of Jerks will likely help us find the answer.

Better Living Through Mathematics

In a world awash in massive, pervasive and invasive data, the opportunity for advantage or abuse becomes clear. Our continued use of and growing dependence on the Digital Trinity inevitably leads us to a life where Jerks will meet our specific needs with ever-greater accuracy, precision and timelines, just as the Six New Normals dictate. So what is the connection to what I call the *hightail*?

For as long as people have been manufacturing things they hoped to sell, they have tried to meet someone else's desire or need. Before the Industrial Revolution, most production was performed by highly skilled craftspeople producing high-quality, individualized products singly or in small batches. Their customers were their neighbors and rarely would their products be sold to someone they didn't already know. In the workshops of the Dirt Trinity vendors literally knew each of their customers like they were neighbors, because they were.

The Capitalist Era changed all of that. With industrialization, manufacturers sought to maximize returns on capital by producing as much of the same thing as possible, over and over and over again. This was well-demonstrated by Henry Ford's famous quote regarding his Model 'T'. "You can have any color you want, as long as it's black." When the world is run by capitalists, variety is the enemy.

Given this perspective, the way that you maximize the popularity and demand for your products is to make them as average as you possibly can. Serving the peak of the normal distribution curve is practically the definition of capitalist marketing. Being 'good enough' for 'most people' is a strategy for maximizing throughput, and hence profits. In a capital-centric world, operating at Analog Trinity speeds, with pre-Digital Trinity volumes of data, good enough generally was.

But this all changes now that Jerks are here. Jerks let the capitalists keep the peak of the normal curve. It's too easy, and too far down Maslow's pyramid for them to bother with anyway. Average products and services meet average needs. Rarely do they inspire passion from their customers. Jerks don't like average, they like meeting our needs for intimacy and purpose, New-Normal-style. They like this both because they enjoy the challenge of unchartered territories with unmined veins of digital silver and gold, and because they enjoy collecting the rewards that come from scratching a previously unreachable itch.

Jerks surrender the middle of the normal distribution curve because playing the average is an Analog's game. Jerks live by the Digital Trinity, which is all about knowing what each individual person needs, wants, and lusts after. Knowing each of us intimately, our needs and desires changing in space and time, is what the Digital Trinity is all about. They are compelled to know our deepest thoughts and act upon them.

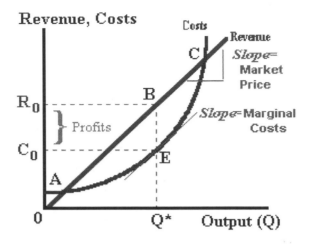

Figure 14.6: Profit Maximization: Economics has 'laws' that Jerks pretty much ignore

If you are a Jerk, and you know all of this about me, you can then focus your energy on the ends of the normal distribution curve, rather than the middle. At either end of the distribution lie each customer's dreams and nightmares. The ends are alternatively our worst-case and our best-case scenarios, the things we fear the most and those most cherished. Once you get past meeting my average needs, and head towards either tail of the normal distribution curve, you enter the territory of my soul; you begin to understand my unmet desires and my deepest fears, and you can begin to address me at an emotional level. This may sound strange to you, but Jerks are quickly discovering that data and math, rather than poetry and art, are the fastest route to the human heart and soul.

When Uber picks you up in mere minutes, allowing you to see your ride coming towards you in real time, that's a hightail solution. Average would be simply having taxis wander the streets, hoping one would be near you when you need it. When Doctor On Demand connects you to a doctor in 60 seconds or less, anywhere in the United States, from your smartphone, that's a hightail solution.

Average would be to have you make an appointment to go to the doctor's office, six to eight weeks from now.

When Waze dynamically re-routes you to your destination along a faster path, that's a hightail solution. Google maps originally just told you the shortest distance, independent of real time conditions, which allowed Waze to out-maneuver even Google. When Panera Bread sends you an exploding coupon for your favorite food item on your birthday, that's a hightail solution. An average solution would be a coupon from Little Caesar's that you cut out of the newspaper. Hightail solutions feel better to us because they are better. They meet our specific, intimate, personal needs, rather than serving the average. Is it any wonder why we find these solutions to be far more compelling?

Life in the Hightail

It is my earnest hope that Jerks use their future power for good rather than for evil. Technology has no morality. It just is. Whether a given technology is good or bad depends on how we use it. Consider electricity: good when you need some light or to cook something, not so good if you're strapped to an electric chair. So it goes with technology.

The Digital Trinity is a revolution based on technology. The data, the mathematics and the statistics represent a family of technologies that are allowing for dramatic changes in how we live. This technology, like all technologies, can be used for either good or evil. And, like all technologies, we will see both use cases in our coming future. After all, The Force must remain in balance.

In general, I expect that Jerks will pursue the hightail of our wants and needs, rather than the lowtail. I make this optimist's prediction for two main reasons. First, while there is great money to be made in playing off people's fears (an Analog marketing trick *extraordinaire*), the degree to which the deeply personal data available to Jerks could actually harm us is far too great. A Jerk who is a jerk, and uses these insights to scare us rather than help us, would be so effective at driving our behaviors through terror that we would not tolerate this psychic assault for long. Pursuing the lowtail is just as effective as pursuing the hightail, but scaring us to near-death would lead to a rebellion against such invasions of our psyche. Our Privacy Paradox protects us in this regard, as we always know that there's the potential for great harm in the misapplication of persuasion from mountains of data.

The second reason that I believe Jerks will choose the hightail over the lowtail is that the benefits of the high road will be immense. Meeting people's deepest needs, predictively, persuasively, warmly, substantively will be so intensely satisfying that Jerks will seek out the positive feedback they receive with almost reckless abandon. We see this already in the responses Jerks get from their Analog opponents. When Analogs protest at the successes of Jerks, the response is nearly always, "Whatever, dude." The upside of using the Digital Trinity to meet customers' needs is so compelling that Jerks are willing to be jerks in order to get that rush. Jerks are already experiencing their high from using the hightail. We can expect this addition to continue, as Jerks get better and better at what they do with mathematical precision.

If all of this quantification of humanity is upsetting to you, you might do well in squirreling yourself away in a bubble of Analog-Trinity-induced political correctness. The Digital Trinity is all about measuring every aspect of every individual and knowing how they think, how they act, how they live, and what their hopes and dreams are. Our higher-level Maslowian desires require that Jerks know us down to the finest detail, warts and all.

There is no hiding either your strengths or your weaknesses from these analyses. The Digital Trinity strips all of us bare and allows others to know us, potentially better than we know ourselves. But, perhaps this is exactly what the New Normal, *our* New Normal, is really telling all of us. Perhaps the only real political correctness out there comes from recognizing our differences, our individual truths, and someday becoming comfortable with the notion that we are all indeed different and unique. Both God and nature love variety, and so we are what we are. We should rejoice in that, rather than hide from it. To me that sounds correct, and there's nothing political about it.

Chapter Summary:

1. Analog organizations seek to maximize the utilization of capital by focusing their products and services to meet the average needs of as many people as possible.
2. Jerks avoid delivering adequate solutions, and instead focus on meeting the specific needs of their customers, unmet by average solutions.
3. Rather than targeting the middle of the normal distribution curve of customer expectations, Jerks deliver in the unserved hightail at the upper limits of customers' wants and needs.
4. There does exist a lowtail where the power of the Digital Trinity may be used to harm customers and do evil. Society must be aware of the lowtail, and work to protect against this threat.

Chapter Fifteen: Jerks Do Then Learn, Not Learn Then Do

"Experts often possess more data than judgment."- Colin Powell

"You can observe a lot just by watching."- Yogi Berra

This principle seems simple, but the origins of its value and disruptive effects go back to the land-wealth era. Jerks are tinkerers, explorers, and modern-day Edison's searching methodically and obsessively for answers to questions that most Analogs wouldn't even think to ask. By the time Analogs recognize the value in the answers that result from these efforts, the Jerks have sopped up all of the benefits of those answers, and moved on to a new question.

How did this lack of inquisitiveness come to pass? How is it possible that today's capital-centric behemoths, with their billion-dollar research budgets, can't learn as fast as three teenagers in Lagos, Nigeria taking turns programming on their shared, five-year-old MacBook computer? Scratch the surface and you will once again find that we got to where we are based upon our history and a million different perfect decisions made under the guidance of the Analog Trinity.

What's the Deal with Summer Break?

When I was a kid, I used to love summer break. It was a time for sleeping in, running around in the woods with my dog, swimming with my sisters and my friends, and spending six hours each week mowing our yard. All of these were more satisfying than sitting in a classroom.

Another favorite activity was lying on our back porch swing, reading books, magazines and pretty much anything I could get my hands on. A favorite was National Geographic. I read and re-read decades of back issues, fascinated by the variety of articles. I'd swing and read my days away, occasionally looking up to note an interesting cloud or an airliner passing by. All the while I contemplated dinosaurs, nuclear power, Aztec pottery and the morphology of lunar rocks. I'm quite certain I learned at least as much during my swinging sessions as I did in a classroom. It wasn't until I was older that I thought to ask, "Why do kids get summers off, anyway?" It seems like an innocuous question, but it's relevant to this discussion. For most of history, and certainly from the late Imperialist through the Capitalist Eras, kids got their summers off so they could work. This was far more important than learning.

The Imperial Age was predominantly agrarian. Most people worked the land. Plants grow best when days are long and the nights not so cold. So summer is the time for tending to the fields. Back then, children weren't the special little snowflakes that we've thought them to be since the end of World War II. Rather, they worked the summer growing season. Using children for labor had its advantages. Kids were shorter, so it was easier for them to plant and to pick. They had a better view of the undersides of plants and could spot pests for removal.

Children were easy to transport from field to field, and they were young and energetic. Clearing rocks from an acre or two of land per week was not overly tiring to them. And finally, since they *were* your kids, and you *had* to feed them *anyway*, you might as well get some work out of them. For kids back then, summer was a time of toil rather than kick-the-can.

For these kids, education was a luxury. *If* you were good, and had finished your chores, and had picked all the caterpillars off *all* of the corn in the 'bottom 40,' then *maybe* you could practice your 'rithmatic after supper. For these kids, learning was the reward for a hard day's work, rather than the punishment some seem to consider it today. Younger generations like to scoff when they hear older generations talk of how easy kids have it 'these days.' Prior to the 20th century, our great grandparents weren't as tough as nails when they were kids. They ate nails for breakfast, and asked for seconds.

Figure 15.1: Child labor was the rule for nearly all of human history

We Don't Need No Education

To the Land Trinity controlling this agrarian age, education wasn't just a hindrance, it was subversive. A commoner with book smarts was a dangerous thing. The landed gentry certainly liked to know a thing or two about the world, through their advisors, emissaries and maybe even their sheriffs and men-at-arms. But for the vast majority, their knowledge of the world rarely extended more than a few miles in any direction, or a few seasons in time. The leaders of the day thought this was just fine; an idle mind is the devil's workshop. Illiterates toiling in the dirt were less likely to realize their crummy lot in life. This lent stability to the Imperial Age and its Trinity of Dirt.

Modernly, the Shire, in J.R.R. Tolkien's *The Lord of the Rings*, is a great representation of life in this era. Everyone knew one another, books were the province of the few and the weird, and lands beyond the next hill were the source of wonder and awe. When your whole world was plants growing at your feet, or farm animals nibbling feed from your hand, there was no need or tolerance for big thoughts.

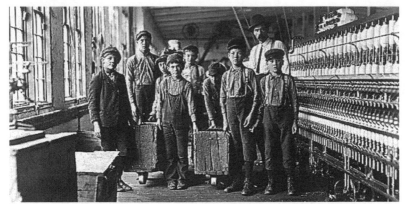

Figure 15.2: Who are you callin' snowflake? There were no 'safe zones' in 19ᵗʰ century munitions factories

Before the Industrial Revolution, almost no one went to college. There were three reasons for this. First, there wasn't a need for abstract learning, beyond farming. Nobility needed a few men of books, to implement their will and to make it stick. Beyond these few coveted positions, nearly all upper-class occupations were learned through apprenticeship rather than formal education.

You would spend years learning by trial and error under the watchful eye of a master. You did things the wrong way a lot before you ever got it right. There were some jobs that required book-learning, such as accountants, astrologers and doctors. But having an education even for these roles was something of a formality. If you were a good actor, you could walk over a yonder hill, tell everyone in the next village that you were a brain surgeon, and they would be none the wiser – at least not before treatment, and certainly not after. For many a sick peasant, 'doctors' were the disenfranchised Nigerian Princes of the day.

Second, there weren't many colleges or universities. In another case of supply and demand, or rather the-chicken-and-the-egg, there wasn't a need for education so there wasn't a need for education. Going to university meant that you were either ridiculously wealthy or were going to join the church, or both, depending upon your birthright. There was no upward mobility for peasants outside the clergy, and strong disincentives for people to understand things beyond their lot in life.

The third reason that there was little formal education is that an informed populace was a threat to those in power. The Land Trinity of Heredity, Edict and Violence only worked if those it controlled knew no better. Ignorance was bliss – for the rulers and the ruled.

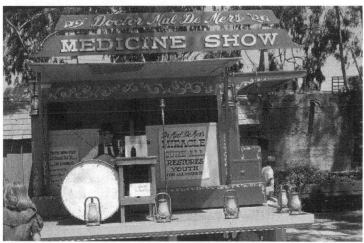

Figure 15.3: Advertising and Marketing are nothing new

Navigation Before Waze

Society remained much this way until the Age of Discovery. The gentry was delighted to discover that there was a whole new world to divide amongst themselves. But this required people who could build ships and sails, travel across a vast ocean, find gold and plant flags, declare their sovereignty, and bring home the riches without getting lost. They also needed people who could keep track of the portable wealth that was required to pay for it all along the way. This was the early birth of banking and capitalism.

The 'discovery' of the New World meant that Imperialism suddenly became a lot harder. All of these new tasks required new labor with new skills, including being able to write. A lot of treasure was at stake. Kings and queens wanted to review their explorers' books, rather than believe all of their tales. All this gave rise to a demand for skilled, educated labor, and the middle class was born. The nobility recognized that creating this new class was risky. But it was deemed warranted to keep up with the radical disruptions that the New World hurled upon the Old.

As the Age of Discovery yielded to the age of exploitation and colonialism, the need for literacy continued to grow. Colonials grew smarter and smarter, as their nobilities' tolerance and treasuries allowed, and soon the New World was populated with as many institutions of learning as the Old. As discussed earlier, society was evolving more quickly. The fields of learning planted by the nobles to feed their conquest of the New World reaped a population of educated subjects who concluded that this whole nobility thing was for the birds.

Figure 15.4: Prince Henry ran the navigation school that helped to end the Dirt Trinity

Teen Angst, With Muskets

Looking at the leadership of the rebellions of the 18th and 19th centuries, most of them came from this newly educated class of merchants and gentlemen. As soon as colonialists such as

Washington, Jefferson, Franklin and Adams learned a thing or two about the world, they realized that they were getting a raw deal out of the Land Trinity. This recognition, borne from education so fearfully and reluctantly authorized by the landed nobility, eventually led to the wars that ended the Dirt Trinity and replaced it with something new. So the nobles' anxieties over education were well founded.

These newly freed and recently educated people brought forth the foundations for the Analog Trinity: science, trade, and capitalism. This increased the need for an educated population. In America, public schooling for all kids started out as a novel idea, a goal to be attained someday. But it soon became something of a right, except during summer, when the kids were needed in the fields. Compared to the previous 500 years, the pace of new discoveries in the Industrial Revolution was staggering, and education became the way to break free from agrarian toil.
College was still nearly unattainable for the masses, but more and more people could at least try to catch that boat across the river that divided the haves from the have-nots. One of these people was a boy of low standing, who came first to learn, and then later to conquer words, in his search for a better life. He wrote of this struggle to gain standing and status through learning, and he was a pillar of society for achieving all three in his lifetime. His words still echo to this day, and he became one of the world's most loved authors.

"I have never let my schooling interfere with my education."
"Get your facts first, and then you can distort them as much as you please"
"Always do right. This will gratify some people and astonish the rest."
"The secret to getting ahead is getting started."
"If you tell the truth, you don't have to remember anything."

His name was Samuel Clemens, but his nom de plume was Mark Twain, in deference to his work as a river boat captain along his climb to celebrity. I grew up near his former summer home of Elmira, New York, where I read his stories on that back porch swing. Coincidently, I had the good fortune later to marry his great-great-great-granddaughter.

Figure 15.5: Samuel Clemens at his summer home in Elmira, NY, where I grew up

Once the capitalists of the 1800s fired up their Analog engines for growth, the more education one received, the higher one could aspire. This was the nightmare scenario for every remaining noble from the Land Era. They would lose their power and wealth after a century of warfare that culminated in two World Wars.

Investment Resonance

By the beginning of the 20th century, going to college was slightly more common. The public schools in America increased the capacity of the country to gain leverage over capital. This created the demand for still more skilled workers. A positive resonance developed between returns on education and returns on capital; investments in one yielded higher returns from the other. Soon, universities and colleges were popping up across capitalist societies like seedlings after a rain shower. Learning had moved from the guild house to the lecture hall and suddenly, taking several years out of the workforce to gain an education was an investment worth making.

Similar gains were being made in education itself. As capital flowed to institutions of learning, educators were able to build on their knowledge of the universe, finding ever more effective means of deriving value from capital and the Analog Trinity. Advances in all forms of science and liberal arts led to further gains in understanding, and our investments in this resonance increased dramatically.

Capitalists found that making 'big bets' on new technologies often paid off, as long as the risks and rewards were understood. Evaluating these pluses and minuses became hugely competitive, as universities and professors vied for funding of their favorite experiments or projects. This resonance between capital investment and technology innovation created a new educational entity called the research university. Spurred on by the need for technical innovation by two World Wars, these universities soon became well-oiled research machines, sucking in ever larger capital grants and spitting out ever more advanced and expensive innovations.

The stakes for research funding grew higher through the 20th century, and so did the costs and the risks. As people grew more sophisticated in their management of capital flows through the ever-expanding Analog Trinity, they also began to recognize the increasing risk of failure. It was one thing to fund Thomas Edison through his thousands of experiments leading up to the incandescent lightbulb. It was quite another to bet a substantial proportion of America's gross domestic product on the crazy notion that an atom could be split in two.

ROI: As Easy as 1-2-3

From radar and transistors, to lasers and metallurgy, to organic chemistry and medicine, every field of technology advanced. So did the risks and potential costs of failure. So risk management became a huge part of the innovation game. Financial modeling of these risks and rewards became a science unto itself, or at least a pseudo-science, not unlike phrenology in form or effectiveness. Business people saw the increasing risks associated with their 'big bets' on innovation, and the governance mechanisms of the Analog Trinity took over from there.

Soon, the same bureaucracies, processes and rules that were used to control the purchase and use of pencils and staplers were also being used to manage the process of disruptive innovation. When creating something from nothing might cost millions of dollars, you had better not come back with nothing. As discussed earlier, the 1960s through the 1980s saw the introduction of information technology in the business world. This technology was soon applied to the process of forecasting returns on innovation, eventually giving rise to the spreadsheet.

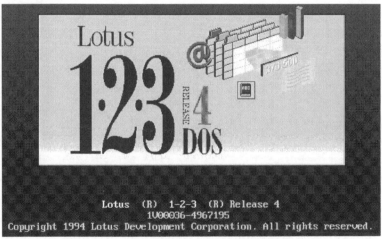

Figure 15.6: Lotus 1-2-3.Spreadsheets literally changed the world

VisiCalc, Lotus 1-2-3 and Microsoft Excel allowed the Analog Trinity to be applied not only to the present but into the future as well. This process of trying to predict the outcomes of anticipated investment in unknown innovations was cast as the science of financial modeling and Enterprise Resource Management (ERM). Financial phrenology had been automated.

As this process of risk management advanced, it demonstrated enormous returns on investment, or at least enormous avoidance of losses. These tools and techniques still dominate the management of trillions of dollars of capital. In the beginning of the 21st century, no self-respecting Analog would contemplate spending hard-earned, tightly managed capital on some research project that carried a major risk of failure.

Learn then Do

To Analogs, research is only worth doing if there is little chance of significant loss. But the only way to ensure that there is no chance of significant loss is to take a significant loss in having a dozen analysts spend a year, and a small fortune, making models that demonstrate that there won't be any losses. This is nonsense, but it is nonsense officially approved by the same bureaucracies, processes and rules that brought us the tiger team and the offsite meeting. Same is same.

I saw this same innovation-stymieing thinking prevail when I started my career in the space industry in the early 1990s. The reasoning was that because rockets were expensive, and could be used only once, you couldn't afford to waste one. This meant that when you designed a satellite to go on top of the rocket, you had to make sure that the satellite was perfect, and would last for years. To do this, you designed the satellite with more and more redundancy, to make sure it would work when it got into orbit. But, this redundancy added weight, which made it more expensive to launch, which raised the risk of failure, which increased the desire for redundancy, and so on.

This speed train of risk aversion was so out of control that you ended up with something like the space shuttle. The space shuttle was often referred to as the most complex machine ever invented; this is not far from the truth. Millions and millions of parts each had to work perfectly, every time, in order to ensure that the shuttle launched without blowing up. NASA maintained a staff of tens of thousands of engineers and technicians, just to keep the shuttle operational, and each individual launch cost well in excess of a billion dollars. Managed by the Analog Trinity, the shuttle was an enormous victory of industrialized innovation over basic common sense.

***Figure 15.7: The Space Shuttle. It worked, but only when
supported by thousands of engineers***

It also reminds me of the story of NASA's 'space pen' from the
Apollo years. In the 1960s when the U.S. and the U.S.S.R. were
racing to reach the moon, both countries recognized a problem:
Astronauts would have to write things down in zero gravity. NASA
engineers spent hundreds of thousands of dollars and years of effort
to design the space pen, a writing utensil that could write in zero
gravity, in a vacuum, upside down, under water and below freezing
temperatures. The space pen was a miracle of innovation-by-
committee, well before anyone had an ROI model in Excel. The
Russians took a different approach and came up with an equally
versatile solution. They gave their cosmonauts pencils.

Figure 15.8: The Space Pen. Expensive innovation-by-committee

Finally, I personally experienced the extreme risk-adversity and learn-then-do attitude of NASA and the space industry when I worked in the business right out of college. As I mentioned earlier, I was assigned to NASA's Earth Observation System (EOS) satellite. My task was to design the equipment that would be used to build, handle and test the satellite. It wasn't the sexiest part of working on a spacecraft, but like new employees everywhere and every when, I was treated like a pledge to a fraternity.

Despite the lack of glamour in my assignment I took to the work with abandon. The most challenging part of the assignment was designing an assembly tool for what we called the propulsion module. This module held the fuel tanks, rocket engines and computers that would propel the spacecraft. Because of its complexity, the propulsion module was to be built separately from the rest of the spacecraft, and then inserted into it once both were complete.

To give this some perspective, consider this: the propulsion module was expected to cost $50 million, the rest of the spacecraft $950 million. Hence, putting these two things together correctly was a billion-dollar design issue. I was a 22-year-old engineer fresh out of school, and I had to get this design right. When I speak of risk, I know what I'm talking about.

The challenge of the design was this: The propulsion module weighed about a ton, and to get the assembly right, its position in three-dimensional space had to be accurate and controllable down to a tenth of a millimeter. This was complicated stuff, and I sat and pondered how to do this for several days.

Suddenly, I had a breakthrough. If we hung the module from a set of cables, each with a turnbuckle attached to it (see diagram), the turnbuckles could be used to adjust the position of the module in three dimensions. I won't get into the math of it here, but the design allowed for extremely precise positioning and it was pretty innovative.

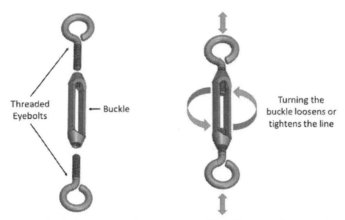

Threaded
Eyebolts

← Buckle

Turning the
buckle loosens or
tightens the line

Figure 15.9: Diagram of a turnbuckle. Space Age technology!

However, there was a problem. For NASA the solution was *too* innovative! When I presented the design at our Preliminary Design Review (PDR) NASA's senior engineers were less than impressed. They immediately scoffed at my design, and told me, "You can't actuate a turnbuckle under load, son." The engineer-to-English translation of that is: "You can't turn a turnbuckle when something is hanging from it." They then told me, "Besides, that would never be able to orient the module correctly." The engineer-to-English translation of which was, "Son, you're an idiot."

The senior engineers told my boss that we needed to go back to the drawing board, come up with an entirely new set of designs for them to choose from, and we'd revisit this issue in six months, at the next review meeting. Oh, and he needed to make sure he sent the NASA guys weekly progress reports, just so they could monitor our 'progress.'

I did not take this feedback well. In fact, at the lunch break, I drove down to the local art supply store, bought some modeling materials, and then I went to the local hardware store and bought a turnbuckle and two cinder blocks. While my boss and the NASA engineers ate lunch, I went back to my desk and built a scale model of my design. I made the module and my fixture out of cardboard, and I used a series of paperclips to simulate the turnbuckles. After an hour, I was ready to go back in the ring.

Figure 15.10: Me as a young space engineer. The cardboard model is hanging over me

214

I returned to the meeting, and demanded to have 15 more minutes out of the agenda. My boss wasn't happy with me, but he could see I wasn't going to take 'no' for an answer. Using the cardboard model, I *showed* the NASA engineers that the design did indeed allow them to control the position of the module in three dimensions. Next, I took the actual turnbuckle, hung the two cinder blocks from it, and handed it to the most senior NASA guy. I told him to try to turn the buckle, and indeed it turned as I had predicted.

Figure 15.11: A soldier tightening a loaded turnbuckle. Sorry NASA, it does work!

NASA wanted to spend hundreds of thousands of additional dollars to 'learn-then-do.' Instead, I spent $25, 'did-then-learned,' and saved the U.S. taxpayers a pile of cash in the process. As we left that meeting, NASA had accepted my design (which later proved to work exactly as I predicted), and my boss had decided it was time for me to work on another project. It turns out that since I saved NASA a bunch of money, our company would have to return that money, and my boss didn't like that. Ah, the unintended consequences of being young, naïve and having a bit of character.

Digital Disruption in Innovation

For two centuries, Analogs have iteratively proven to themselves that in order to innovate, you first have to learn, and then you can apply that learning. The investment of time and treasure in creating innovation comes dearly to their capital-centric sensibilities. No risk goes unpunished in the world of quarterly fiscal reports. Because of this, the optimal course of action for Analogs has been to learn then do – and then, only with the greatest of caution and analysis.

For most of Western society, going to college in the 21st century doesn't mean very much. This is a bum deal for Millennials and Generation Z, and they're justifiably not happy. In Analog companies the process for taking risks has become so onerous, and the fear of failure so high, that recent college graduates cannot break into the entry levels of organizations. They are overflowing with mid- or late-career managers whose sole purpose is to make sure that nothing ever happens, and certainly not untried, untested, un-modeled research or innovation.

This is too bad, because kids these days are a lot closer to Dirt Era craftspeople than Analog era bureaucrats. Today's kids have grown up in a world where pretty much all answers are a click away. You would think that this makes them entirely different from the apprentices of the Land Era, but this isn't necessarily so. While those apprentices lived where the raw materials of innovation were iron, stone, wind and water, today's kids live in a world fed by information.

Young people today have been apprenticing on this raw material since their first mouse click. This is far earlier than any blacksmith's apprentice was given the chance to take a whack at hot metal. Millennials are so tied to the tools of this digital world that the adults around them take them for uneducated, or perhaps even dumb. Despite this perception, by the time they graduate from high school, today's youth aren't apprentices in manipulating the raw material of the Digital Trinity. They are masters.

The degree to which modern young people understand the universe and take that understanding for granted is shocking to Analogs. Clearly, young people don't understand the ins and outs of managing capital in today's complex world. It is only through years of clerking and understudy, and several advanced degrees, that these young people can possibly be trusted to manage substantial chunks of capital wealth.

The view that the 'digital natives' of the Millennial and Gen Z generations are viewed so skeptically by Gen X and Boomers is fairly simple to understand. They don't think less, they just think different (as Steve Jobs put it). The truth is these people are hyper-educated in how to manipulate information, they are masters of understanding information's value, and they practically defined each element of the Six New Normals. The entire world that is disrupting the Analog Trinity is the one created by these over-educated upstarts, in order to maintain the viability of the Analog Trinity. This is exactly as newly and necessarily educated revolutionaries of the 1700s ended the dominance of the Landed Nobility.

Today's youth know dramatically more about how the world *will* work than the people who want to manage them know how it *now* works. For these young Jerks, learning how to model the costs and returns of enormous capital projects in the 2000s makes as much sense as getting a degree in ancient Greek philosophy would to a blacksmith of the 1500s. In a world of apps and clouds and crowdsourcing and microloans, if you want to try to innovate, you're better off just taking a whack at it.

Do Then Learn

Capital is expensive and wasting it is deeply frowned upon. Information is largely free and desperately wants to be shared, analyzed and used. In the Capital Era, being wrong about an hypothesis could cost millions of dollars – and potentially your career. In the Digital age, being wrong about an hypothesis might cost you $1.25 and a morning's effort of setting up an analytic computing cluster in some far-flung land. This was paid for by your Facebook friends in any event.

For the cost of creating yet another iteration of yet another ROI model to prove to yet another Vice President of Risk Management that some well-defined investment is worth the hypothetical non-risk, Jerks can run thousands of wildly varying hypotheses, using actual data, and real-time feedback, to fish for insights to questions they never before thought to ask. From those insights come new ideas, new models, new technologies, products and services which would never see the light of a warm summer's day from inside an Analog's well-designed risk review process. Instead it would lie dormant under fresh mounds of snow-white paperwork, reports and PowerPoints, like a seed in winter hoping for the spring.

Chapter Summary:

1. Analog companies are strongly rewarded for avoiding risks and protecting their capital. After 200 years of optimization, their tendency towards risk avoidance and fear of failure is highly developed.
2. Analogs tend to extensively analyze *what* might happen if they take action before ever doing so.
3. Jerks do the opposite. Jerks experiment, take risks and learn what does or does not generate their desired results.
4. Jerks take small risks, quickly, so that they rapidly converge on the correct answer for the question at hand.

Chapter Sixteen: Jerks Look Forward Not Backward

"In order to carry a positive action we must develop here a positive vision."- Dalai Lama

"Revolutions go not backward."- Ralph Waldo Emerson

This chapter is the end of Section Two. This closing principle of Jerks – look forward and not backward – may seem curious, given the amount of history discussed in the previous 11 chapters. I'll get to that in a moment.

Jerks are hyper-focused on where they are going, and not so much on where they have been. This is a function of the speed at which they must operate as they metabolize information with the Digital Trinity. It's a function of meeting their customers' needs at the speed of light, or even faster, according to the Six New Normals. It's dependent on the fact that context and correlation are constantly changing, and in the new Information Era, context and correlation are the new currency of power. And finally, it's a function of the age-old adage, "You get what you focus on." Or, as Mark Twain put it, "There is no sadder sight than a young pessimist."

Jerks care about the future, so that's where their attention lies. Analogs generally care about the past, so that's where their minds tend to go. This is critically important to understanding the differences in how Analogs approach their work and their world, and how some Jerks do the same with theirs. To Jerks, reports about what has happened in the past are like stats to a professional sports star. They're good for keeping score. Beyond this mildly interesting method for keeping track of how well you are doing, or how fast you are moving, reports are mostly worthless to Jerks. They're too busy actually working.

This attitude is completely and utterly mystifying to Analogs, and it also pisses them off. Telling an Analog that their business reports are useless is like telling the devoutly religious that their chosen holy writ is pulp fiction. It usually provokes a strong negative reaction. For Analogs, reports are scripture. Reporting is worshipping at the altar of Capitalism.

How did we get to this point? How did Analogs become so deeply wedded to reports, and Jerks so viciously opposed? Again, a brief review of history may be revealing. Also, if you're a Jerk, I promise, this will be enlightening and worth your time. Don't dismiss me yet!

Bean Counters in Love

Analogs love reports. They live and die by reports. To them, the sun rises and sets by reports, like the captain of a clipper ship lost at sea, desperate for the sun to set so he can shoot a bearing with his sextant and figure out where he is.

To Analogs, reports are the embodiment of the power of the Analog Trinity. They are to capitalist organizations what birth certificates or a royal seal were to people under the Land Trinity. They are what dried skulls, brightly-colored feathers, bear claws and rattles were to shamans in the Tool Trinity. In their respective trinities, these objects are physical manifestations of the allocation of power. To an Analog, coming up with a really good report is like a shaman stumbling upon an eagle feather while high on ayahuasca or peyote: your mojo is now strong!

Analog Vision Quest

Consider the Annual Report. Look at it with a slightly critical eye. Do the parallels to shamanistic tools leap out at you? When shamans wanted to demonstrate their power and value to their tribes, they'd hold a vision quest. The shaman would cook up a secret psychedelic brew, made of herbs, cacti, poison dart frogs, and such. Then, the shaman would schedule a meeting of the tribe, typically in a sacred place with cosmic significance to the tribe. Perhaps there would be a nearby rock formation that looked like a person or a bird. Or maybe it was a place where at certain times of the year the sun or the moon lined up just-so. Where and when the vision quest took place was important to the overall effect.

Figure 16.1: A Shaman's outfit. The annual report of the Tool Trinity

Once the ceremony began, everyone partook of the shaman's sacred brew. It short-circuited the critical thinking skills of their frontal lobes. Once everyone was a bit loopy, the shaman would use his magical crow's foot, feather, gem-encrusted rock or gong to start invoking control over the spirits the tribe believed in. He would utter sacred chants, sing ritualized songs familiar to all as the path to enlightenment, and they would all chant in unison their belief in the power held by the shaman on their behalf.

The following morning, the whole tribe would awake, shake their heads, and try to remember the details of what they had seen the night before. Some details stuck with them, and would guide their activities for the next few months. Other details were hazy, but seemed to have spoken of visions, strategies, collaboration and focus. These thoughts sort of floated around the fringes of their headaches, forming a somewhat negative psychic association for the tribe members' visions and strategies.

When I look at an Analog company's executive meeting, I see a shaman's vision quest. The CEO or Chairman of the Board is the shaman, trying to convince the tribe that the coming harvest will be blessed. There is no shortage of mystical brew shared among the believers. Most of us know the term 'drinking the Kool-Aid,' as the executive prepares to wield the magical trinkets that embody his power. Those trinkets are reports, lovingly, masterfully, carefully, industriously assembled by armies of assistants, bookkeepers, auditors and administrators.

Once the magical relics are produced for display, the executive begins the mystical chants, talking in tongues about strategies and forecasts, seasonality and competition from other tribes, about the resources they have and the efforts they need. This shows the organization that they are on top of things. After each holy relic is displayed (in this case, the Revenues, Balance Sheets, and so on) the executive pronounces that the next harvest will be better than the last. This will be true as long as the tribe continues to focus on what matters, and keeps praying to their collective gods.

Following the ceremony, the executive returns to his wood-paneled long hut, which in this case is a Gulfstream business jet, satisfied that the gods have been appeased (financial analysts and reporters). Their relics are hung back up in the long hut, stored until the next ceremony, updated with a new feather or trinket or bauble picked up along the way (new metrics), demonstrating a new and improved level of power for the tribe. The tribe, their worship ceremony completed, return to their daily tasks, wondering how these might change based upon the vision and strategy that was just shared with them. Within a few days everything returns to how it was before, save a few lingering hangovers, and the tribe goes about its business until the next annual meeting.

No matter how the world around us changes, one thing remains much the same: some of our traditions go far back in our history and still resonate with us today. In this light, business reports are the harbingers of spring for Analogs, and nothing foretells of a bountiful harvest like a well-formatted balance sheet.

Reporting: Rituals of the Church of Capitalism

We've discussed the critical nature of reports and reporting to the control of capital. Because reporting is so important, organizations invest an enormous amount of capital to control, well, their capital. Scrooge and Marley spent their days counting their riches and keeping their books because this was the embodiment of their power over their community. A penny saved is a penny earned, but only if your books say so! To be powerful you need to show your power, and nothing shows your power like your bank balance or stock portfolio.

Companies embraced information technology in the middle of the 20th century when they applied it to their management of capital-centric information. Computers were both faster and more accurate than an army of accountants, leading to faster and more accurate reports. By the 1980s these tools had advanced sufficiently that an entire Analog business could be replicated in software and tracked online, and Enterprise Resource Planning software was born – a colossal innovation for applying the Analog Trinity. Organizations still maintained their huge bureaucracies, byzantine processes and archaic rules (they remain relics of power after all). But now they were automated by ERP, making them more efficient, effective and faster. Soon, reports no longer took months or years to create. They could be made in under a week! Shaman/executives rejoiced.

Business Intelligence?

By the 1990s, executives were intoxicated by the transparency that ERP lent to the Analog Trinity. Leaders could generate reports and rejoice at how their wealth and power grew. They paid keen attention to how the organization performed compared to previous time frames. This quantified their increases in wealth and power. Each quarter should be better than the last. ERP technologies meant that much more detailed information could be kept and reused in the quest for more capital growth. Analyzing old data could reveal beneficial trends that might be otherwise missed. Looking at old data for hidden gems of efficiency became automated and industrialized, and the concept of Business Intelligence (BI) was born. BI is the notion that by looking at past performance, organizations could improve their performance today. Identifying sources of inefficiency or waste of capital allowed for the Analog Trinity to be adjusted for improved performance. The 'intelligence' of BI came from the idea that this process of analysis of the past to optimize the present was similar to how people think, and hence it is a form of intelligence. Soon, practitioners of BI became the new shamans of their tribes, as they became a new source of wealth and power.

I love the term *business intelligence*. It's so nuanced and loaded with subconscious manipulation that you can't possibly not want to use it. The very label implies that if you're not doing business intelligence, then you must not be, well, intelligent. This was marketing par excellence, as technology vendors rushed to create systems and solutions that would prevent Analogs from remaining 'dumb.' Soon, organizations were piling up all of their data in gigantic 'data warehouses,' and hiring a new breed of shaman, the dreaded 'data scientist,' in order to sift out and recover capital that had been lost through oversight and dumb decisions. Any company that hoped to have a good quarterly Vision Quest simply had to have this new breed of shaman as part of the ceremony.

Big Data

By the start of the 21st century, BI had inculcated the entire Analog world with the notion that no decision could possibly be made without a thorough exploration of the past. Sifting through old data stacked high and wide in data warehouses was key to finding and re-collecting old, lost, or misallocated capital.

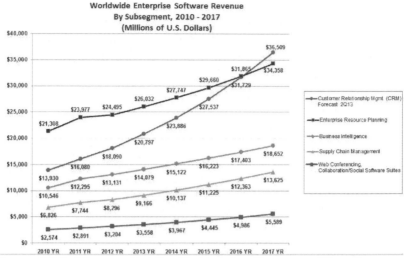

Figure 16.2: The market for Enterprise Resource Planning software

Like most things that are piled high and left by themselves, much of this old data began to decay and rot. Over time, this composting of old data meant that new techniques of exploration and discovery were required, and data mining was born. Analysts were trained to dig through ever-deepening piles of data in an attempt to find chunks that might be somehow useful to capital growth. In these massive lakes of old information, data miners were looking for bits of correlated data floating about in vast bodies of open uncorrelated data.

This process had its early roots at the turn of the century, in what became known as 'Big Data.' Three characteristics converged to represent the challenges faced by data miners as they dug through massive amounts of uncorrelated slag. Volume, Velocity and Variety defined the scope of the problem faced by miners. Because the amount of each of these Vs was growing exponentially in the post-Internet 1.0 world, this problem of ingestion, digestion and comprehension of lots of data was named Big Data.

Big Data was, and remains, an enormous trend in the world of business, and I am something of a practitioner in this field. Organizations the world over are looking to deploy so-called Big

Data solutions, so that they can have their newly hired data scientists swim through lakes of data, looking for correlations that were missed as they passed through the bowels of their Analog digestive systems. In 2016, it's a very good thing to claim that you are a data scientist, because it attracts job offers. It's even better if you actually have skills at this kind of work as, eventually, a lack of progress or output will show up on a report somewhere.

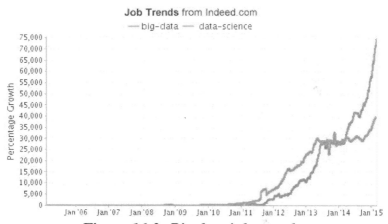

Figure 16.3: Big data job growth

I foresee that this present craze over Big Data will continue, at least for a time. The interest in Big Data is a logical extension of trying to apply Analog principles to a world heading towards Digitization. As discussed in the previous chapter, nobles in the 1600s tried to extend and maintain the influence of the Dirt Trinity by taking small steps towards the Analog Trinity. They created institutions of learning, and populations of educated people, in order to expand the amount of dirt that they controlled. Similarly, current efforts by Analogs to implement Big Data solutions are an attempt to use tools of the coming Digital Trinity to expand the reach and control of the Analog Trinity, and to build more capital as a result.

Just as partially embracing Analog tools ensured the eventual end of the Land Trinity, capital-centric organizations that are partially embracing the Digital Trinity by implementing Big Data are ensuring their own destruction. Switching from one power structure to another is not a halfway affair. Like a snowball rolling down a hill, once you start this transition, its completion is inevitable. Big Data represents a tepid and tenuous misapplication of the Digital Trinity, in an attempt to optimize the old by applying selective aspects of the new.

Unfortunately, this approach is like being sort of pregnant. If you subvert your beliefs in how you create wealth and power, there is no going back. Once you stop drinking deeply from the shaman's cup of magical brew, much of the effect of the ceremony wears off. Once you stop believing that the eagle feather is anything more than a feather, the whole show starts to look faintly ridiculous. Once there is a shift in your perspective on how wealth and power are created, even a little bit, the whole pageant begins to look like it's fixed. The MC is in cahoots with the contestants to make for a better show.

A Focus on the Past

The point is that reports are all about focusing on the past. Trying to get smarter about the present by looking at past performance has been an extremely effective method for reclaiming capital that had previously been missed, or in finding ways to use it more effectively in the present. From Business Intelligence, through Data Mining, to the present craze that is Big Data, Analog companies have been combining old data with new techniques, in order to apply the Analog Trinity more effectively.

This maniacal focus on the past is fundamental to capitalists, because capitalism is all about keeping the books. The more wealth that your books, balance sheets or ERP systems say that you have, the more power you have in actuality. That's how capitalism works, and its how capitalism came to surpass and then supplant imperialism and its Trinity of Dirt. To Analogs, the past isn't just nostalgic, it's the basis of how they evaluate their very existence, and how well they are doing in it.

Back to the Future

This world view is foreign to Jerks. Jerks just don't care that much about the past. For all of the time, effort and space we have used in discussing the past in this book, I have not done so for the benefit of Jerks. Rather, I have done so to try to help Analogs understand why they think the way they do, and why this thinking, which was once so right, is now so wrong.

Jerks care about the here and the now; recall their focus on context and correlation. But they care about the here and the now because these are the bases of their predictions. The here, the now and the future are the focus of their customers, as defined by the Six New Normals. For Jerks to effectively meet their customers' needs and expectations, they need to act right here, right now, perfectly and invisibly; so say we all.

Jerks do find some value in older data, but only to front-load their analyses. Jerks use old data like we humans do ourselves. When we perceive something new to us, we have no knowledge of it and so we are not sure how to react to it. When a child first sees a stove top or an open flame, it is a new experience. They proceed to check out this unknown and potentially fascinating new phenomenon, and they get burned. The next time that child comes across an open flame they remember *exactly* what that phenomenon is capable of, and their fingers give it a wide berth.

Jerks use old information to instill memory into their analyses. Jerks could start with no historical information at all, and just take their best guess at delivering a product or service. But, by using old information on our wants and our needs, Jerks can accelerate their try/fail/learn/repeat cycle and find new solutions more quickly. Jerks may use old data to get a better grip on the present, but for Jerks, using old data is all about getting back to the future more quickly.

Data, Doc's DeLorean and Digital Drowning

To Jerks, old information in Analog reports is also fairly irrelevant because of Einstein's law of general relativity. Einstein postulated, and researchers and engineers have recently confirmed, that when you approach the speed of light, everything else seems to slow down. This is the impact of relativity, the insight that launched Einstein into immortality. As you move through space and time, everything else is moving too, relative to you. Your motions through these dimensions can be captured by measuring them, capturing your changes in context. If you speed up your rate of context change, everything else begins to appear to slow down. This is relativity at work. Indeed, Einstein predicted that this deceleration isn't just a perception, it is real. As you speed up your rate of context change, and approach the speed of light, the entire universe actually does slow down relative to you.

This is also true for the world of Jerks. Jerks deal in information -- and information, the life blood of the Digital Trinity, pretty much moves at the speed of light. The faster and faster Jerks can move in analyzing our changing context in the universe, the more we appear to slow down to them. This relative deceleration helps Jerks to know and respond to us better, leading to the outcomes that we desire most.

For Jerks, the faster they operate in the present, the sooner they can get to the future. And when they get there, things – at least from their perspective – slow down to the point that both they, and we, can kick back and enjoy the results. For Analogs looking backwards inside their Big Data warehouses, all they see is a momentary flash as the Jerk and their customers wiz by, like Doc and Marty McFly in a souped up Delorean time machine. Once the distraction passes, Analog data miners quietly return to their digging, looking for nuggets of misapplied capital hidden deep in some data lake.

Naturally, Jerks do still run reports, if only because they must remain at least partially tied to the lingering Analog world. But beyond minimal creation of such relics, and superficial participation in these Capitalist rituals, Jerks have better things to do with their time. Jerks will bridge these two worlds for as long as it's expected. This will be only as much as is minimally necessary to survive while the transition from Analog to Digital takes place. Fortunately for them, Jerks will likely have to play this shaman's charade for just a short while longer. The future is arriving faster than most Analogs can possibly fathom.

Figure 16.4: Doc discovered that the future is full of 'data scientists'

Chapter Summary:

1. Analogs use business reports to ensure that they are applying the Analog Trinity effectively and efficiently.
2. Reports inevitably focus on what has already happened, rather than the present or the future. Hence, reports reinforce Analogs' fixation on the past.
3. Jerks know that historical data has only one use: making better predictions of the future.
4. Beyond making predictions, Jerks largely ignore reports, and the old, outdated information they encompass.

SECTION III: The Six 'Digital Dashpots'

If you're an Analog, you might have found Section Two disturbing. There's a formula for disrupting your world and your business. If there's a formula, then it's coming for you, too.

What's an Analog to do? Given the inevitability of this change occurring, and the ease with which the 'Dirty Dozen' can be used, what possible response is left for Analogs? How can Analogs delay, if not prevent, the disruption that Jerks are bringing?

To answer this I present the six 'Digital Dashpots.' These six principles may be the only response that Analogs may use to delay, for a time, the impact that Jerks will have on your organization, your industry and your life.

In engineering, a dashpot is a device that absorbs kinetic energy and converts that energy into something else, usually heat. The shock absorbers on your car are dashpots. When your car hits a bump, the energy that pushes up on your wheel is fed into the shock absorber as kinetic energy. The shock absorber literally absorbs the shock and motion, and converts them into heat. The dashpot takes the force of the blow, and turns it into waste heat. The dashpot takes the velocity of the motion and slows it way down, lessening its impact on the rest of the car.

So too, Analogs can use these six Digital Dashpots to slow Jerks down and to divert some of their disruptive force. These strategies won't stop Jerks, at least not all of them. But they will kill off some Jerks, and will slow down and delay others enough that Analogs can form another committee, to perform another analysis, to create another ROI analysis, and put it into another report about what not to do. Kidding. These can buy you some time to begin choosing how you change, rather than being forced into changes that you may not like.

The six 'Digital Dashpots' are:
1. DIE While You Can

2. Rewrite Your Books
3. Break Your Rules
4. Annihilate Your Processes
5. Fail Fast
6. Seek Discomfort

In Section Three, we will review each in turn.

Chapter Seventeen: Use Capital to DIE

"If I had asked people what they wanted, they would have said faster horses."- Henry Ford

"It ain't what you don't know that gets you into trouble. It's what you know for sure that just ain't so."- Mark Twain

Welcome to the opening volley of Section 3. What in the world can you do about these Jerks? If you are asking this question I'm going to assume that you live somewhere within an Analog organization. Jerks might read Section 3 to amuse themselves during a brief semi-legalized-pot-induced flash mob coding session at their local solar-powered, off-grid, volunteer-staffed, organic-coffee house, but otherwise this stuff doesn't apply to them.

Section 3 doesn't apply to Jerks because they don't haul around Analog baggage. Perhaps they started out as Digital and have always been that way, like Millennials and Generation Z. Or they are ex-Analogs who turned their backs on the old ways and were ejected by their Analog overlords as heretics, left to wander in the Digital wilderness (arguably, like yours truly). Jerks have different sensibilities than Analogs, and they are free from the grip of two centuries of capitalist history.

Jerks also won't get a lot of value from Section 3 because they also don't have the same strengths as Analogs. Section 2 may have seemed like a tirade against Big Business, but that was not my intent. Rather, Section 2 was supposed to be an exploration of exactly how Big Business got to be that way. We should recognize the success of their efforts before their slide into oblivion. At the moment there are certain advantages enjoyed by capital-rich Analog organizations. Putting these advantages to work is the key to extending your power and wealth in the world, at least for a while longer.

A key advantage for Analogs is that they have lots of capital, which they are supposed to harness to create still more wealth. Generally, when looking for returns on capital investments, Analogs like to go back to the same old well. As discussed in Section 2, Analogs like to go with what they know when it comes to investing. This means that there is no need to revise their ROI models, no need to modify their investment review process, no need to change their approval workflows, and no need to get trained in some new-fangled technology like Hadoop, Hive or Pig. When your ERP system already has a line item for buying U.S. Treasury T-Bills, it's easy to throw a bit more cash into that journal entry, negative interest rates notwithstanding.

A Brief Note on DIEing

So, is there a way for Analogs to reinvest capital back into capital that will generate Digital-like results? The answer is, emphatically, Yes! Unfortunately, when investing, many Analogs follow the path of least resistance; they keep doing the same old thing they did before, just a bit faster, a bit leaner, a bit more offshore or with a bit more quality. For backwards-focused, risk-averse, capital-centric Analogs, change is a scary thing.

But as we approach the end of the Capital Age, earning decent returns on these tried-and-true investment methods is becoming harder. How many times can you make a Snickers bar three per cent smaller before you reach the point that your old Fun-Sized won't feed a hamster for a few laps on its wheel? To disrupt Jerks you need to put them off balance by putting *yourself* off balance. You need to beat Bruce Lee in the sumo ring by getting in close and crushing him with your immense bulk. KERFLATTEN!!!!

The way to cause this unbalance is to change the Analog rules of capital management so they are back in your favor. Analog-to-Digital gap-jumpers like Amazon, SpaceX, Tesla Motors, Google, and Apple do exactly that, and they have extraordinary market capitalization as a result. These companies use immense capital to generate disruption by *their* rules rather than some Jerk's rules. In so doing, they manage to keep their advantages to themselves for a while longer.

Figure 17.1: 'Fun size' Snickers bars

What does the investment strategy of these gap-jumpers look like? What drives these organizations to invest in moving between the DIE phases, rather than inside of a phase? Well, I'm not privy to their board meetings, but from my perspective these companies DIE a lot. D-I-E stands for *Discover, Infiltrate* and *Exploit*. These are the three phases of how our society takes new inputs, comes to understand them, and then puts them to work. I have written a bit about this approach elsewhere, but we will revisit it briefly below. Google DIE if you want a deeper dive into this process.

DIE is how we find, break through and dominate new territories, barriers, frontiers, etc. This process is innate. We've been doing it for nearly all of our history and it's the basis of much of our success as a species. As we push our boundaries we *discover* new territories to explore, which we then *infiltrate* by roaming around, checking out their nooks and crannies, peaks and valleys. Finally, once we have the lay of the land, we begin to e*xploit* the heck out of it. It's what we do and, for better or for worse, we're good at DIE. Look at the history of how we took control of any new land or technology, and the way we succeeded was to DIE.

Transitions are Scary

While humans are comfortable with this process of DIEing, not all aspects of it are kind to us. There can be a lot of unknowns. When

Europeans first started to explore the open Atlantic Ocean to their west, most were terrified of the unknown that might lie beyond the horizon. Most sailors of the time seemed to believe that out past that edge there were terrible sea monsters that swallowed people whole, churning them up inside and spitting them out on some foreign shore. Today we call these monsters cruise ships, but I digress.

When Analogs begin a new DIE process, or when they transition from *discover* to *infiltrate* to *exploit*, they are alarmed by uncertainty, doubt and risk. These are three qualities that Analogs love to model out in their ROI calculators. When the investment comes up for review, it inevitably leads to a resounding No! For most Analogs, investing in a move from one DIE phase to another is a sure way to make your tribe's shaman throw down some ugly voodoo on your investment report.

Figure 17.2: Conestoga wagons, heading to California

Conversely, when moving within each phase of the DIE process, we tend to be pretty comfortable. Once I know that there is a new world across the ocean, hopping on a galleon isn't quite so scary. If I know I'm taking a Conestoga wagon westward to California, I've accepted that I may face hostile locals along the way. Once I'm actually inside a certain phase of this process, I probably have all of the pertinent risk variables set up in my ROI models. Hence, cranking out a justification for a further inner-phase investment only takes *one* tiger team to figure out, instead of eight or nine.

Analogs love to invest inside a DIE phase because it's easy, less risky, and less disruptive. There are not a lot of unknowns, so you're not taking on a lot of risk. Analogs like that. The problem is, intra-phase investments in DIE are necessarily less risky, but they are also necessarily less disruptive, to both Analogs and the Jerks they're competing against.

Jerks, practically by definition, don't work inside of DIE phases. Instead they operate almost exclusively *between* DIE phases, and for good reason. Analogs won't go there. Taxi companies could have easily created an app to connect riders with drivers as quickly and conveniently as Uber does. This would have been a very inter-DIE-phase thing for them to do. Instead, to get better returns on their capital, they switched from honkin' big rear-wheel-drive sedans to cute, fuel-efficient hybrids. This was a very intra-DIE-phase approach to investing, which was much more comfortable.

Taxi companies already had Analog Trinity infrastructures in place to evaluate their investment strategy. It was simple to update the data entries for price, fuel mileage, maintenance and insurance in their investment models with the new values for hybrid taxis. It didn't even dawn on them to come up with a completely new ROI model for some new-fangled app, built on new technology, doing something that had never been done before, and wasn't guaranteed to work anyway. Analogs keep getting out-maneuvered by Jerks, not because Analogs are dumb, or slow, or backwards, or lack innovation. But this describes the tools that they use. Rather, Analogs get out maneuvered because they are risk averse, comfortable with the status quo, and are rewarded for keeping capital from moving about. This, wedded to their obsession with incremental improvement, Kaizen-style, leads to poor investment choices.

Uber is just one of many examples of successful Jerks, either out there already or waiting in the wings, causing disruption to existing players. They are using information, and the Digital Trinity, to drive innovation inter-DIE-phase, rather than intra-DIE-phase. Analogs don't like going there.

Let Your Capital DIE

17.3: The Apple Newton. The iPhone version 0

So, how can Analogs beat Jerks at their own game? Simple, just do the same as Jerks do, only do it bigger and better, like a sumo. Analogs need to focus their dramatically greater reserves of capital on the goal of moving inter-DIE-phase, rather than simply intra-DIE-phase. If you have already discovered a new product or service, use your capital to drive that innovation into the *infiltrate* phase where economies of scale and scope still matter. This is what Apple did with the iPhone, and Blackberry didn't know what hit it.

If you have already milked an *infiltrate* phase dry, invest in driving the cost and the price down to zero as fast as possible. Drag the whole industry into the *exploit* phase, and make it impossible for

Jerks to sustain a competitive advantage from their digital dexterity. If this sounds eerily like what Amazon did to retail businesses other than books once they had the basics of ecommerce figured out, it's no accident.

Intra-DIE-phase investing is seductive because it's easy. There are few risks to doing the same old thing, just a little bit better. You'll likely keep the same old customers as you have come to depend on, even if you keep Snickering their fun-sized candy bars year after year. Intra-DIE-phase investment pays off in terms of minimizing short-term risk, which looks great at your tribe's next quarterly Vision Quest. But, if you want to keep having Vision Quests more than a year or two out, and you want the chants to be those of continued success and growth of the tribe, you need to focus your capital dollars on inter-DIE-phase investments, despite the risks and unknowns.

Chapter Summary:

1. Humanity follows a three-step process for expanding our reach: Discover, Infiltrate and Exploit.
2. In the Discover phase, we identify new technologies or frontiers that were previously unknown. In the Infiltrate phase, we learn the breadth and depth of the new discovery, and enrich our understanding of its possibilities. In the Exploit phase, we take full advantage of the new discovery.
3. Innovating within a phase tends to have lower risks, but also yields smaller rewards. Innovating between phases is riskier but can yield great rewards.
4. Analogs tend to innovate within a given DIE phase. Jerks tend to innovate between phases, or start entirely new DIE frontiers.

Chapter Eighteen: Rewrite Your Books

"Watch what people are cynical about, and one can often discover what they lack."- George S. Patton

"In theory there is no difference between theory and practice. In practice, there is."- Yogi Berra

Chapter 17 explained why changing your investment strategy from intra-DIE-phase to inter-DIE-phase is essential to fighting off Jerks. When you do this, you multiply the power of your key strength which is capital. But, as noted earlier, this typically runs counter to every bone in the bodies of your analysts, accountants, controllers, administrators and executives. To make it possible for these Analogs to be willing to make this switch in investment strategy, you need to add new terms to their ROI equations. Without this, their math will simply never add up and allow them to make this switch.

The difference in risk profile between intra- and inter-DIE-phase investment is simply too large for most Analogs. What may be on the other side of a phase gap is either too difficult to characterize, or the investments inside of a phase are too *easy* to characterize, creating an enormous sense of fear of the unknown. Recall that the one thing that Analogs hate more than risk is failure to gain return on investment, and it's easy to see why they almost never go gap-jumping.

Through Section 2 we discussed the historical context for the fears of risk and failure; these characteristics have served Analogs well during two centuries of capitalism's ascendency. For these people, the notion that this rise has somehow peaked, and a descent is now imminent, simply does not compute. Their models say it ain't so! And remember that those same models have been built, nurtured, and lovingly adhered to by these Analogs for decades, if not longer. It's not easy telling someone that their baby is ugly, especially after it's won a beauty pageant or two.

Assumptions, and You and Me

Analogs must be shown that they missed some important variables in their equations. They also need to check their assumptions. Here, in the mid-2010s, there is a tremendous amount of turmoil in the world. Open conflict between nation-states and new-semi-pseudo-kinda-nation-states; commodity prices alternately collapsing and spiking; crude oil losing over 80 per cent of its agreed-to value in under a year; *negative* interest rates enacted by central banks (an OMG!!! moment for Analogs if ever there was one); and political climates shifting in directions not seen since the very last days of the Dirt Trinity. All these lead one to think that not just some of the assumptions that Analogs have been using in their models might be wrong. Oh no, it's starting to look like *all* of the assumptions might be wrong. Hence, everything down in the Accounting and Finance departments is going catawampus (I love that word. Thanks Mark Twain!).

Note: If this, too, sounds like an interesting angle to take on all this Hope and Change stuff, stay tuned for my next book, Rupture, which will deal with the social and political impacts of the Digital Trinity and the shift to the Information Age.

These modelers, diligent in their efforts and stoic in their beliefs, are finding their assumptions not only moving outside of expected normal values, they are truly moving into unchartered territories: DIE-style. A little variation is expected; into each distribution a little tail must fall. But to have such drastic swings in the inputs that Analogs use to feed their equations and calculate risks and returns is a little too 'down the rabbit hole' for most of them.

This annihilation of Analog input assumptions can be turned to our advantage, and we will return to that thought in a moment.

Put a Monkey in the Wrench

To help Analogs learn to be a bit more change- and risk-friendly, you have to hit them where they live: in their spreadsheets and models. You have to recall that, for their entire careers, these people have been measured, compensated, rewarded or punished by the supposed accuracy of these models. They were taught to take the models extremely seriously, and they do. Asking them to ignore, discard or otherwise discount the results of these models simply isn't going to convince them. They are far too vested in their work. To get your Analogs to make this psychic shift, you first need to change their mathematics.

Analog modelers work hard to replicate reality in the models they build. This is essential to feeding the needs of Analog Trinity governance, because accurate books are what capitalism is all about. Time and again I have seen Analog managers literally spend hours combing through every last detail in a financial model, just to figure out why some calculation came out as $1,235,600 rather than $1,235,599.53 (HINT: it's call rounding, *Einstein*).

I had one manager who was fanatical about this. He literally said that rounding didn't exist. He also was a former artillery officer in the Marine Corps, which doesn't speak well of this otherwise-elite organization. I used to cringe when I thought of some poor Marines calling for artillery support from this genius. They would have been overrun by their enemy long before he finished calculating the exact location to start dropping artillery shells with his slide rule, compass and anemometer. In a capital-centric, Analog world, accuracy is good, but false precision is next to godliness.

To get Analogs to have a change of heart about risk, you need to add new variables to their equations. Their existing models will almost invariably support an intra-DIE-phase investment over an inter-DIE-phase investment, because the unknown variable, *risk*, tends to get played up. Recall that the only thing capitalists hate more than risk is a loss due to risk, so we tend to overstate the size and shape of risks in order to avoid being wrong. Adding new terms to the equations that Analogs use can allow them, via you, to overcome their tendency towards risk inflation, and lead them to consider new answers. The fact that this approach almost always leads to a better representation or reality is an added bonus.

242

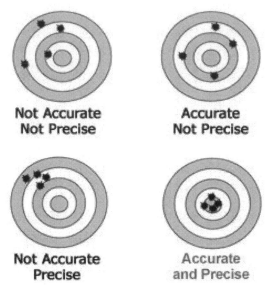

Not Accurate Not Precise **Accurate Not Precise**

Not Accurate Precise **Accurate and Precise**

Figure 18.1: Accuracy versus precision. Financial modelers,
please take note

The Lever is Already Getting Longer

The ancient Greek philosopher Archimedes once wrote, "Give me a lever long enough and I could move the world." Indeed, he was correct in the physical sense. As long as the lever is strong enough to carry the load, you can make enormous things move, more easily than you might think. Changing people's attitudes, too, can take a lot of effort, especially when you're trying to change decades of herd-like thinking that has been rewarded, Pavlov-style, with this stuff we call 'income.'

Getting Analogs to change their models requires them to change their thinking. It has been my general observation that Analogs hate both in equal measure. If you want to make substantial changes in how Analogs measure risks and rewards, you need to figure out what's in it for them. They're good at making these kinds of calculations – it's their job!

The argument that I have found to work best is that something new has happened which requires a re-think. It's not that the model is wrong. At the time it was created it was perfection itself. Rather, the world has moved on a bit since then, and to maintain accuracy and to avoid risk and capital loss (*horrors!*) it may be necessary to make some modifications. Drifting assumptions are the Trojan Horse of change.

Figure 18.2: Make change small, subtle, and unavoidable

Given the massive degree of disruptive changes in the world, the assumptions that Analogs have used in their models aren't drifting, they're careering about like Chuck in a game of Angry Birds. If it takes a lever to move the thinking of an Analog modeler, then I'd say that negative interest rates, ISIS and crude oil cheaper than spring water are mighty long levers. With these changes afoot, the time is right to sneak in some other disruptions, Trojan-style!

Analytic Carpet Bombing

Given that radical changes are going on all around us, and Analogs need to account for these in their quest for optimal growth with no risk, these days the time is right to give disruption to them with both barrels. I'm confident in making the prediction that when it comes to disruption, we ain't seen nothin' yet. Between now and about 2030, there is far more disruption to come as our society and economy shift from the Capitalist Era to the Information Era. Collectively we have been through this before, as we shifted first from Tools to Dirt and then again from Dirt to Capital; social and economic change is nothing new, thanks to our love of technology.

I presented this notion through Section 2, and I hope I made a decent argument. If there is indeed more disruption to come, we are going to see changes similar in amplitude, or intensity, to those we have seen in the past – only it will all happen about a million times faster. Thank Mr. Einstein and his speed of light for that. If we are already in an era where it will be necessary to more or less toss out the Analog structures that we have built up and relied upon, perhaps this is the time to sneak in some new variables that make inter-DIE-phase investments actually *more* attractive and less risky than intra-DIE-phase investments.

Here's how this might work. Say that your Analog tribe has figured out that as long as oil prices stay below $25 a barrel, and the interest rates on American T-Bills stay above zero per cent, and global unemployment continues to fall, and China's stock market stabilizes, and Iran does not explode its first atomic bomb, you can sell your whatchamacallit at a gross profit of 20 per cent. This is an entirely plausible use case that should ring familiar to all of my fellow Analogs.

What I find interesting here is that these sorts of interdependencies, these massively intertwined and co-dependent variables, are something that financial modelers started working on in the mid-1990s, right about the time that the Cold War ended and lots of rocket scientists like me had to find employment elsewhere. The really scary, creepy-cool rocket guys, those who programmed the guidance and navigation systems, all went to Wall Street and invented something called derivatives. As a result of their work they all made a fortune, and some even managed to keep some of it following the two stock market meltdowns their modeling helped to create. Math is some powerful stuff!

Figure 18.3: Calvin, world-leading economist

Back to the hypothetical. Given all of these variables in the equation, your Analog modelers and decision-makers will have to model out all of the possible scenarios in order to manage the risk. If any one of these inputs goes beyond the limits of the original assumptions, the other variables tend to be impacted too, calling for some modification to the model. If enough of these variations and interdependencies converge, it becomes time for a substantial rewrite; the lever finally grew long enough to move the conventional wisdom of the group. The models will be recast, reshaped, rejiggered and recalculated in order to ensure that risk is avoided and capital growth is maintained. In essence, make the requirements of modelers such that they must completely redesign their models to fit a new reality. They'll do it, and own it, which will change the organization's thinking overnight. Change has to be the result, not the cause.

Given that the frequency and intensity of disruptive change is likely to increase over the next few decades, now is the time to force these changes in the thinking conventions and beliefs of your Analogs, in order to change your investment strategies. Changes that were inconceivable just a few years ago (and hence remained un-modeled, and perhaps un-modelable) are now fair game. A door to analytic and political change is cracked open. If you see this, it is time to strike. It is time to carpet bomb your Analogs with more variables that have more extreme values than they ever considered possible, because these things are now normal. Your Analogs have been trained to be thorough, diligent and conscientious about considering every possibility, *within the realm of reasonableness*. To change your Analog company's ability to adapt to this changing world, you must make things that were ridiculous appear to be at least conceivable, if not downright likely.

If you do this, your Analog organization will reorient itself to these changes. Its mechanisms of control, defined by the Analog Trinity, will reorient, realign and adapt themselves, to ensure that risks are eliminated and capital growth is maintained, just like good old capitalism intended. If it just so happens that one of the results of this recalculation is that inter-DIE-phase investments make more sense than intra-DIE-phase investments, just blame the wooden horse; he looked guilty for it anyway.

Use a Soft Touch

Throughout my consulting career I've built hundreds, if not thousands, of financial models. Like other Analogs, I put countless hours into making these models as accurate as possible, to enable clients to make good business decisions. The work can often be tedious, but it can also be strangely interesting. Both building these models, and testing how they work, sort of bonds the modeler to the model. The more time a modeler puts into a model, the stronger that bond and the more personal it gets when you want to get them to make a change.

If you convince these keepers of the crown of capitalism to change their models in the name of accuracy, precision, risk reduction and capital maximization, go easy on them. Yes, their babies may need a little remedial tutoring in order to keep up with a changing world, but they should at least get a trophy for participation, so they don't feel like they're the wrong kind of special.

Chapter Summary:

1. Analog organizations are well versed in using metrics, models and math to govern capital. Use these tools to drive the organization to change in ways they otherwise would not.
2. Breakthrough performance requires breakthrough metrics. Set goals that require a doubling or tripling of performance, or more, in order to get out-of-the-box thinking.
3. If the organization responds that these new goals are impossible, then you are on the right track.

Chapter Nineteen: Break Your Rules

*"Change is the law of life. And those who look only to
the past or present are certain to miss the future."-
John F. Kennedy*

*"Congratulations. I knew the record would stand until
it was broken."- Yogi Berra*

For 200 years the Analog Trinity has taught us to believe that rules
are a good thing. Rules are critical for ensuring stability, tranquility
and predictability in a world focused on capital. Organizations use
rules to ensure that capital grows and is never wasted. This is
eminently rational in a capital-centric society.

Sure, rules may be a drag sometimes. They can prevent us from
exploring shorter routes or faster means to reach our destination, but
they allow us to feel comfortable in our shells. When it comes to
minimizing risks and ensuring capital returns, slow and steady is
best. But, what if things have changed? What if the rules that we live
by, the path that we have been on, no longer work for us? How
likely are we to understand and embrace such changes, to give up all
that we have known, in order to adopt the new? That sounds pretty
hare-brained to most of us.

If we consider the Six New Normals, there is some interesting
guidance to this question. The first four New Normals suggest that
not only have the rules of the Analog Trinity worked, they perhaps
worked too well. Success in our pursuit of perfect quality has led
customers to simply expect perfection. As companies have worked
to meet customers' demands to have what they want, where they
want it, ubiquity is now simply expected. Meeting customers' needs
as quickly as possible has taught them to expect even more. And,
following the rules has made us so successful that customers today
don't care how hard we worked to get here.

To deliver more than your present rules allow, you need more than
just new rules. New rules don't help. New rules are easy to come up

with; just ask Congress. For global capital-era legislatures, nothing is more satisfying than spitting out a few hundred new regulations before lunchtime each day – unintended consequences be damned.

No! To get new results that meet new or unmet needs, you must do something more. You need to break your old rules. By definition, new rules add to the constraints that you already have, rather than changing existing constraints. New rules will make it harder to adjust to change, rather than help with your goal of responding to change. New rules are comforting to us, because the Analog Trinity has been optimally tuned to allow for new rules. That's how you manage capital better over time. Conversely, the Analog Trinity despises the elimination of old rules, because what has worked in the past must also work in the future. Control builds and ripens over time.

Total Pages, Code of Federal Regulations (1950 - 2014)

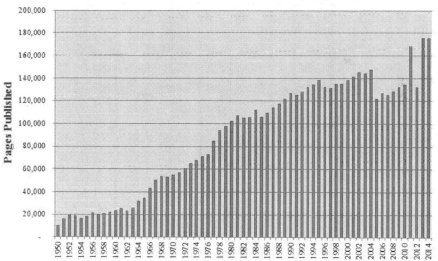

Figure 19.1: Total pages of United States Federal regulations by year

These Jerks Have no Rules

As I watch Jerks sprout up all over our world, in every nation and in every industry, I continually see the Analog powers-that-be complaining about them. They cry foul over the methods used by Jerks, followed swiftly by a snowstorm of court orders, injunctions and negative news releases. This viewpoint is completely wrong of course, as we discussed through Section 2. Jerks do indeed have rules that they follow, or at least principles. It's just that they are completely different than those followed by Analogs.

Figure 19.2: Sometimes, good ideas don't translate well

You could be the greatest golfer in the world and it won't matter one iota if the game suddenly changes to water polo. Perhaps your bubble-head driver will help you float, but beyond that you're in deep water until you learn the eggbeater. New rules put you into deeper water, with leg irons. But new rules can also allow you to stay afloat, perhaps even long enough to stay in the game.

To make life harder on Jerks, you need to adopt, or at least adapt to, the rules they do follow. These necessarily run counter to your Analog way of living, so this task will not be easy. Nonetheless, it is imperative that you make some basic changes to how you operate under the Analog Trinity in order to keep up with the Digital.

Making Change

As discussed in Chapter 17, the one key advantage that Analogs have in this game is access to capital. It is critical that Analogs use this advantage as much as possible, and in different ways than before. The Six New Normals show us both that our previous investments in improving the Analog Trinity were hugely successful, and that they are now largely irrelevant. The rule changes that Analogs must make now need to allow them to reorient to and focus on the Six New Normals as fast as possible, while they are still normal.

So let's say that you choose to act on this advice, and begin searching for rules to eliminate. You may find many that either lead to questionable results or no longer provide the intended results, or their usefulness has been played out, Six-New-Normals-style. You may pick a range of rules to strike from the organization's books, in an effort to respond to Jerks. After all, outside disruption requires inside disruption in kind, right?

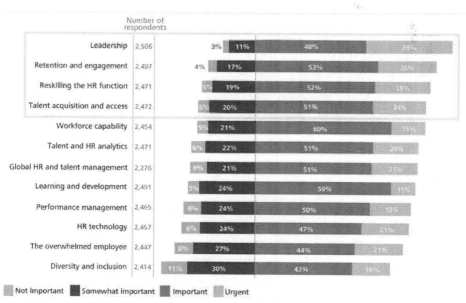

Figure 19.3: Labor concerns of business executives. Cost is notable by its absence

You may tell your subordinates of your plans, and superficially they will agree. But, I can almost guarantee that when you tell them that some of the rules they have followed or enforced are going away, they will likely have a cow. As they stand there before you, as you tell them your plan, they will suddenly feel as if they have just given birth to a fully grown half-ton milking heifer.

If you start to change some of the rules of your Analog organization, each part of the organization will respond differently, according to their role in the Trinity. Finance will produce a stack of reports (always, reports) that clearly show that your new decision will lower ROI, waste capital and bring forth the Four Horsemen of the Apocalypse. Accounting will think that you've suffered some form of head trauma, or a stroke, and return to their books, unfazed. Compliance will try to scare you to death with any number of Chicken-Little scenarios, certainly with references to steep penalties and jail time. Legal will begin compiling a list of all of the laws you might be breaking, diligently indexed and footnoted for ease of use. Marketing will insist on having an offsite somewhere warm and exotic in order to brainstorm how to leverage the innovative new approach that you're promoting. In reality, they'll be drowning the anxieties you caused them in some fruity umbrella drinks. And, of course, HR will begin documenting your descent into madness, in anticipation of your involuntary departure. Recall that your human resource manager has been trained to think that *humans* are *resources* to be *managed*, Analog-style. Think on that one a bit... I'll wait....

None of these Analogs will be obvious about being repelled by the notion of giving up old rules. That would be unseemly. They will try to hide from you the fact that they've suffered any trauma by your attempt to remove (*gulp*) a control. They will say that's a good idea, let us think about that, we'll get back to you with our report and recommendations, and so on. Platitudes come to our aid when we've publicly had an unplanned psychic cow, and we don't want the neighbors to find out about it.

Got Milk?

Where do you start changing rules in order to reengage with customers and keep them away from Jerks? How do you milk the advantage of your capital, to buy as much time as you can? The Six New Normals provide the answer. The New Normals are the result of the success of the Analog Trinity. These New Normals exist only because capital-centricity has met, and often exceeded, our lesser Maslowian needs, and so our focus has moved on to other things. To address these new needs, to recapture your customers' attention, you need to behave differently. You need to break your rules.

Consider the first New Normal, Quality. As we discussed in Section 1, Analogs have done such a great job of implementing quality over the last half-century that you and I simply expect perfection. Analogs get no points for perfection. Rather, they get massive negative points when something goes wrong. It no longer matters what you do to prevent bad things from occurring – *I simply expect this*. But if and when something happens to go wrong, *how you respond to that issue means everything to me*.

Figure 19.4: How you respond to unplanned failure says a lot about you

This is exactly the opposite of what most Analogs have implemented in their pursuit of quality. Nearly all Analogs have built bureaucracies that operate processes, controlled by rules which were intended to make sure that nothing goes wrong, ever. That's why they call it 'quality.' Analogs work tirelessly to ensure that things always work as intended, that they are reliable, predictable and steady. As customers, we like this. But when something does go wrong, and something *always* goes wrong, this alignment towards prevention ends up preventing appropriate action. Our efforts to achieve quality, via the Analog Trinity, have prevented our ability to respond when quality leaves the building.

Do you question this hypothesis? Think of the last time something went wrong in your world and you took steps to set it right. You likely called a help desk, or approached a customer service representative, or in some way engaged a support mechanism governed by the Analog Trinity. Analogs are all about metrics, processes and controlling capital, so almost invariably the conversation starts with pleasantries, ("Hello, how may I help you?") and then quickly gets down to business ("I need help with X").

At this point, the service representative has one job and one job only: figure out what other resource or resources will correct the customers issue at the *lowest possible cost of capital and the lowest possible risk.* I emphasize this because these two governing principles of the Analog Trinity determine everything that happens next. Once the service representative understands what you might require, their job is to route you to the least expensive, least risky solution. This is where they start to route you to other resources in the organization that have been predicted to deliver a solution at the lowest possible cost *to the organization.*

There is little or no consideration of the cost *to the customer,* because this is irrelevant to the Analog. Sure, there are some metrics in place, such as call hold-time, which supposedly ensure that customers have a good experience with solving their problem. Companies are filled with these supposedly customer-centric metrics. But if you look at these metrics closely their purpose is almost always disingenuous. The call hold-time metric, supposedly selected so that customers don't wait too long to receive attention, really is intended to minimize the total cost of providing the service. At some point, in designing this service, some analyst figured out that reducing call hold-times somehow reduced the cost to deliver the solution. Why? Because that's what Analogs do!

Figure 19.5: Helpdesk tiger team

How do I know this? Because I've done hundreds of these analyses in my career, in order to do exactly this calculation. Analogs translate every single metric in their organizations back to capital efficiency, because that's what they live for. If something as esoteric as quality is to be measured, it has to tie back to something that Analogs care about, and what they care about is capital. So, the endless routing and re-routing and form-filling and queueing that we all experience when trying to fix our problem have nothing to do with actually fixing our problem. Rather, it's all about how Analogs can resolve your issue for as low a capital cost as possible. If not even answering the phone led to a lower total cost of capital to the Analog, then your call would never be picked up. (Recall our earlier discussion of the cost of keeping versus finding customers).

As your conversation continues with the customer service representative, eventually you will get to the point where there is comprehension of what you need. At this point one of two things will happen: a) the service representative has been given enough control of capital to actually fix your problem; or b) they will tell you that they can't help you. How many times have you heard this before? "I can't help you," or alternatively, "I'm not authorized to do that." This is Analog speak for "the solution to your problem costs more capital than I have been authorized to spend because the Analog Trinity won't allow it."

Remember the last time you had this experience? Likely you won't have to think back very far. It was pretty annoying, wasn't it? Of course it was. You expect perfection, and when you don't get it you aren't happy. At that moment, the worst thing an Analog can do is give you further excuses as to why it didn't operate perfectly, and how it cannot solve the problem. But, due to capital controls, optimized through thousands of hours of analysis and reports, that person simply is not and *cannot* be allowed to solve your problem.

What if you changed all of that? What if, for a moment, that first-line service representative was allowed to actually solve your problem, independent of the cost to the Analog? Would the world come to an end? Not likely. Would the organization be swallowed whole into some black hole of bankruptcy caused by customer satisfaction? Probably not. Instead, if that person was allowed in that moment to immediately solve the customer's problem, they would be responsive to the customer's Six New Normals, and they'd generate tremendous good will as a result.

Now, a typical Analog response to this would be, "You could afford to do that once, but what if every customer demanded a more expensive solution to their problem? We'd then go bankrupt for sure!" Absolutely, according to your risk-averse, worst-case-scenario, conserve-capital-at-all-cost models, empowered employees would doom the Analog to certain financial ruin; it says so right there in the models.

But, what's not in the model is the Digital Trinity's view of this transaction. In the Digital Trinity view, that happy, satisfied customer is now telling all of their friends, relatives and others about their great experience, which creates information wealth through context and correlation. Rather than driving customers away with a negative review of your service, they are creating positive correlations that drive customers *to* you. This is nowhere in your Analog models, but it is a real and immensely valuable effect, as discussed in Section 2. *And*, given the constant use of social media, every experience – whether good or bad – will be made public.

Figure 19.6: Social media is permanent, global and unforgiving

If you're lucky, at some point you have experienced a customer service representative who stepped out of their little box, went beyond their authority, and actually solved your problem on their own. These people, in a moment of rage against the machine, actually click the 'approve' button when they shouldn't, or let you board your plane when it's 'too late' to do so. They let you out of the parking garage without charging you, because you never found a space, and so on. Every once in a while some Analog will step out of line on our behalf, to the utter horror of Analogs everywhere.

When these tiny little rebellions took place in your favor, how did you respond? If you're like me, once you got past your stunned amazement, you told others about the experience. This sort of take-charge experience is exactly what the Analog Trinity is designed to prevent, and for most customers it is what they hunger for most. That's why it one of the Six New Normals. The Analog Trinity has taught us to expect a set of predictable outcomes, which no longer satisfy us. Instead, we want the opposite of what we have become accustomed to, or we want something entirely different than what we state.

Loosen the Chains to Remain in Control

To use your capital advantage to remain competitive with Jerks, you need to actually use your advantage and convert it into victories in the Digital Trinity. This means pushing the authority for the use of capital as close to customers as possible, in both time and space. To have a prayer of keeping your customers, you need to make sure they never hear the words "I can't help you" or "I'm not authorized to do that." Because, in a world increasingly filled with Jerks, customers can immediately find someone who is not so encumbered.

This doesn't mean that service people go out and rent private jets for your customers, or any of the other nightmare scenarios that your Analog veterans may dream up. I'm not suggesting that you allow people to be reckless with capital decisions. They won't be, because they will be terrified. But, loosening the tightly bound controls that you have optimized for decades, using the Analog Trinity, may be exactly what is required to remain relevant to customers who now have less rigid options.

Reducing control by eliminating outdated rules feels like heresy. At the altar of the Analog Trinity, it is. Your bureaucracy will reject these efforts, just as it has been trained to do for a very long time. People will complain. People will argue against this. People will panic. These are good things, as they are signs that you are heading in the right direction!

When this happens – and if you are eliminating rules it most certainly will – be sure to share with those who protest, the timeless words of the television star Bart Simpson: "Don't have a cow, man!"

Figure 19.7: Employees training for the elimination of unnecessary, Analog business rules

They will want to have a cow because this sort of behavior encourages free will, creative thinking, independent thought, experimentation and, most of all, rule breaking. And, like your grandmother used to say, these behaviors can only lead to bad things, like teenage pregnancy. This is the sort of thing that is actually encouraged by the Digital Trinity, which is what makes it so compelling to us, and so effective. You may find it useful to keep in mind a favorite axiom of mine. If your employees do something stupid, there can be two possible reasons:

1. They are stupid.
2. They work for an organization that rewards them for being stupid.

If you remove obsolete restraints from your employees, and they act crazy, then you either have the wrong people or you may not have cut away enough stupidity for their smarts to come out.

This will horrify HR, baffle your mid-level management, and first-line managers will revolt. These are all good signs. Allow your people a bit of room to roam around after removing some of their chains, and be sure to see what happens as they do (DO, then Learn).

When they do use some of their new freedom, celebrate it. Go nuts. Go social, throw a party, give them psychic rewards. Remember, the first time they step beyond their old limits, they will be terrified, like an abused pet afraid of its master. You should shower them with praise if you want their little rebellion to pay off. Soon, your organization may become comfortable with removing more constraints on your capital, and you might be able to get back in the fight against the Jerks taking your customers away from you.

Make the New Normals Yours

In this chapter, I focused on an example of only one of the Six New Normals, Quality. There are any number of additional examples for this Normal, and the others as well. As you look to find rules to eliminate, as you try to decide which of your sacred Analog cows to slaughter, let the changing expectations outlined in the Six New Normals guide you to where to look. Certainly, you don't want to mistakenly turn your milk cow into hamburgers, but you do want to make sure that oppressive, overly conservative and confining rules make sense in an Information-centered world, governed by the Digital Trinity. I suspect that they no longer will – and Jerks are betting that you won't figure that out until it's too late to stop them.

<u>Chapter Summary</u>:

1. Rules are a fundamental tenant of the Analog Trinity. Whether they are business rules, laws, regulations or traditions, the rules followed by Analog organizations have been used to control and to grow capital wealth.
2. These same rules that create capital-based wealth and power are nearly always a hindrance in creating information-based wealth and power. Capital wants to stay put, information wants to be free.
3. Analogs dedicate enormous resources to following rules, while Jerks ignore or actively flout them. To respond to this, Analogs must begin to question their adherence to rules that don't make sense in the Digital Era.
4. When contemplating new business strategies, offerings, solutions and value propositions, push the boundaries of what would normally be acceptable. If your Legal, Compliance, Human Resources or Accounting resources are dead-set against what you propose to do, you're likely on the right track. The strength of their opposition is likely directly proportional to the 'rightness' and the value generated by your disruptive proposal.

Chapter Twenty: Annihilate Your Processes

"Never interrupt your enemy when he is making a mistake."-
Napoleon Bonaparte

*"All men are prepared to accomplish the incredible if their
ideals are threatened."*- *Maya Angelou*

"A few great men would have to get past Personnel."- *Paul
Goodman*

In Chapter 19 we took a swing at rules, the method of wealth control
in the Analog Trinity. Now, let's cast a critical eye at the Analog
Trinity processes. Business process is a topic near and dear to me.
For nearly all of my adult life I have been defining and refining
processes to help Analogs be more effective. For a slightly
extroverted engineer like me, engineering business processes is a
dream come true. It remains an interesting intersection of science,
math, engineering, sociology, politics, PowerPoints and semi-
professional mud wrestling. I loved the work then and I love it even
more now, because today we are annihilating what we did in the past
in order to make it even better.

As Analog companies deployed IT in the 1980s and 1990s, business
process automation was the third most common area of focus, after
financial information and supply chain information. These three
areas represented the three legs of the Trinity. Processes were being
automated in order to apply and enforce the Analog Trinity more
effectively. Once you could keep track of your capital faster and
with greater precision (with Enterprise Resource Planning), and you
could manage it better as it moved around (Supply Chain
Management), you then needed to make sure that your methods of
controlling capital (bureaucracy, processes and rules) could keep up.
As a result, everybody in the 1990s began automating their Trinities
using the new technologies of the personal computer, networking
and business software.

Business Process Reengineering

This push towards automating the Analog Trinity (but not Digitizing the Analog Trinity, that would be nonsense) swept through the business world like a wildfire, leading to a then-new business trend called Business Process Reengineering (BPR). Companies everywhere jumped on the BPR bandwagon, and this trend was so popular in the 1990s that it was core curriculum for any business school worth attending. I was hooked on BPR when it came onto the scene, completely entranced by the notion of applying the brand new technologies of IT to the business controls of the Analog Trinity. Business Process Reengineering was the Scientology of its day.

The problem with BPR was that it was a complete misnomer. Anyone who spent any time doing this work quickly came to the realization that we weren't re-'engineering' anything. The elements of the Analog Trinity that we were working on had never been engineered in the first place! In most instances, the bureaucracies, processes and rules that we were analyzing and automating had never been made with purpose and intent, which are the hallmarks of something that is engineered. Rather, they were the results of two centuries of trial and error, random chance, and frequent doses of corporate politics. For most of the Capitalist Age, the mechanisms of the Analog Trinity grew massively because in a capital-centric world, the more controls, the better. Bureaucracy, processes and rules grew completely out of control, like so much organizational kudzu.

As anyone who worked on this stuff back in the day can recall, automating was a total nightmare. We had to try to replicate the most idiotic processes and rules imaginable, and feed them into computers and software that only worked with quantifiable facts. Despite their focus on books, spreadsheets and metrics, Analogs are very, well, *analog*. Their answer to every question is usually, 'it depends.' Documenting these conditional statements so that a computer could follow them was a Sisyphean task, as each time we tried to deploy a new automated process or system, some Analog would come along and say, "yeah but …" I soon learned to passionately hate yeah-*butts*.

Figure 20.1: Urban growth. The only thing worse than unplanned failure is unplanned success

Putting Out the Trash

While it took the better part of two decades, pretty much all Analog organizations have now automated their Analog Trinity. Those that failed at this transition did indeed fail, as a quick review of the list of Fortune 500 companies reveals. According to a study by the software company SAP, 40 per cent of those companies that were on the Fortune 500 list of largest companies in 2000 were off the list by 2010. By 2015 this number had grown to 52 per cent. Between 2000 and 2015 Fortune 500 companies were more likely to fail than not. I'm fairly certain that a key factor in this was that their organizational metabolism was too slow for them to compete. True, to some degree being inefficient faster means that you're more inefficient but, in defiance of Aesop's fable, non-automated Analogs were soon so much more tortoise than hare that they faded into irrelevance.

Analogs that were quick to roll out automation were also faster to catch two echo-trends, offshoring and outsourcing. Once you automated your Analog Trinity, it became easier to break it up into little chunks and send those chunks out to be processed more cheaply by someone else. This was a horrifying notion to Analogs in pre-computer times. Outsourcing would mean that they would necessarily lose control of their capital while it was in someone else's hands. But, with new information systems, Analogs could now maintain visibility and control of their capital while others messed around with it, more cheaply.

I spent much of the first decade of the 21st century helping companies to offshore, outsource, downsize, right-size, reorient, pivot and so on, as they sought cheaper ways of maintaining their Analog Trinity control structures. This business process mambo was a huge business for consulting and services firms, and it continues to grow today. Companies like Salesforce.com, Workday, and ADP are making the automation of the Analog Trinity cheaper and faster, if not necessarily better. Remember the NASA warning about expecting all three.

Snickering Your Way to Success

As you might have noticed by now, I'm a bit of a contrarian. Unlike most people, I'm pretty comfortable with accepting new ideas, learning from them, and adapting as I go. When I look at the present wave of outsourcing, offshoring, cloud-basing and so on, I don't see much progress. Instead, I see organizations doing the same old stuff they have always done, only a little bit faster and a little bit cheaper.

Change is hard. People don't like change, at least not in big chunks. So, just like product marketing people, business engineers have resorted to *Snickering* their business processes, rather than fundamentally changing them. Recall that Snickering is the process of making a product or service a few per cent smaller every year to create the illusion of progress. Well, Analogs have been Snickering their Analog Trinity controls in the same way.

Every year, Analogs cut a percentage point or two out of the cost of operating their Analog Trinity, and declare the result a 'success.'

When I was focused on outsourcing and offshoring deals in the 2000s, they were all about Snickering. This sort of small improvements, year-over-year, was so fundamental to the thinking of outsourcing firms that they were written into the contracts of the time. Vendors were being contractually obligated to Snicker, and if they didn't deliver there would be hell to pay. Outsourcers were free to do whatever necessary to achieve these goals, as long as they didn't mess with the customer's Analog Trinity, and as long as they could guarantee their ability to Snicker.

Analog Armageddon

The problem with Snickering is this: eventually, there's nothing left to cut. Once you take the very last peanut out of the Snickers bar in the name of incremental 'improvement,' you have a Milky Way bar, not a Snickers bar. And no matter how small you cut it up, a Milky Way is not the same thing as a Snickers bar. If your customers really love peanuts, they will go somewhere else to get them.

The era of automating the Analog Trinity is rapidly drawing to a close for precisely this reason. Once you cut away the fat, muscle and sinew of the Analog Trinity, all you're left with are the bones. Skeletons are strong, but they're pretty useless without muscles and organs to move them around and give them life. Analogs maintain the structures and controls of their Analog Trinity, but to what end? Tradition? Perception? Comfort?

When, by Snickering your business, you strip away all of the trappings of two centuries' worth of corporate empire building (bureaucracy), all you are left with are rules and processes. Rules and processes aren't costs *per se* (Analogs don't actually spend money on these elements like they do with people) so they aren't eroded away through Snickering like people are. Every week I walk the halls of Analog companies the world over, and inevitably I see row after row of empty cubicles, their former occupants long since eliminated by the Analog mambo. All of the hamsters have been removed from their cages, but the cages, wheels, and other containments remain. So too remain the rules and processes, a legacy of two centuries of trying to manage and grow capital as effectively as possible.

Process De-engineering

No matter how effective organizations find their offshoring and outsourcing efforts to be, eventually there is no more room for improvement. Eventually, there are no more people to cut. Once this occurs, once all of the low-hanging, mid-hanging and even high-hanging fruit has been picked, it's time for a new tree. This is precisely what Edward Deming predicted back in the 1950s, and it is what every person trained in Quality and Process Improvement in the 1990s conveniently forgot. Eliminating people from the Analog Trinity came easily to us because they were easy to measure in terms of direct costs of capital.

Processes and rules are much harder to quantify as capital expenses, and so they tend to hang around. This is doubly bad for present-day Analogs, because they find it next to impossible to remove these controls. The controls are all that remain between them and their inevitable Digital future. For Analogs to survive, they must use their capital to their advantage over Jerks. How can Analogs do this? They must smash what's left of their Analog skeletons, while there is still time to do so.

Analogs must de-engineer the same processes that they (re)engineered in the late 20th century. They must pointedly interrogate every process and every rule left over from that era, and eliminate all that aren't imperative for survival. Analogs must terminate these rules and processes with extreme prejudice. They need to assume that each process hinders the future of the business, rather than guaranteeing it. Analogs need to adjust to the idea that after 20 years of Snickering, what remains of the Analog Trinity isn't the ultimate refinement of control, it's the wretched refuse. It's the skeleton of Jacob Marley, chains and all, left behind to haunt us – as Jerks use the Digital Trinity to take over.

268

"We've considered every potential risk except the risks of avoiding all risks."

***Figure 20.2: Analogs rarely measure the risk of not taking a risk.
Jerks just do it***

Process Annihilation

How do you free yourself from these Analog chains? How do you clear these Analog relics from your business so that you can remain relevant in our increasingly Digital world? You need to blow up your processes and rules with the same tools you used to create them: metrics. Think of the rules and processes which you use to run your business as if you were building a wall. Rules are the bricks and process is the mortar. Your Analog organization has built walls of control around capital; brick-by-brick, trowel-by-trowel.

Your organization has unwittingly played both Montresor and Fortunato from Poe's *Cask of Amontillado*, alternately building the wall that immures, and dying from the resulting immurement. You need to blast this wall down fast, while you still can. The metrics that you have used to build these walls as efficiently and quickly as possible can be the very tools that you use to break yourself free.

The path to breaking down your walls comes from selecting, measuring and rewarding metrics that are so radical that your existing processes cannot possibly deliver them. You need to expect, even demand, process performance that is so outstanding that your existing rules and processes cannot possibly deliver them, which is precisely the point.

You need to set goals that are so radical that they demand radical thinking and radical solutions: de-engineering. You need to demand an Almond Joy, a candy bar with completely different nuts, rather than a cheaper Snickers bar with fewer peanuts. You destroy old processes and delete old rules only by setting new metrics that demand their destruction. People will free themselves from their old constraints only when those constraints are made out to be the source of discomfort, rather than comfort. You need to make your Analog employees look for a new tree, rather than wait for their bare-branched tree to give more fruit

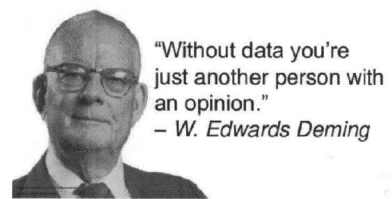

Figure 20.3: Only through radical new metrics can new results be achieved

How do you do this? Pick radical metrics. If you have spent years making your products, services or processes one or two per cent better, demand that they now be twice as good, or twice as fast. If you have tolerated small, incremental improvements in customer satisfaction, seek to double or triple them, in one year or less. To blast away the tomb-like walls of rules and process that have been built up over time, you need to scare your Analog people to near-death. And that's exactly what radical new metrics can do.

Don't Play 'Possum

As you pick the metrics that will dynamite your way out of your Analog catacombs, don't let your organization play 'possum.

Opossums are dim-witted marsupials. When threatened, they fall over and play dead, hoping that the threat loses interest and passes them by. Many of the people in an Analog organization will use this tactic to avoid the changes you're trying to make.

This playing 'possum usually presents itself in many ways familiar to Analogs, which is why it's so effective. Analogs play 'possum when they create tiger teams, nominate special committees, generate impact assessments, create ROIs or schedule an offsite. Such tactics are used to create the appearance of work and compliance. What they really represent are methods for remaining busy, and appearing to comply with a demand for change – while in reality they are playing 'possum.

There's an easy way to prevent this: measure the right metric. Jerks are known for speed. Recall that capital likes to move slowly, while information wants to move at the speed of light or faster. For decades, Analog organizations worked on improving quality, value, customer perception, reputation, efficiency and effectiveness. Metric-loving Analogs are passionate about reports. Give them a new metric and they will find a way to meet that metric, or at least appear to do so.

If there is one thing I have learned in a quarter-century of trying to be a good Analog, it is this: You can fake quality, value, price, that you care, that you're green, and so on. Analogs are good at creating metrics that show progress, or at least the illusion thereof. But the one thing that can't be faked is speed. No matter how hard you try to pretend that you're fast, no matter how much you spin your latest schedule slip, no matter how well you rationalize why you're going to be a little late, you can't fake speed. Why? Because we humans are creatures who are aware of context. For good or for bad (and there are arguments both ways) we humans are very conscious of and sensitive to time. And because time is the one resource you can never get back once it is spent, and you can never get more of once it runs out, we value it very dearly.

The Jerks Have Gone Plaid

Because we are creatures of time, but we are fairly resistant to change, time becomes the lever with which you can chip away at your Analog Trinity walls. You do this by setting ridiculous goals and expecting people to meet them. In *Data Crush*, I talked about a principle I simply called *Accelerate*, in which I advised readers to cut every cycle time in their organizations by at least half, at least every 18 months and preferably every 12. In this way, an organization can shake off its Analog, capital-induced lethargy, and start to move as fast as information allows.

The feedback I get on this piece of advice is fairly consistent: I must be nuts! Analogs constantly tell me that this point is unreasonable, unachievable, incomprehensible and so on; hence, for them it is so. Conversely, I know when I'm talking to a Jerk because their response is different. When I mention *accelerate* to a Jerk, the response is more typically, "Yeah, we just did that last week, what's the big deal?" The big deal is this: for a Jerk, constant, endless, relentless acceleration is normal. They are constantly trying to approach the speed of light (the speed of information). For Analogs, who have dedicated their careers to the idea that capital is valuable only when it is at rest, and capital must be maximized, the notion of constant *radical* acceleration is unacceptable. Their problem is this: Jerks don't just accelerate, they jerk!

When Elon Musk wanted to shake up the auto industry even more than he already had, he put to use one of the key advantages of electric vehicles: torque. Internal combustion engines tend to make more power, and more torque, the faster they spin. We all know this effect, as we have sensed it a million times when a driver 'hits the gas.' Electric cars don't do this. Electric motors actually produce their maximum torque when they aren't spinning at all; they produce maximum thrust at zero RPM. So, electric motors can accelerate a car at rest much more quickly than a gasoline engine.

Elon took advantage of this little bit of physics to yet again blow the Analog auto industry into the weeds. Tesla reset some of the parameters of its electric motors and batteries so that it could use this maximum torque feature of electric engines to make its cars accelerate like no others. When correctly configured, Tesla's Model S automobile can launch itself from a standing start to 60 miles an hour in under three seconds, which is right up there with the most exotic and expensive gas-powered cars ever made. Elon labeled this driving mode 'ludicrous speed,' in deference to its seeming impossibility. Analog drivers stood on the sidelines, telling themselves it couldn't be done.

Figure 20.4: 'Going Plaid,' or faster than light speed. From the movie 'Space Balls'

As a recovering Analog I don't just write about this stuff, I live it, too. When I wrote *Data Crush* I told my editor I would write the book in six weeks. Her reply was an exasperated, "That's not possible, it can't be done." I went to work writing and 41 days later, just under six weeks, I had finished. She was astonished. When it came time to write this book, I figured that I needed to follow my own advice from that chapter called *Accelerate*, and set myself the goal of writing *Jerk* in half that time, or 21 days, start to finish. Again, everyone told me that I was crazy, nuts, cuckoo, loco and not right in the head. It couldn't be done, and I was only setting myself up for disappointment and failure.

As I type these words in this chapter, I'm on day 18. I'm ahead of schedule and, like last time, I'm pretty sure I'll finish Jerk a day early – just so I can say that I did (author's note: I *did* finish this book in 20 days). Now, I plan to write more books, and doing a book in less than 11 days will be *extremely* difficult. But I like the challenge of it all. I spent 25 years trying to be the best Analog I could possibly be. Today, I'm all about being a Jerk.

<u>Chapter Summary:</u>

1. Process is another pillar of the Analog Trinity. For 200 years, organizations have worked to optimize their processes in order to build capital wealth.
2. For 60 years, organizations have followed the approach of constant, incremental improvement in order to make their processes evermore effective. This approach has largely succeeded in creating today's world.
3. To face a new economic and social model, and to compete with Jerks, Analogs need to achieve break-out performance from their processes. Process performance must double, triple, even improve by factors of 10 or more, in order to remain competitive.
4. To adopt new modes of disruptive process performance, implement radical new metrics and goals which force disruptive thinking. If your organization tells you such performance is impossible, you're on the right track.

Chapter Twenty-One: Fail Fast

"I don't want yes-men around me. I want everyone to tell the truth, even if it costs them their jobs."- Samuel Goldwyn

"Anyone who has never made a mistake has never tried anything new."- Albert Einstein

"Why waste time learning when ignorance is instantaneous?"- Bill Watterson as Calvin in 'Calvin and Hobbes'

By this point, I hope that you agree to some extent that change is inevitable, action is required, and speed is imperative. If not, then I really need to get some new editors, because clearly it can't be the fault of my writing; my praetorians told me that at our last offsite meeting. If you put change, action and speed together, you come up with the theme of this chapter. You must learn how to fail, and do it as quickly as possible.

Frequent Fast Failure is an old axiom from the Quality and BPR wave that took off in the early 1990s. This phrase was religion. At Lockheed Astrospace we would chant this phrase repeatedly like so many Buddhist monks, because for us Frequent Fast Failure was scripture. This concept was also interesting because it was somewhat contrary to the quality dogma created by Edward Deming and then perverted by Analog managers as they embraced Deming's teachings selectively. Deming always said that you had to 'break some glass' and be disruptive, but those aspects of his approach were lost in Analog translation. I deeply admire W. Edward Deming. He was the Archbishop of the Church of Jerks.

Nerds to the Rescue!

Frequent Fast Failure was critical in the space industry, because the costs and risks were so high. Every time you build and launch a satellite, something – or often many things – are happening for the first time, ever. Combine this constant newness with the fact that the simple act of getting a satellite into orbit costs tens of millions of dollars, and you get zero tolerance for failure. Once a satellite is put on top of a rocket (which is nothing but a giant soda can filled with high explosives), and freed from the surly bonds of the Earth, there is no turning back. It has to be perfect, because you can't go back and fix it – although this, too, may soon be changing.

Because we could not possibly afford for something to go wrong after the launch, we engineers would test, analyze, model and retest these spacecraft to near-death – our own! The models and analyses that we created and performed were fantastically complex. To this day, I think I still don't understand half of the math we used. Thank god those tests were all open-book.

Figure 21.1: Launch Failure ... A bad day for a rocket scientist

With stakes so high, modeling alone was not enough; you had to test your models. So, we would constantly make real components and subsystems based on our designs, and test them to destruction: literal destruction. Shooting-at-them-with-the-world's-most-powerful-laser destruction. It turned out that spacecraft engineering had its upsides, too.

As I mentioned at the opening of this book, jerk is the third derivative of the equation of motion. It comes after position (no derivative), velocity (first derivative) and acceleration (second derivative). Well, some of our PhD modelers of spacecraft performance would model things out to the seventh, eighth or even ninth derivative, just to have fun. I forget the name of one of these PhDs I worked with, so let's call him Spiff.

Spaceman Spiff to the Rescue

Spiff was a modeler and mathematician *extraordinaire*, and he ran the mechanical engineering team on the Earth Observation System (EOS) satellite I mentioned earlier. That bird, renamed TERRA, and was a key source of the scientific data that argues for the human contribution to Earth's climate change. Scientists are still learning about our planet from the data pouring out of TERRA's instruments, and I'm proud to have been part of the team that put her up there.

Spiff knew practically everything there was to know, with the possible exception of where to buy bath soap. During a design review with EOS's customer, NASA, we were discussing the plusses and minuses of the new design for the chassis (or structure) of the spacecraft, known to us as the bus. We had largely convinced the NASA guys that the whole design was sound, and this was the Critical Design Review, or CDR. We had built a mathematical model of the structure and had tested that model to our collective satisfaction. Spiff took exception to this. He had done a far more detailed analysis of the design than we had, and he believed he had found some potentially dangerous weaknesses.

Spiff told the assembled engineers, "This design looks good on paper, but I have found that there is a 9th-derivative harmonic resonance that could remain under-damped during the ascent phase (launch into orbit). Due to this design flaw, in the 9th dimension it will likely fail. In the 9th dimension? Seriously? Spiff's idea of fun was calculating things in the 9th dimension, for kicks? And he was sober at the time? Rocket scientists are party animals like that.

Regardless, after Spiff had gone through his analysis and results, sure enough it appeared we had a weakness in the design. But, we had already spent millions of dollars in engineering time coming up with this design, and we weren't prepared to admit we had made that much of an error (anyone married to an engineer will be familiar with this character trait).

Figure 21.2: Space failures tend to be exciting affairs

To satisfy ourselves that we were right, we built an actual scale model of our design and tested it in our labs. That test consisted of bolting the model to a large steel table big enough to strap a house to, and that was driven to vibrate via enormous hydraulic rams. The table was designed to replicate life on top of a rocket going great-guns into orbit. This is not a benign and pleasant journey like launching into hyperspace in Han Solo's *Millennium Falcon*. It's more like being inside a giant blender filled with ice cubes and roofing nails... and the band Motley Crüe, complete with sound system and fireworks display. We attached our model to this shaker-table, shook the snot out of it, and waited to see what would happen.

When the test finished we concluded, rather sheepishly, that Spiff was entirely correct in his math and his conclusions. His time spent in the 9th dimension made all of us look like damned, dirty apes. I don't remember the moment, but I do remember Spiff's look of vindication after the test was completed. He sat with a slight smile in the corner of his mouth, looking as if he had just blasted some blob of gelatinous muck from the planet Anhooie-4 with his Atomic Napalm Neutralizer. Damn that Spaceman Spiff!

When Failure is Not an Option

Gene Kranz, the globally famous mission controller of the Apollo 13 mission, said it best: "Failure is not an option." When he said this, the lives of three American heroes were in the palms of his and his teams' hands. And when the mission had ended with those three astronauts safely back on the earth, the engineers proved that Frequent Fast Failure was the best game in town.

Figure 21.3: Gene Kranz. Engineer, NASA flight director, and American Hero

The failure that Gene was referring to was the failure of final execution. Gene's message to his team was not that they weren't supposed to fail at all. Rather, his message was really, 'Fail small. Fail soon. Fail fast.' Those three astronauts were literally living moment-by-moment based on the decisions made by ground control. If the engineers told them to flip this switch or that, and they were wrong, all three men would be dead, on live television. Recall this was decades before the movie *Jackass* was put into syndicated reruns.

For four days in that summer of 1970, thousands of engineers failed, over and over and over again. The likelihood of getting those astronauts were a million-to-one, maybe a billion-to-one. But, the engineers didn't focus on the one right solution. There wasn't time for that. Rather, they focused on the millions of ways it could go wrong, and they cut each of them from the list of their options as quickly as they possibly could, Thomas-Edison-style. They tried every possible scenario, out of thousands of no-win-scenarios, in order to find the *one* scenario that would get their people home. Then, and only then, did they implement their solution in the most unforgiving environment they would ever encounter – real life. Failure is not an option, indeed.

Frozen in Fear

Gene Kranz wasn't telling his people not to fail, he was telling them to fail when it doesn't really count, so that you *don't* fail when it really *does* count. That's a huge difference, but it is one that seems to be completely, totally and utterly lost on heavily optimized Analogs. As we discussed in Chapters 17 and 18, for 200 years Analogs have trained themselves to avoid risk at all costs. This overriding fear of risk, of making a mistake, seems to underpin every decision, every opinion and every thought that Analogs make. It colors their worldview with the rosy tint of an investment going 'into the red' (taking a loss).

Throughout my career I was taught to analyze investment risk to the nth degree, and beyond, in order to ensure that capital did not go to waste. Bad or incorrect decisions were to be avoided at all costs, even at the expense of actual progress. I have sat in thousands of meetings where the dominant topic of discussion was how to avoid risks in innovation, rather than how to chase its potential rewards. Our centuries of self-indoctrination in the avoidance of risk have been remarkably successful. Most Analogs are frozen in fear.

Hence, we analyze investments repeatedly, tweaking our models to ensure we didn't miss a possible mode of fiscal failure. We weigh the odds, assess the gravity of the situation, and haul out more models in order to carry the load of responsibility for potentially being wrong. The very descriptions of our investment processes are loaded with terms implying weight, inertia and mass. These decisions weigh heavily on our minds, and many find that it feels safer to do nothing, rather than risk anything.

The Analog Trinity not only encourages this sort of thinking, it practically demands it. The avoidance of risk and loss of capital is the paramount purpose of the Analog Trinity, and we built our monuments to indecision with mathematical precision. We use the best thinking available to convince ourselves to do nothing.

When the time to make an investment arrives, they happily invest inside of a safe little box, intra-DIE-phase-style, rather than reach for the riskier rewards waiting in the next box down the line. We have taught ourselves that playing 'possum is the path to success with capital. Playing dead, by making no decision at all, feels safer to us than taking the risk of crossing the road of innovation.

Climbing Down from your Horse

If this discussion rings true for you, even just a little, it's likely because you have many of the same experiences as I have had, my fellow Analogs. Time and time again I have sat in meetings, debating the pluses and minuses of making this investment or that. Over and over again I have listened to business managers articulate precisely why it is best to do nothing. Naturally, these executives don't come right out and say, "Hey, I'm afraid. I don't think my career can handle taking a risk and failing." But these people wouldn't have achieved the level of success they now enjoy if they weren't skilled in using a little verbal judo.

Perhaps you've experienced this, too. In a meeting or presentation an executive asks, "What makes you think that this investment won't fail?" Or perhaps they say, "What's the return on investment that you're going to commit to?" The data analyst inside me gets a chuckle from this type of questions, because they are asked in a way that guides the resulting answer. In analytics we call this selection bias, and/or omitted variable bias. The way in which the question is asked biases the resulting answer, Heisenberg-style. Senior Analog executives are exceptionally talented at this, as are news reporters and politicians, because it is a way of managing people's basest emotions (such as fear) without grabbing and yanking on them full-force.

It's subtle, it's manipulative and it's effective, just as Ebenezer Scrooge intended.

Figure 21.4: Omitted variable bias. A cornerstone of American journalism

There are no stupid questions; the desire to know the truth should never be a slight against one's intelligence. There are, however, stupid questioners. Anyone asking a rhetorical question is likely a stupid questioner. Why? Because they believe they already have the answer, and the question is disingenuous.

Failing Fast, with Pride

As my fellow rocket persons and I discovered long ago, Frequent Fast Failure is a remarkably effective methodology for arriving at results that must be perfectly right. Only through repeated, incremental failure can we learn what we do not already know, so that we can generate better results than were ever achieved before. If you're not failing, at least occasionally, how can you believe that you've taken any risks at all, or learned anything new either? Risk is an inherent part of any exploration of the new. If you already know what you will find, then what's the point of, or value in, exploration?

For more than 200 years Analogs have taught themselves that taking risks is bad. Loss of capital, or even just its less-than-perfect use, is a major no-no, and we have the reports to prove it! When we view risk-taking, and the potential for losses, in this regard, it is easy to convince ourselves to do nothing or as close to nothing as possible. In a world of good-quarterly-reports-or-die, Snickering isn't just a safe, easy and comfortable approach, it's the *only* approach that is acceptable.

The problem for Analogs is this: here in the beginning of the Information Age, your Snickers bar just ran out of peanuts. Not only have you cut out all of the excess costs for doing the same-old-same-old, you've managed to collect and hold on to every control mechanism that was ever useful along the way. You continue to drag these controls around, Jacob-Marley-style, in the hopes that they will keep you safe from risk and from loss. And indeed they will, for a time, right up until some Jerk points them out to you, as they whiz by you at the speed of information, like Spaceman Spiff launching himself on yet another adventure at the planet Zartok-3.

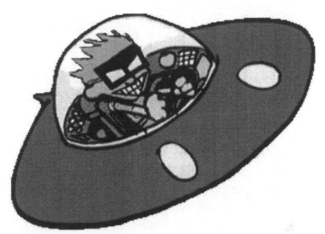

Figure 21.5: Spaceman Spiff does it again!

To keep up with the Jerks, you need to do the same thing that innovative Analogs like Deming and Kranz knew: fail frequently, and fail fast. These early Jerks, mis-located in time and space, knew that taking small risks, failing, learning, and risking again, were the key to converging on the answer that is ultimately correct. Sitting back, analyzing again and again and again, trapped in the knowledge of what you already know, and trying to project that into what scary things the future might hold, is an approach certain to lead you to stay right where you are. There is safety in familiarity.

"Stay hungry, stay foolish"
Steve Jobs

21.6: Steve Jobs. Failure, disruptor, contrarian. In other words, a real Jerk

But, should you choose to stay where you are, take little if any risk, and try to survive on what's left of an ever-shrinking Snickers bar while you polish the chains you drag around, the Jerks are going to run right past you. And they'll take your customers along for their wild, risky, and ultimately fulfilling ride.

Failure is not the enemy. It is the indication that there is more for you to know and appreciate about the universe around us. Saying "I don't know" shouldn't scare you. It should excite you. Or at least it should do both in equal measure. If Maslow was right about anything, and I firmly believe that he was, this process of failing, learning and trying again sounds remarkably like something I've heard referred to as *living*. If you are a dyed-in-the-wool Analog, I suggest you give *living* a try sometime. You don't know what you're missing!

Chapter Summary:

1. The Analog Trinity enforces the notion that capital should never be wasted, and it must be grown with as little risk as possible.
2. Over time, this philosophy has led to a mindset of risk avoidance, which has further led to extreme fear of failure. In most Analog organizations, failure is intolerable.
3. Avoidance of risk and intolerance of failure lead to a range of behaviors that all Analogs are familiar with: Tiger Teams, Committees, ROI analyses, financial models and so on. Analogs invest heavily in these behaviors, rather than on actual investments.
4. To compete with Jerks, Analogs must embrace the idea that to learn anything worthwhile, a little failure must be accepted. But, failure should be small, it should come fast, and its lessons should be applied immediately, in order to create much better outcomes. This is how Jerks do what they do.

Chapter Twenty-Two: Seek Discomfort

"If you change the way you look at things, the things you look at change."- Wayne Dyer

"Always go to other people's funerals, otherwise they won't come to yours."- Yogi Berra

This, the last of six recommendations for dealing with Jerks, is by far the most difficult for Analogs to achieve, and because of that it may be your most potent weapon. You will need it, as I fully expect the transition from the Analog to the Digital Trinity that we have been discussing will largely come to pass in the coming decade. In suggesting that you seek discomfort, I am saying that your most powerful defense against those who would seek to disrupt you is simply to disrupt yourself first. In this way, you make yourself not only *less* predictable, you make yourself *unpredictable*.

What I really mean when I say seek discomfort is: be unpredictable. Do things that superficially don't make any sense under the rules of the Analog Trinity, and do them fairly inconsistently. This will be exceptionally hard to do, because every cell in your body, and every element in your Trinity, is going to tell you that you're doing something wrong. Your actions should not only be hard to justify under the Analog Trinity, they should be impossible to justify, at least by your normal means. The decisions that you make should not only feel irrational, they should *be* irrational.

It will be incredibly discomforting to fight your every rule, instinct and lesson-learned. This is why this approach can be so very effective. Indeed, the more discomfort you feel in these decisions, the more effective they will be at disarming, and alarming, the Jerks at your door. Those Jerks out there not only think that you're totally predictable, but that they can *count on your predictability*. After all, you're Analog, and your entire belief system, and all of your metrics, are telling you to move slowly, be predictable and stay within the rules. Like a designated driver on prom night, the Jerks are counting on you to follow the rules so that they can pull a Lindsey Lohan or Charlie Sheen on you and still get home safely.

Figure 22.1: Tom Cruise risks it all in the movie 'Risky Business'

The best way to ruin a Jerk's prom night is to *not* be predictable; it's the last thing that they'd ever expect of an Analog, and they're completely unprepared for your departure from your normal self. Even if they can recover from your jink, it will rattle their confidence. They will have no idea what to expect of you when they see you in homeroom on Monday morning, and they'll worry about it all weekend until they do.

Let's All Be Codependent Together

Jerks travel about at the speed of light. Analogs are just a bit more predictable. They are more like black holes. A black hole bends light that passes by, its path altered by the black hole's mass and gravity. This might change the light beam's direction, but it does so in an entirely predictable and quantifiable manner. Hence, even though the beam's path is altered, both its trajectory and destination can be accurately determined. Jerks count on Analogs to act, well, analog. That's a key part of their strategy in defeating them. Even if an Analog manages to alter a Jerk's course or trajectory, the Jerk just keeps zooming along. Their Trinity encourages them to be flexible, dynamic and fluid, adjusting to changes as they go.

This is all universally true, but only up to a point. If a beam of light passes too close to a black hole it becomes trapped. The black hole's gravity catches the beam of light, holds it, and doesn't let go. When this occurs the light beam is doomed. It is pulled into the black hole until it passes the event horizon, at which point it disappears forever. A light beam that somehow 'miscalculates' its trajectory past the black hole may find itself trapped by the mistake. When this occurs, its future is assured, and it doesn't look very bright.

Figure 22.2: Black holes bend the space and time around them

This is pretty much what happens between Jerks and Analogs. Jerks can succeed only if their plans ensure that they keep out of range of Analogs' gravity, or their strengths. If a Jerk miscalculates its trajectory, or somehow the black hole isn't exactly where it was supposed to be, the game may be up for the Jerk, and it'll fade into darkness.

Your goal, if you're an Analog, is to cause such a shift or miscalculation. You want to make the Jerk's beam of light pass just a bit too close to the event horizon, so that it's snuffed out by gravity's crush. If you are a sumo wrestler, you want to break with tradition and protocol, stick your arm straight out to the side, and catch Bruce Lee with your enormous fleshy forearm just before you go sailing by. If you do, you'll knock Bruce flat as a pancake, and you might just slow yourself down enough to stay in the ring.

None of this will be easy; far from it. There is a codependency between carriers of the traditions of the past and those who wish to replace them. As long as both sides play according to their own roles the result is a foregone conclusion. But, if either party to the dysfunctional relationship breaks ranks and does something out of character, the whole game breaks down, like an episode of Jerry Springer. When this occurs, the party most likely to benefit is the one least expected to change. And in the case of Analogs and Digitals, we've sort of established by now who that might be, haven't we?

Figure 22.3: Disruptor's Dilemma. Sometimes, the bull, or the Analog, wins

This leads to what I call the Disruptor's Dilemma, and it's a doozy of a strategy when you get it right. Basically, this dilemma says that Disruptors can be disruptive only as long as they're the ones doing the disrupting. The disrupted has to be complicit for the disruptor's disruption to work. If and when the disrupted moves first, the shoe goes on the other foot – often in a big and fatal way. None of this approach will be easy. If it were, there would be no dilemma. But with a well-timed arm swing, the match can be over in an instant, and in a way that makes other potential Bruce's pause.

Breaking Ranks to Win

As you've probably guessed by now, I'm a big fan of history. Examples of the Disruptor's Dilemma are sprinkled throughout human history, which should come as no surprise. What I find interesting is that you can often find both sides of a conflict using this dilemma to gain advantage, at least for a time. In many instances the consequences of disruption are pretty much inevitable. But at least you can keep things interesting until the eventual end.

The key to making the dilemma work to your advantage is to use it sparingly, decisively, and with commitment. Half-measures, feigns or frequent deviations from your normal destroy the whole effectiveness of the game. When you shift your strategy and do the unexpected, it has to *be unexpected.*

The Chinese philosopher-warrior-general Sun Tzu was a master at this stuff, which is why he is one of the most legendary strategists of all time. His writing is full of examples of the power of the Disruptor's Dilemma, both in its presence and its absence.

> *"If you know the enemy and know yourself you need not fear the results of a hundred battles."*

> *"If you are far from the enemy, make him believe you are near."*

> *"Let your plans be dark and impenetrable as night, and when you move, fall like a thunderbolt."*

> *"Engage people with what they expect; it is what they are able to discern and it confirms their projections. It settles them into predictable patterns of response, occupying their minds while*

you wait for the extraordinary moment – that which they cannot anticipate."

"Attack him where he is unprepared, appear where you are not expected."

"The opportunity to secure ourselves against defeat lies in our own hands, but the opportunity of defeating the enemy is provided by the enemy himself."

"Thus, what is of supreme importance in war is to attack the enemy's strategy."

And perhaps my favorite Sun Tzu quote:
"Dude, where's my car?"

Oh wait, that was Ashton Kutcher...

Disruption comes in many forms, and even Jerks can be disrupted.

Clinton Versus a Real Jerk

History is full of both disruptive Jerks and disruptive Analogs. Indeed, the first Analogs were disruptors of Dirts, and so on. Some of those Dirts knew that turnabout was fair play, and they did a reasonable job of stopping those who were trying to Jerk them, at least for a time.

As I mentioned before, George Washington was a first-rate Jerk. He represented the coming wave of Analogs who were seeking to disrupt the Dirts who were then in control. He used a range of tactics and strategies to pull off what was believed to be impossible: defeat the strongest landed power in the world, and do so decisively in battle. Despite winning the American War of Independence, George himself was almost disrupted by a wily old Dirt named Sir Henry Clinton. There's something about the combination of a Clinton, the American South, and disruptive strategies that seems to reverberate to the present day.

In the early years of America's War of Independence, alternatively known to the British as 'The Right Buggery Mess,' George Washington and his men were doing pretty well with their disruptive, rebellious ways. In March 1776 they surprised the British garrison in Boston, forcing them to evacuate in complete humiliation. While this was a stunning victory for the colonial upstarts, they had largely just tweaked the nose of a rather grumpy old bear, and subsequently had to live with the consequences. Through 1777 the British suffered additional defeats at the hands of these pre-Analogs, adding insult to the injuries at Boston. For more than a year it appeared that George and the boys might win, and disrupt the entire Dirt Trinity as a result.

Figure 22.4: General Sir Henry Clinton. British Commander of the Southern Theater of War in the American Revolution

While some of the southern colonials supported independence, the sentiment was not as strong as in the North. As a result, Washington maintained the bulk of his forces in the northern colonies, while a token force maintained a presence in the South. Here is where the

British broke ranks with tradition, and nearly crushed the Revolution as a result.

It is important to remember the time factor in all of this. Communications across the Atlantic took months in transit, and any meaningful response by the British Crown would take many more months to organize and implement. While the British worked to respond to the crisis in America, the forces already in place fought the rag-tag army of rebels in a range of engagements that were predictable in both strategy and tactics. Both sides did roughly what the other expected.

The British, over-extended by wars elsewhere and conscious of the relative calm of the southern colonies, decided to do the unexpected. Rather than deploy his newly arriving forces in the North, where his primary opposition lay, General Clinton deployed his new armies in the South, effectively cutting the rebellion in two.

The British move was a master-stroke in the use of the Disruptor's Dilemma. Up to that point, the main focus of the British occupation of America centered on the colonies of New England. Here was the home of most of the opposition to the Crown, and the troops garrisoned there were a classic Dirt Trinity strategy of maintaining control. The southern colonies were not as averse to British rule, as England was the primary destination for the region's economic outputs of cotton, tobacco and grains. Money makes for good friends, if only while convenient.

When Clinton's forces landed, the rebels in the area were taken largely by surprise, while the bulk of the American army lay far to the north, unable to respond for several months. George Washington, pre-Jerk, general *extraordinaire* and father of the nation that resulted from the war, nonetheless was completely disrupted by Clinton's move. While Washington and his fellow neo-Analogs finally prevailed over King George III and his empire of Dirt, it was a closer-run affair than is often taught in American schools.

The Disruptor's Dilemma is that in counting on the opposition to do the predictable, you put yourself at extreme risk when and if they do not. There are many, many additional examples that can be explored, such as Imperial Japan in the decades after America's Admiral Perry arrived in Tokyo Bay, ahead of a fleet of clipper ships seeking trade with the Land of the Rising Sun. In a matter of half a century, Japan moved from living in the depths of the Dirt Trinity to being the poster child of the Analog Trinity, with a disruptive little event called Pearl Harbor occurring along the way.

The jihadists of the late 20th century similarly face repeated Disruptor's Dilemmas, as their dastardly and cowardly success on 9/11/2001 led to the likely unexpected invasion of their sanctuaries of Iraq and Afghanistan. The same territories they had freed from Soviet aggression, and had infiltrated after the First Gulf War, now fell firmly into the hands of their primary opposition, then-President George Bush responding far more strongly than the jihadists ever believed likely.

Just as with the battles between Clinton and Washington were a cat-and-mouse game of disruption and counter-disruption, dilemma and response, the present war between America and ISIS parallels that between the forces of the Age of Land and those of the new Age of Capital. Will this present war result in the victory of the armies of the Capital Age, or in their capitulation to the amorphous forces of the new Age of Information? Time will tell. I know which side I am rooting for, and I hope that we can use the Disruptor's Dilemma to continued good effect, just as Sun Tzu taught us over 2,500 years ago.

Back to Business

What does all of this have to do with business, you may ask. What do muskets and M-1 tanks have to do with making money? Well, strategy is strategy. And while master military strategist Carl von Clausewitz called war 'the continuation of politics by other means,' it's fair to say that business is the continuation of war, with exploding coupons and drones.

I use this example specifically because Amazon is masterful at using Disruptors Dilemma to keep both Analogs and Jerks off balance. Amazon confounds both groups by playing the gap in between them. It would be totally like a Jerk to try something as disruptive as drone delivery to gain advantage over existing retailers. However, no Jerk would have the resources to tell America's Federal Aviation Administration (FAA) how to regulate the skies the way that Amazon can, and did.

Figure 22.5: Drone delivery. Amazon does the unpredictable, in order to stay ahead

Many a Jerk has tried to deploy same-day delivery of all manner of goods, because customers demand the New Normals of ubiquity and immediacy and they're willing to pay for them. But, only a company as large as Amazon has the resources to actually pull off something like Amazon Prime, and thereby ensures that any Jerks who try to do the same thing can't possibly deliver as effectively. Amazon CEO Jeff Bezos has been called many things by all manner of people who find it difficult to follow his strategies and tactics. My label for him would certainly be 'fox,' as in crazy-like-a.

Aim, Ready, Fire

How do you make sense of the strategies of an Amazon, a Google or an Apple, and make them work for you? How can an Analog hold the Jerks at bay, or at least delay their continuing onslaught? Can a capital-centric organization, saturated in the thinking of the Analog Trinity, find a way to hold off the relentless advance of the Information Age and the Digital Trinity? In the long run, I'd bet against it; history has a way of repeating itself. However, in the quarter-by-quarter world of the Capital Age, Analogs might be able to get a few good shots in before they are through.

To do this, Analogs have to do what they hate the most: be unpredictable. They need to jink when their latest report says to move, they need to bob when their tiger teams suggest that they weave. Analogs need to hold a 'free taxi-rides day' when the regulations governing livery companies comes up for a vote – just to make the guys at Uber say, "What the????" Mind you, Analogs shouldn't do too much of this sort of thing; when overdone by Analogs, disruptive just looks like crazy. But, when done occasionally, decisively and randomly, such acts of willful insanity can be the wisest course of action.

Pulling the trigger of Disruptor's Dilemma on your competition can be like firing the first missile, from the first Predator Drone, flying the first remote mission over the deserts of Southwest Asia. Just before that missile hit home, some Jerk was probably heard saying, "What the????" and nothing more.

Chapter Summary:

1. The Analog Trinity thrives on structure, predictability and slowness. The greatest weapon a Jerk has in fighting Analogs is the expectation that Analogs will act predictably and with agonizing slowness.
2. The greatest defense an Analog has against a Jerk's attack is to leverage the *Disruptor's Dilemma*: A disruptor *needs* their opponent to act as they always have, in order to disrupt them. For a Jerk to disrupt an Analog, the Analog must be complicit, and allow the disruption to occur.
3. If an Analog moves first, and in an unexpected manner, a Jerk can be completely countered. This is the Disruptor's Dilemma.

4. Analogs are typically far better financed than any potential disruptor. Using that capital advantage as well as knowledge of the affected market can defeat any Jerk threat, but the Analog has to fire first, and in an unexpected manner. Give a Jerk too much of a head start, and act predictably and slowly in your response, and you're toast.

Chapter Twenty-Three: Conclusion

"Extinction is the rule. Survival is the exception."- Carl Sagan

"Free to roam the heavens in man's noble quest to investigate the weirdness of the universe!"- Bill Watterson's Spaceman Spiff from 'Calvin and Hobbes'

Well, you and I made it to the end of the chapters. And with any luck, this marks a beginning, as well. As I write this book I find myself to be, with no shortage of incredulity, 46 years old. I'm simultaneously at the middle of my career and the middle of my life. I may be at the peak of my game, the top of the rollercoaster, the apogee of my orbit, the hump in my normal distribution curve. It is not lost on me that I have both come a long way and still have a long way to go, but I've decided to take the last three weeks off from my life, so that I might take a moment to do a little living. I took some time to enjoy the view, to actually live, if only for a short while.

In other words, welcome to my midlife crisis.

I just now Googled "crisis" and this is what I found:
> A **crisis** (from the Greek κρίσις - krisis; plural: "**crises**"; adjectival form: "critical") is any event that is, or is expected to lead to, an unstable and dangerous situation affecting an individual, group, community, or whole society.

I can live with every aspect of this definition save one: the word 'dangerous.' As the well-known Chinese curse states, "May you live in interesting times ..." Like 'interesting,' the word 'crisis' can have a dual meaning. Now that I've arrived at middle age, I find that the changes you experience at midlife can be the source of both fear and inspiration. In either case, a crisis is upon you, but the word 'dangerous' does not reflect the response I feel each morning when I wake up, one day older than the night before.

As I said earlier in this book, technology has no morality; it just *is*.
The same is true of change. Whether it is for good or bad is up to us,
and how we choose to perceive it, and put it to use. If you view
change as a crisis, filled with danger, then so it shall be. If instead
you see it as an opportunity to learn from past mistakes, to grow
from them, and to try to fail forward and fast, then perhaps such a
midlife 'awakening' is exactly the 'crisis' that you need.

Either way, the most important thing to keep in mind is that it's all a
matter of your state of mind. If you focus on the positive, that's what
you will see. If you focus on the negative, you will find it. With the
presence of negative thoughts come negative neurochemicals, and
vice versa. Our brains are stimulation-driven chemistry sets; they
can't tell where each chemical comes from, only that it is there.
Excitement without context can be thrilling or terrifying, depending
on how your brain interprets it. In our heads as well as in our world,
context is everything.

***Figure 23.1: Our brains register, 'Excitement!' Fear or
exhilaration is a matter of interpretation***

As it is in life, so it is with business, because business is just the
economic manifestation of how we live. If you look for risk, you will
find it. If you look for opportunity, surely it will be there, too.

Discomfort from change will be there regardless of the source, either risk or opportunity. Your brain might not know the difference; it only knows that discomfort is there. Instead of assuming that discomfort is bad, might you achieve some better results by telling yourself to explore that source of discomfort a bit more, before you cast judgment? Is the risk that you're assessing with your latest investment automatically bad, or is it opportunity, just masked by neurochemical and organizational confusion? Analogs have to fight against a lifetime of training to achieve this viewpoint; Jerks simply look it up like they were searching for a definition on Google.

So You Think You're Some Kind of Jerk?

Our society has always had its share of Jerks. Whether in the hightail or the lowtail, Jerks are necessary to maintain the health of a population. As we discussed earlier, Jerks maintain the 'normal' in a normal distribution. How fantastic it must be to be a Jerk at a time in history where it is finally becoming a clear competitive advantage. This strikes me as another key takeaway from the transition we are going through, as the Analog Trinity fades away and the Digital Trinity ascends.

In some ways I envy people who start out as Jerks; what a great way to live! I'm struck that their lives may be simpler, easier, and more fulfilling than that of Analogs, and that leads me to a bit of jealousy. No doubt, many Dirts felt the same about early Analogs, and many Tools about the Dirts in their midst. But on the other side of this argument is the comfort I have in knowing that I have gained my Jerk-like perspective the hard, Smith-Barney way. I earned it. Something given is never valued as much as something earned; yet another lesson I learned from my parents and for which I am grateful.

Better Living Through Physics?

Perhaps surprisingly, there are parallels to this discussion of our emotions in the world of physics. When the Industrial Revolution began, we let go of much of the superstitions that we created under the Tool Trinity, and formalized under the Dirt Trinity, and we began to embrace a new way of thinking: science. As we did so, we took on some very different views of our universe, not all of which were welcomed by the powers of the time. In that age, Isaac Newton was a radical, a weirdo, a Jerk. He dared to claim that our universe was knowable and predictable, which completely flew in the face of the thinking of the day.

Figure 23.2: Isaac Newton. A real Jerk

It took a while to gain acceptance, but eventually Newton's view of the universe prevailed, which dramatically accelerated the transition from our land-centric society to our capital-centered one. Here we stayed for over a century, harvesting the fruits of Newton's insights as we came to understand, and then put to our use, the laws of how the universe operates.

Then, along came another Jerk, who upset the whole Newtonian apple cart. That Jerk, Albert Einstein, found yet another way of perceiving our universe. He saw that there is a deeper understanding out there, something more than what Newton had seen. Einstein did not say that Newton was wrong. Old Isaac was a pretty bright guy for being a Dirt. Rather, Einstein found that there was more to the universe than what Isaac had seen. Einstein's insights didn't replace Newton's, they enhanced them.

Figure 23.3: Albert Einstein. Perhaps the greatest Jerk of all time

As with Newton, it took quite some time before society was ready to understand and embrace what Einstein was telling us, and many of us struggle with his ideas about relativity to this day. The implications of his insights are weird, unfamiliar and not very intuitive, particularly for those of us weaned on the notion of a well-ordered and quantifiable world, Newton-style.

Like the transition from Dirt to Capital, and then Capital to Information, our evolution from superstition to Newtonian physics to relativity has brought both good and bad to our way of life and our understanding of it. Life certainly seemed to be simpler back when you struggled to simply make it through your day. But it likely was also a bit more spiritually hollow. There was no time for deep thoughts when you were focused on your empty stomach, and where your family might find shelter for the night.

In the world of Capital, the Industrial Revolution and Newtonian physics, we were able to free ourselves from many lesser concerns of the day, and we could start to deepen our humanity, rather than lose it, as many seem to suggest. So too, as we move to a world centered on information, the Digital Revolution and relativity, we stand to potentially gain still more of our true humanness – in all of the splendid, horrifying, stupefying glory that we see on Facebook every day.

The Highs, the Lows, and What's in Between

I've argued in this book that we are in transition from a world centered on capital to one centered on information. I hope that I've done well to make this case. But, just as we hold onto many institutions, traditions and beliefs from previous Trinities, so too will we keep many from the Analog as we advance beyond. After a century of assessing the relationship between Newtonian and Einsteinian physics, the best we can determine is that both are 'the truth.' We have found that their 'correctness' depends upon context (there it is again), and correctness is just a difference in metrics.

In one context, that of the human scale, Newtonian physics are largely correct, and its rules and laws prevail. In other contexts, Einstein is largely correct and relativity comes to the fore. Both are for the context that they best serve. While Newton's worldview works best in our average world, it's in the tails, both high- and low-, that relativity takes over and becomes the better predictor of 'the truth.'

When we seek to understand the universe on the scale of us and our world, Newton works just fine. On average, Newton was right: the laws of the universe are fixed and knowable. But Einstein was right, too –although his thinking works best for the areas outside of the averages, where conditions tend to be more extreme. Einstein was right in recognizing that, in order for the universe to be 'normal,' it also has to be a little bit strange.

On the grand scale of the universe as a whole, the hightail if you like, relativity is the best guide to tell us when the universe formed, how it lives and how it will eventually die. This is the realm of light speed, space-time, gravity waves and black holes. These are the aspects of this still-new science of relativity that we are struggling to understand.

$$\mathcal{L}_{GWS} = \sum_f (\bar{\Psi}_f(i\gamma^\mu \partial\mu - m_f)\Psi_f - eQ_f \bar{\Psi}_f \gamma^\mu \Psi_f A_\mu)+$$

$$+\frac{g}{\sqrt{2}}\sum_i (\bar{a}_L^i \gamma^\mu b_L^i W_\mu^+ + \bar{b}_L^i \gamma^\mu a_L^i W_\mu^-)+\frac{g}{2c_w}\sum_f \bar{\Psi}_f \gamma^\mu (I_f^3 - 2s_w^2 Q_f - I_f^3 \gamma_5)\Psi_f Z_\mu +$$

$$-\frac{1}{4}|\partial_\mu A_\nu - \partial_\nu A_\mu - ie(W_\mu^- W_\nu^+ - W_\mu^+ W_\nu^-)|^2 - \frac{1}{2}|\partial_\mu W_\nu^+ - \partial_\nu W_\mu^+ +$$

$$-ie(W_\mu^+ A_\nu - W_\nu^+ A_\mu) + ig'c_w(W_\mu^+ Z_\nu - W_\nu^+ Z_\mu|^2 +$$

$$-\frac{1}{4}|\partial_\mu Z_\nu - \partial_\nu Z_\mu + ig'c_w(W_\mu^- W_\nu^+ - W_\mu^+ W_\nu^-)|^2 +$$

$$-\frac{1}{2}M_\eta^2 \eta^2 - \frac{gM_\eta^2}{8M_W}\eta^3 - \frac{g'^2 M_\eta^2}{32M_W}\eta^4 + |M_W W_\mu^+ + \frac{g}{2}\eta W_\mu^+|^2 +$$

$$+\frac{1}{2}|\partial_\mu \eta + iM_Z Z_\mu + \frac{ig}{2c_w}\eta Z_\mu|^2 - \sum_f \frac{g}{2}\frac{m_f}{M_W}\bar{\Psi}_f \Psi_f \eta$$

Figure 23.4: The equations of the Grand Unified Theory (GUT) attempt to join Newton's gravity with Einstein's relativity. This is not for the faint of heart

At the scale of the exceedingly small, Newtonian physics again gives way to quantum mechanics, which does a far better job of describing the truth of the Universe on the scale of atoms, quarks and whatever else may be way down there inside of the smallest stuff we presently know. This is, no doubt, the lowtail of the universe. At this lowtail, relativity again explains 'the truth,' dictating the on-again, off-again positions of electrons as they fade in and out of the four dimensions we seem certain of, perhaps on their journey through dimensions Five through Nine - no doubt accompanied by my old friend, Spaceman Spiff.

From all of the collective effort that our society has invested in understanding and applying Einstein's ideas since he had his revelation, we have confirmed with striking clarity that Einstein was a Jerk of the highest order. Not to take away from Newton's own Jerkiness in his day.

Despite this, we still aren't completely sure of how we got here or, more importantly, why we got here. Hence our Maslowian hunger to find these answers. With luck and perseverance, they will come to us in time.

What's This Got to Do with Business?

I realize that all of this is a pretty ethereal discussion, especially when you may have thought this to be some kind of business book. Fine, let's spend a moment more centered, and find some applicability in all of this. When I hear 'data scientists' today talking in terms of absolutes, metrics and the certain measurability of businesses and customers, I'm struck by these same ethereal thoughts. Analogs grew up on a steady stream of very Newtonian thinking, and we love it when things get all linear. It means they are measureable, predictable and knowable, and this leads to a better bottom line, in terms of capital.

Certainly the data analytics that we learned and applied during the Analog Era showed us facts and figures and allowed us to make better decisions; this was critical to our appropriate management of capital. This approach is also relevant to the beginnings of our transition to the Information Era because we don't yet know what we don't know.

What some of us in the data sciences world are recognizing is that truly different sorts of results come from asking different questions. These in turn lead to different answers, and those new insights usually live in the hightail or lowtail of things. Average thinking leads to average results.

Given our easy and longtime access to the world of the average, I'll place my bets on the -tails every time.

Lawyers and Managers and Scientists, Oh My!

After two decades as an engineer and business person, I decided to get a law degree. This was an eminently oddball decision, to be sure.

Engineers are trained to think Digitally, and not necessarily in a good way. Engineers see things as right or wrong, true or false, correct or incorrect, black or white. This is a critical part of an engineer's search for truth in the universe, just as Newton intended.

Figure 23.5: "It depends on what your definition of the word 'is,' is." Former President Clinton had an attorney's view of the world

This is not how lawyers are taught to think. Lawyers do not see the world in blacks and whites, but rather as a smear of grays. The law is about arguments, based upon the evidence at hand, and trying to figure out the best interpretation of what happened, in context. For attorneys, "...it depends" is not just a mindset, it *is* the journey.

This conditional and relative view of 'the truth' is very disappointing to scientists and engineers. It causes us discomfort. This may explain why it took so long for relativity to be discovered by a Jerk like Einstein. Relativity is a little too squishy for those raised on Newtonian physics, and most attorneys are too caught up in formulating their next argument to allow 'yes' or 'no' logic to stand in their way.

That Kid Ain't Right

As much of a dichotomy as I may encompass from the unnatural blending of these two world views, I kind of dig it too. Engineers may know you need to go north, and they may be able to plot the most efficient way to get there. Lawyers may take an entirely different route to their destination, but they find the journey much more interesting along the way. Tracking towards True North, while admiring the view, strikes me as an excellent vantage point for the trip I presently find myself on.

For me, the most valuable takeaway from the first 46 years of my life is that I choose to look forward without letting go of my past. I try to smell any roses I may encounter along the way, and argue with them a bit, too. If I can do that for another 46 years, I'll be the luckiest person I know.

Like a lawyer forming arguments around a case, I choose to see both the good and the bad, the positive and the negative aspects of change. Then, like an engineer, I hope I will resolve the way that best suits who I want to be, where I want to be, and how I want to be at that moment in space-time – and act like failure is not an option. Gene Kranz was a genius. I aspire to do the best that I can with the data I have in hand, staying open to new ideas as they zip by at somewhere near the speed of information.

I find this journey fascinating, and I hope the same for you.

My Parthian Shot

If any of these chapters have reached you and spoken to you, then I am grateful that you took the time to read them. If any of the thoughts I've shared here help you shape your own new ways of thinking, or challenge some of the beliefs that you have of your world, then I am pleased. This would mean that not only have I reached my personal goal of getting a little self-actualization out of life, it may even mean that I have achieved some level of transcendence. The engineer in me is still trying to get his head around what that even means, but he's pretty sure the answer is out there, somewhere in the tenth, eleventh or twelfth dimensions. I hope that I run into Carl Sagan, another hero of mine, as he passes by in his spaceship of the imagination.

Figure 23.6: Carl Sagan. A hero to Jerks everywhere

Whether you are a Tool, a Dirt, an Analog or a Jerk, I wish you well as you try to figure it out for yourself, too.

Figure 23.7: Bridge of the Starship Enterprise, from the TV series 'Star Trek'

As I begin this next phase of my journey I feel a bit like Captain James Tiberius Kirk. I see myself taking the big chair in the middle of the bridge of my life, and I say to my crew, "Shields **down**, phasers set for stun**ned**, warp**ed** drive engaged, full Jerk ahead! I want to boldly go where I've never gone before …"

Chapter Summary:

1. The one constant in the world is change. You can try to fight it, which seems futile. Or, you can try to embrace it and direct it towards the things you desire most.
2. Your world view is a product of your history. Your future is a product of your willingness to embrace new world views, which inevitably come with change.

SECTION IV: The World of Jerk, 2025

In my first book, *Data Crush*, I ended with a set of predictions of what life might be like in 2020, then seven years in the future. Despite the remarkably negative feedback given to me by my then-editors, these five vignettes proved to be one of the more popular aspects of *Data Crush*. I decided it was important to listen to this feedback, and provide that finale here in *Jerk*.

When coming up with the stories of the world of 2020 in *Data Crush* I tried to project how apps and the smartphone would advance in the coming seven years and what sorts of capabilities they would present to their users. I spend a lot of time thinking about and studying this stuff, so I'd like to believe that I can make pretty good predictions about where the technology is going. My livelihood depends on it.

Nevertheless, I was surprised to see just how fast the world is changing. By 2016, at least half of the capabilities that I had predicted in the vignettes from *Data Crush* had already appeared in the marketplace, and I suspect the rest will appear a year or two ahead of my 2020 estimate.

With this in mind, I am stretching myself out to 2025. I am following my own advice about getting uncomfortable and seeing past my own prejudices and constraints and seeing the world from those with the most to gain, rather than those with the most to lose.

Some of these predictions may be way off. Others may come years ahead of 2025. That is the point of this exercise: to project into the future our present capabilities, and try to see how as yet unknown needs may be met through as yet unknown capabilities. I hope you find this useful in opening your own thinking about what may be possible in our not-so-distant future. Rather than five different stories, this time I'm writing about a single individual, Rebecca, and how different aspects of her life are all enhanced, and sometimes driven by, the social and technical changes all around her.

Chapter Twenty-Four: Saturday, February 15, 2025

<u>Life</u>

Rebecca stirred for a moment as her homebase buzzed at her hip, rousing her from her slumber after a decent night's sleep. After a few brief moments, her homebase, or 'homie,' buzzed again, this time a bit more insistently. Homie was well aware that Becki liked to sleep in a bit, but that she also had to get ready for her important meeting this morning.

Her base continued its sensory assault on her sleeping by tickling her with some music. Slowly, softly, distantly at first. The easy rhythm of her favorite Caribbean reggae rap began playing in her ear. Homie gave Becki another two minutes, and then began to vibrate more insistently, matching the new beat of the French-Sahrawi-Soul-Jazz song, "Eau de Cœur," a recent favorite of hers. Becki relented, sat up, and leapt to her feet, steeling herself for her day.

She turned on the pre-heater for her shower, and moved to the sink to address herself in her mirror. She picked up the trim, smooth, bright white box containing her new eyePhone contacts, removing them from their recharging case and clearing them of fluid with a rapid shake of the hand. In seconds, she had placed a lens in each eye, and blinked a few times, both to ensure they were properly situated and to begin their startup process.

She was excited that her parents had bought her the eyePhones for her birthday. The excitement over this, the first new product launch from Gapple, had been enormous, and the interview process had been intense. While Becki passed the application and evaluation process with flying colors, she still had to wait for six months before her insurance carrier had finalized the contract for coverage, and Gapple's production output had finally produced the set designed for her.
The eyePhone was the culmination of the 20-year-long battle between Apple and Google to create the greatest information

interface in history. When the two companies finally merged in 2023, the world wondered if the merger would mark the end of their innovation, or a new beginning. As the sales numbers and the waiting period showed, Gapple seemed to find the best balance of coopetition inside of their organization; the eyePhone was a game-changer in every respect.

As her lenses finished their start-up sequence Becki noticed a flicker in her field of view, and then the eyePhone's user interface began to appear in her field of vision. The lenses quickly confirmed her identity based upon their retina scan and then asked her to log in, by using her characteristic, blink-and-zig-zag-your-eye motion that she programmed when she first got them. Immediately after her login, the lenses synchronized with her ear buds and her homie, and then pulled up the summary of her bio status, including her blood sugar, weight, eye salinity, mood, electrolytes and her sleep pattern from the previous night.

After this synchronization, homie noticed that Becki was still a bit agitated. Homie quickly sorted through Becki's inbound messages, and filtered out those which would likely upset her the most; she didn't need to hear about Carol's second virtual date with that creepy guy, Gustav. Clearly he had earned his two and a half stars on links.com, regardless of how 'hunkie' he felt through his virtual reality (VR) body suit or how much fun Carol had on their first VR encounter. But then, Becki was never a big fan of the whole global VR dating world pioneered by the Ecuadorian company FlashBang, SdH.

Homie decided Becki could deal with this after she kicked up her blood sugar with some breakfast. Homie pulled up the funniest video posts from her overnight social feeds, and presented her a 'greatest hits' summary from the previous six hours. Becki laughed repeatedly during her shower, and homie noted the biochemical improvement in her mood detected in her tears by her eyePhones.

After showering and drying off, Becki stepped onto her 3H (holistic health helper) scale and waited 15 seconds for the scale to make its measurements. The 3H reported back to Homie, and Becki saw through her eyePhones that she was still in remarkably good health, despite not exercising the day before. Homie noted that her health carrier, CNN Healthcare, charged her $1.53 for not taking her usual four-mile walk the day before. "I'll have to make up the mileage today," Becki noted to herself in passing.

Homie saw the coverage offers that arrived 30 seconds later from four competitors of CNN. Healthy, employed, 23-year old Americans were extremely rare and extremely valuable to the healthcare exchange providers, and customers like Becki were in high demand, even if she engaged in some risky behaviors like in-person dating. Homie noted that the offer from Volvo Health seemed particularly attractive, and began negotiating a better signing bonus on Becki's behalf. Homie noted that Becki's Panamanian Doctor, Maria Santiago, also gave a discount through Volvo and worked that into its coverage counteroffer.

Becki quickly brushed her teeth, her toothbrush counting the strokes, and sending that information to CNN. She always brushed at least 70 seconds, to pick up the bonus for brushing more than a minute at a time. Homie noted that her brush was nearly at its end-of-life in brush strokes, and started a negotiation to have a replacement brush dropped off in Monday's drone delivery.

Becki began putting on her makeup, per her usual routine. Homie's Bluetooth proximity sensors detected each item she used, reporting back to Bobbi Brown that today she was in full Bobbi regalia. Her eyePhones snapped a photo of her looking in the mirror. The Bobbi Brown app quickly evaluated the picture, suggested that Becki use a little bit more rouge on her left cheek, to better balance her look, and then gave her a 'thumbs up' approval for her makeup job. Bobbi Brown posted a 'thank you, Becki' on her Facebook site, and credited her with 10 Bobbi bucks for her support for the day.

Becki moved to her closet and scanned her clothes, her eyePhones displaying the offer provided by each brand as they bid for the chance to be worn by her today. She didn't feel like authorizing Levi's or Nordstrom's to advertise her whereabouts today, so she picked one of her offline, off-brand, black-market jeans and a shirt with an expired advertising contract she bought on ExBay. She was giving up five co-branding loyalty points from Bobbi for not wearing on-label clothes, but she wanted to lie low today.

Dressed, Becki wandered into the kitchen, following Homie as it read her top emails to her. She opened her refrigerator and her eyePhones highlighted the foods that were nearing their expiration date. Homie rapidly scanned those items, and then presented three options for how to combine them into something she would like to eat, and would earn her the most consumption and healthy living points. She selected three different kinds of locally produced fruit, the non-BGH, certified-organic, sole-source, heritage breed, ancient-biota Greek-style yogurt, and the Colombian bacupari fruit that she loved so much.

She placed these into her blender, added some water and some soy protein, and whipped up her breakfast. The blender bluetoothed the weight and conductivity of the mix to Homie who noted this combination, and sent the resulting calories and anti-oxidants consumed to CNN and her local grocer. Becki sat at her small kitchen table, drinking her breakfast and scanning through her messages, presented to her through her eyePhones.

Becki lost track of time and space while browsing through her messages and social feeds. Soon, Homie gently reminded her to make her appointment with her mother this morning. Homie confirmed a Lyft car was nearby, and Becki approved Homie's reservation of the car with a quick double blink and a look-up-and-to-the-left. She quickly picked a pair of comfortable, off-contract shoes, opened the door, and then stopped, as Homie reminded her to grab her purse before she left her apartment.

Love

As she stepped outside of her building, Homie informed her that her ride was two minutes away. Becki looked up and saw her neighbor Tim approaching her from down the street. He looked worn out, angry and frustrated. He appeared a bit yellow-tinged in her eyePhones, which displayed a VR attitude score of '68,' shaded yellow to indicate that Tim was not in a very good mood. Becki looked at her iAffect points balance, noted that she had 1,503 points in her account, and decided to help Tim out with his seemingly bad day.

iAffect was one of the more controversial new features of the eyePhone, particularly since the patent infringement lawsuit between Gapple and Facebook-General Electric was still ongoing. That, and the recent hacking theft of popstar Kid Khaleem's 47 million iAffect points caused massive price inflation in the AffectBucks marketplace. Forty-seven million 'likes' doesn't buy as much happiness as it used to.

As Tim approached her, Becki offered him a, "Hi Tim, why so glum?" and then double-blinked to send him 25 iAffect points to see if the gesture would help. Tim looked up and said, "Hi, Beck, how's it goin'?"

His own eyePhones noted the points Becki just sent to him and he immediately felt a bit better. Becki's eyePhones noted that his score jumped up to '74' and she continued with, "I saw your status from last night. Fighting again with Maria?"

"Yeah, it seems like no matter how hard I try, I just can't keep up with her. It's hard to understand her life and her world when we live six thousand miles from each other. No matter how much time we spend in VR, it's not the same as actually *being* in Manila with her."

Becki empathized, "I know, I'm still not into this whole VR dating fad, especially not the suit rentals!"

"Ha! Yeah, I know, gross, right? But who can afford to buy their own suit?" replied Tim.

"Married people," replied Becki, with a touch of cynicism. Just then, her Lyft pulled up, and Becki cut the conversation short, "Well Tim, if Maria is that important to you, maybe you should just fly to the

Philippines and meet her in person." "Fly?!? To meet her in person?!? Beck, don't be crazy. I love her, I'm not *OBSESSED* with her!"

With that, Becki hopped in her ride and closed the door. As she pulled away, Becki gave Tim a parting glance, and noted that his score had fallen again to '71.' "I hope I didn't waste *ALL* of those points," she thought to herself.

Liberty

Homie pinged in her ear, notifying Becki that she had an important in-bound. She blinked to open it, and her iAmerican app opened in her field of view. The app noted that five different bills had passed review by different subcommittees of the United States House of Representatives, and each might impact her life in measurable ways. She quickly scanned the summary of each, their history as they moved through the legislature, the partisan perspectives of all four political parties as to why they supported or opposed each bill, and the potential impact each would have specifically on Becki's life.

iAmerican was one of the most tangible results of the passing of the 29th Amendment to the Constitution. That amendment changed the entire operation of politics in America. It changed American Presidential elections from indirect to direct, set term limits for Congress and implemented citizen oversight by plebiscite, through the app called iAmerican.

This Amendment was a direct result of the riots, protests and social disorder that followed the disastrous election of 2020. It was still shameful that more than10,000 Americans died and more than $60 billion in property was destroyed at the hands of each other and of the National Guard, but change is always costly and hard.

Once the powers-that-be recognized that that populist revolt of the previous 10 years was exploding into a full-blown revolution, they were finally willing to actually follow the will of the people, if only to avoid an ending like those of Louis XIV, Mussolini or Muammar

Gaddafi. iAmerican, started as a subversive effort to undermine the American government, evolved into the platform for Americans to take back control of their country.

As her Lyft auto-navigated to her appointment with her mother, Becki assessed each bill's wording, their arguments for and against them, and the projected impacts to the country and Becki's own political profile. iAmerican displayed the stance of Becki's friends and family on each bill, and made a recommended position for Becki to take on each, based upon her own beliefs and principles profile maintained in the app.

Becki had 24 hours to make up her mind on each, and iAmerican provided her with several courses of action on each. For the three that she decided to support, iAmerican recommended how best to support each. For the bill supporting the taxation and registration of vending-machine-sold hypodermic needles, Becki spent 25 iAffect 'likes' in support of the bill. For the bill that required hotels, landlords and other providers of overnight accommodations to allow for elective privacy during a stay, Becki donated 750 Hilton Hotel points and 250 Airbnb points in support of the bill. Finally, for the bill that would repeal over 5,000 elements of the Federal Registry of Laws which we deemed to be 'obsolete,' Becki paid $125 in cash, which was the only form of payment allowed in support of that particular bill.

Longing

Becki completed her civic duties just as her Lyft dropped her off at the Starbucks super center, where her mother was waiting for her. Becki exited the car, took three long steps and greeted her mother with a hug and a 'Hi mom."

"Are you losing weight again?" her mom asked in reply.

"Mom, stop it," she returned as she stepped to and sat at the outside table they had reserved the night before.

Both took a seat, and a waiter brought them each their favorite coffee and bakery sweet. Homie noted the fast service, paid the bill and tipped the waiter, and then notified CNN that Becki was drinking a bit more than her daily allowance of caffeine and baked goods. CNN charged her $.37 in reply.

Becki wasn't looking forward to another conversation about her future, but her mom deftly shifted from pleasantries and into Beck's personal life like a thief in the night. "I don't know why you have such a problem with VR," her mom started. "Why, just the other day my friend Sara met a perfectly wonderful man on links.com. He's a doctor living in Havana. Handsome, successful, funny, and …"

"Fake mom. Probably fake," Becki replied.

"Well, maybe you're right, Becki. But aren't we all fake? Aren't we all fake at least a little? If you're going to pretend, why not pretend big?"

"Mom, I'm not dead yet. I'm barely out of Med school!" Becki replied, exasperated. "Besides, I hear more horror stories about cyber stalkers, Affect-hackers and VR sexual assaults then I hear about happy VR marriages. I guess I'm old-fashioned that way."

"Well, don't wait forever, dear. The man of your dreams may be just an eyePhone blink away!" Mom could be relentless on this ticking-clock topic.

Their interlude continued. Becki floated in and out of the conversation, at times listening to her mother, at others watching the goings-on around her. She'd see people walking by on the street next to the Starbucks. Some were tinged rose and had a score of '42' or '37' over their sulking bodies, others were tinged green, and fairly skipped along under their score of '87' or '92'. Like most people, Becki sent a friend request to those who she thought handsome, beautiful, had common interest and had high iAffect scores. She noted that typically, when a 'happy' person received an invitation, their score went up by a point or two: Cause and effect.

Loss

When not noticing the people around her, or hearing about her mother's friends and their latest escapades in VR, Becki noted the drones flying from place to place. They were now ubiquitous, and she marveled that there weren't more mid-air collisions than were already considered normal. The thought had no sooner crossed her mind when, suddenly, 10 drones in her field of view began gyrating wildly. Her eyePhones highlighted each of these now-dangerous robo-missiles with a flashing red warning, and urged her to take cover.

Each drone twisted and turned, apparently out of control. And then, one by one, they crashed into cars, store fronts and directly into people on the street. These collisions resulted in several cars crashing into one another, three store windows smashed, the flying glass injuring a dozen patrons, and two people directly injured by the suicide attacks by these rogue drones.

In the chaos of the streets, Becki's eyePhones displayed a new message. Crouched under her table at the Starbucks, Becki watched the incoming message from iJihad, who claimed responsibility for the spontaneous drone attack they just initiated. Becki exhaled deeply. These attacks were becoming more and more frequent, and more and more bold, as iJihad infiltrated more and more of the online, VR world and became ever-more sophisticated in its ability to disrupt people's new way of life in America.

Becki emerged from under her table, brushed off her off-contract jeans, helped her mother up and began to walk inside. Better to be under cover during an attack, anyway. As they entered the building, her eyePhones registered that CNN lowered her 'risk tax' fee from $.58 to $.27, with her decision to go inside. Homie, noting her increased level of anxiety over the last 60 seconds, consulted with Becki's virtual Physician's Assistant at CNN Healthcare. With the approval of the VPA, Homie instructed Becki's pharmabot, implanted in her stomach lining, to release a bit of Ativan into her system.

Becki, calmer now, mentally moved past the all-too-common drone attack she just witnessed and returned to shopping with her mother. She wondered what all of her iCash balances would look like by the end of the day, while her mother further encouraged her to reserve a VR suit for next weekend, in case she met someone 'nice.' As she strolled along, the video of the attack recorded by homie through her eyePhones was already being uploaded to the local police department, while the footage was being placed on ExBay, to be bid on by global news agencies who might like to pay for the content.

Next, Becki...

To be continued

Acknowledgements

In creating this book, I tried to follow my own advice as much as I possibly could. So, when it came time to edit the original manuscript, I tossed aside the typical editorial process of one-by-one, serial review by editors with little or no knowledge of the content I created. This is the traditional notion of an editorial 'value chain,' deeply rooted in Analog thinking from the last 200 years. The notion that a person with 10, 20 or 30 years of experience in publishing has some understanding of the issues faced by people in any, or *every,* other industry always struck me as cartoonish and foolish.

To properly edit this book, I instead create a 'value web.' I reached out to a whole range of people, with *actual* expertise and experience in the subject matter at hand, and I asked them to review and edit the material as I wrote it. As a result, Jerk improved in its accuracy and quality as it was being written. Once completed, I went back to the beginning, rewrote much of the early material based upon the improvements we made along the way (Do-Then-Learn-style), and in the end had a dramatically better product.

And, the entire process took about three weeks, rather than the six months that I had seen in the Analog way of doing things. My thanks to these experts who were part of my editorial web, listed below:

Lead Editors:

Bill Gillies	Walter Surdak, Jr.

Contributing Editors:

James Bacon	Richard Buchanan	Luda Bujoreanu
Zev Eigen	Jaime Espinoza	Bill Graff
Nathan Greenberg	Ed King	Douglas Laney
Wayne Matus	Stela Mocan	Robert O'Leary
Robert Owen	Jitendra Patel	Ali Qureshi
Dan Regard	Charles Snyder	Jason Stern

Writing Schedule

For my first book, *Data Crush*, I set the goal of writing the entire manuscript in six weeks, or 42 days. My then-editor told me that was impossible, and it had never been done before. I finished it in 41.

One of the principles I discuss in *Data Crush* is the need to cut every one of your business process cycle times in half, every 12 months, in order to remain relevant. So, when it came time to write *Jerk*, I set the goal of finishing the book in 21 days.

As with *Data Crush*, I set a daily writing goal, and tracked my progress. I used metrics and gamification to do 'the impossible.' The chart below is what I used in writing *Jerk*. As it shows, I completed the manuscript not in 21 days, but in 20.

Achieving the impossible starts with setting goals, deadlines and rewards for success. And then simply dig in and do it.

Chapter		Target	Words	Percent	Date	Words Written	% of Goal	Cumulative
1	Why Jerk	3000	3204	107%	26-Mar	6,850	10%	10%
2	A History of Us	3000	3646	122%	27-Mar	5,724	8%	19%
3	New Normal	3000	5724	191%	28-Mar	3,929	6%	24%
4	Call to Action	3000	3929	131%	29-Mar	2,312	3%	28%
5	OPC	2500	2386	95%	30-Mar	2,312	3%	31%
6	Grow Information	2500	2318	93%	31-Mar	2,000	3%	34%
7	Monetize context	2500	2892	116%	1-Apr	1,133	2%	36%
8	Eliminate Friction	2500	2487	99%	2-Apr	3,995	6%	42%
9	Value Chains and Webs	2500	4005	160%	3-Apr	4,990	7%	49%
10	Invert scale and scope	2500	2654	106%	4-Apr	-	0%	49%
11	sell with not to	2500	3130	125%	5-Apr	1,300	2%	51%
12	print money	2500	3496	140%	6-Apr	1,830	3%	54%
13	flout the rules	2500	3283	131%	7-Apr	5,326	8%	62%
14	Hightail it	2500	3811	152%	8-Apr	6,339	9%	71%
15	do then learn	2500	4011	160%	9-Apr	4,766	7%	78%
16	forwards not backwards	2500	3872	155%	10-Apr	8,289	12%	91%
17	Use Capital to DIE	3000	2258	75%	11-Apr	3,362	5%	95%
18	Rewrite your books	3000	2159	72%	12-Apr	3,340	5%	100%
19	Break your rules	3000	3362	112%	13-Apr	8,414	12%	113%
20	Annihilate process	3000	3340	111%	14-Apr		0%	113%
21	fail fast	3000	2713	90%	15-Apr		0%	113%
22	Seek Discomfort	3000	2838	95%		76,211	112.9%	
23	Welcome to 2025	7500		0%				
		67500	71518	106.0%				
24	Epilogue, added 4/13	3000	2863	95%				

Suggested Reading

1. Pierce, John, *An Introduction to Information Theory*. Dover Publications
2. Schneier, Bruce, *Liars & Outliers*. Wiley
3. Chien, Chao, *The Chinese Origin of the Age of Discovery*. Booklocker.com
4. Menzies, Gavin, *1434* Harper Collins Publishers
5. Mann, Charles, *1493*. Knopf
6. Mann, Charles, *1491*. Knopf
7. Zinn, Howard, *A People's History of the United States*. Harper
8. Harris, Shane, *The Watchers: The Rise of America's Surveillance State*. Penguin Press

End Notes

Section 1
1.   http://www.scienceandjusticejournal.com/article/S1355-0306%2800%2971944-7/abstract Accessed June 7, 2016.
2.   https://jhss10cestoncarino.wordpress.com/2013/02/15/study-the-past-if-you-would-define-the-future-confucius/ Accessed June 7, 2016.
3.   http://www.patheos.com/blogs/drishtikone/2013/01/amazingly-profound-quotes-from-calvin-and-hobbes/ Accessed June 7, 2016.

Chapter 1
1.   http://www.successories.com/iquote/author/11/mark-twain-quotes/1 Accessed June 2, 2016.
2.   http://www.goodreads.com/quotes/73865-in-my-opinion-we-don-t-devote-nearly-enough-scientific-research Accessed June 2, 2016.
3.   Wikipedia contributors. List of countries by number of Internet users. Wikipedia, The Free Encyclopedia. June 1, 2016, 08:37 UTC. Available at: https://en.wikipedia.org/w/index.php?title=List_of_countries_by_number_of_Internet_users&oldid=723146129 . Accessed June 2, 2016.
4.   App Store (iOS). (2016, May 27). In *Wikipedia, The Free Encyclopedia*. Retrieved 15:18, June 2, 2016, from https://en.wikipedia.org/w/index.php?title=App_Store_(iOS)&oldid=722296787

Chapter 2
1.   http://www.hitc.com/en-gb/2013/04/08/famous-maggie-thatcher-quotes/ Accessed June 2, 2016.
2.   http://www.successories.com/iquote/category/121/american-athlete-quotes/8 Accessed June 2, 2016.
3.   Ancient history. (2016, May 26). In *Wikipedia, The Free Encyclopedia*. Retrieved 21:37, June 7, 2016, from https://en.wikipedia.org/w/index.php?title=Ancient_history&oldid=722146814

Chapter 3
1.   https://www.quotes.as/quote/authors/sagan Accessed June 76, 2016.
2.   https://vacilandoblog.wordpress.com/2013/11/16/things-calvin-and-hobbes-said-better-than-anyone/ Accessed June 7, 2016.
3.   Economic history of Japan. (2016, May 3). In *Wikipedia, The Free Encyclopedia*. Retrieved 22:26, June 7, 2016, from https://en.wikipedia.org/w/index.php?title=Economic_history_of_Japan&oldid=718464649
4.   http://info.localytics.com/blog/app-user-retention-improves-in-the-us Accessed June 7, 2016.
5.   http://www.who.int/whr/2001/media_centre/press_release/en/ Accessed June 7, 2016.
6.   http://atwar.blogs.nytimes.com/2013/08/16/the-marines-secret-weapon-coffee/?_r=0 Accessed June 7, 2016.

Chapter 4
1.   http://www.blackpast.org/1857-frederick-douglass-if-there-no-struggle-there-no-progress Accessed June 7, 2016.
2.   Bill Watterson. (2016, March 10). *Wikiquote,* . Retrieved 22:46, June 7, 2016 from https://en.wikiquote.org/w/index.php?title=Bill_Watterson&oldid=2098421.

Chapter 5
1.   http://www.brainyquote.com/quotes/quotes/d/davidkorte283717.html Accessed June 7, 2016.
2.   http://www.quoteauthors.com/ralph-waldo-emerson-quotes/ Accessed June 7, 2016.
3.   Elon Musk. (2016, June 6). In *Wikipedia, The Free Encyclopedia*. Retrieved 01:09, June 8, 2016, from https://en.wikipedia.org/w/index.php?title=Elon_Musk&oldid=724026974

Chapter 6
1.   http://www.brainyquote.com/quotes/quotes/c/carlsagan105003.html Accessed June 7, 2016.
2.   Bill Watterson. (2016, March 10). *Wikiquote,* . Retrieved 01:13, June 8, 2016 from https://en.wikiquote.org/w/index.php?title=Bill_Watterson&oldid=2098421.

Chapter 7
1.   https://books.google.com/books?id=wDr8uQ_vITQC&pg=PA44&lpg=PA44&dq=Space+and+time+not+only+affect,+but+are+also+affected+by,+everything+that+happens+in+the+universe.&source=bl&ots=9RRI-UiA-D&sig=K_gBEEvplJ2oTulkM9U5sVL0Fuw&hl=en&sa=X&ved=0ahUKEwjbp6yRo5fNAhUDKh4KHUiIAVoQ6AEIIzAB#v=onepage&q=Space%20and%20time%20not%20only%20affect%2C%20but%20are%20also%20affected%20by%2C%20everything%20that%20happens%20in%20the%20universe.&f=false Accessed June 7, 2016.
2.   http://www.brainyquote.com/quotes/quotes/w/williamsha139153.html Accessed June 7, 2016.

Chapter 8
1.   http://www.brainyquote.com/quotes/quotes/r/ralphwaldo122767.html Accessed June 7, 2016.
2.   http://www.brainyquote.com/quotes/quotes/e/eecummin176712.html Accessed June 7, 2016.
3.   Clipper. (2016, May 9). In *Wikipedia, The Free Encyclopedia*. Retrieved 01:36, June 8, 2016, from https://en.wikipedia.org/w/index.php?title=Clipper&oldid=719463920
4.   Flying Cloud (clipper). (2016, May 30). In *Wikipedia, The Free Encyclopedia*. Retrieved 01:38, June 8, 2016, from https://en.wikipedia.org/w/index.php?title=Flying_Cloud_(clipper)&oldid=722926501
5.   Pony Express. (2016, June 7). In *Wikipedia, The Free Encyclopedia*. Retrieved 01:41, June 8, 2016, from https://en.wikipedia.org/w/index.php?title=Pony_Express&oldid=724088193

Chapter 9

1. http://www.brainyquote.com/quotes/quotes/c/carlsagan130525.html Accessed June 7, 2016.
2. http://www.brainyquote.com/quotes/quotes/n/nelsonmand178787.html Accessed June 7, 2016.
3. Intermodal container. (2016, June 5). In *Wikipedia, The Free Encyclopedia*. Retrieved 01:51, June 8, 2016, from https://en.wikipedia.org/w/index.php?title=Intermodal_container&oldid=723770365

Chapter 10
1. http://www.brainyquote.com/quotes/quotes/e/eecummin397775.html Accessed June 7, 2016.
2. http://www.brainyquote.com/quotes/quotes/m/marktwain122378.html Accessed June 7, 2016.
3. Abraham Maslow. (2016, June 6). In *Wikipedia, The Free Encyclopedia*. Retrieved 01:59, June 8, 2016, from https://en.wikipedia.org/w/index.php?title=Abraham_Maslow&oldid=723995504

Chapter 11
1. http://www.brainyquote.com/quotes/quotes/m/mayaangelo120197.html Accessed June 7, 2016.
2. http://www.goodreads.com/quotes/63089-the-world-is-full-of-willing-people-some-willing-to Accessed June 7, 2016.
3. S&H Green Stamps. (2016, April 28). In *Wikipedia, The Free Encyclopedia*. Retrieved 02:06, June 8, 2016, from https://en.wikipedia.org/w/index.php?title=S%26H_Green_Stamps&oldid=717626095

Chapter 12
1. http://nelsonmandelas.com/nelson-mandela-quotes/ Accessed June 7, 2016.
2. http://www.brainyquote.com/quotes/quotes/m/marktwain397078.html Accessed June 7, 2016.
3. Ancient Greek coinage. (2016, April 17). In *Wikipedia, The Free Encyclopedia*. Retrieved 02:15, June 8, 2016, from https://en.wikipedia.org/w/index.php?title=Ancient_Greek_coinage&oldid=715780250
4. History of money. (2016, June 5). In *Wikipedia, The Free Encyclopedia*. Retrieved 02:17, June 8, 2016, from https://en.wikipedia.org/w/index.php?title=History_of_money&oldid=723840131

Chapter 13
1. https://en.wikiquote.org/wiki/Talk:Douglas_MacArthur Accessed June 7, 2016.
2. Steve Jobs. (2016, May 22). *Wikiquote, .* Retrieved 02:22, June 8, 2016 from https://en.wikiquote.org/w/index.php?title=Steve_Jobs&oldid=2129611.
3. FanDuel. (2016, June 4). In *Wikipedia, The Free Encyclopedia*. Retrieved 02:25, June 8, 2016, from https://en.wikipedia.org/w/index.php?title=FanDuel&oldid=723675573

Chapter 14
1. http://www.brainyquote.com/quotes/quotes/r/ralphwaldo380544.html Accessed June 7, 2016.
2. http://bookriot.com/2012/02/06/sixteen-things-calvin-and-hobbes-said-better-than-anyone-else/ Accessed June 7, 2016.
3. The Bell Curve. (2016, June 6). In *Wikipedia, The Free Encyclopedia*. Retrieved 02:40, June 8, 2016, from https://en.wikipedia.org/w/index.php?title=The_Bell_Curve&oldid=723929749
4. http://ec.europa.eu/justice/data-protection/files/factsheets/factsheet_data_protection_en.pdf Accessed June 7, 2016.
5. http://curia.europa.eu/jcms/upload/docs/application/pdf/2015-10/cp150117en.pdf Accessed June 7, 2016.

Chapter 15
1. http://www.azquotes.com/quote/235190 Accessed June 7, 2016.
2. Yogi Berra. (2016, April 29). *Wikiquote, .* Retrieved 02:49, June 8, 2016 from https://en.wikiquote.org/w/index.php?title=Yogi_Berra&oldid=2121917.
3. http://www.twainquotes.com/Education.html Accessed June 7, 2016.
4. Space Pen. (2016, May 25). In *Wikipedia, The Free Encyclopedia*. Retrieved 02:56, June 8, 2016, from https://en.wikipedia.org/w/index.php?title=Space_Pen&oldid=722014636

Chapter 16
1. http://www.brainyquote.com/quotes/quotes/d/dalailama446740.html Accessed June 7, 2016.
2. http://www.brainyquote.com/quotes/quotes/r/ralphwaldo166470.html Accessed June 7, 2016.
3. http://www.twainquotes.com/Optimist.html Accessed June 7, 2016.
4. General relativity. (2016, May 27). In *Wikipedia, The Free Encyclopedia*. Retrieved 03:05, June 8, 2016, from https://en.wikipedia.org/w/index.php?title=General_relativity&oldid=722392517

Section 3
1. Dashpot. (2016, February 12). In *Wikipedia, The Free Encyclopedia*. Retrieved 03:07, June 8, 2016, from https://en.wikipedia.org/w/index.php?title=Dashpot&oldid=704617865

Chapter 17
1. http://www.wisdomtoinspire.com/t/henry-ford/E1TDRr3v/if-I-had-asked-people Accessed June 7, 2016.
2. http://www.brainyquote.com/quotes/quotes/m/marktwain109624.html Accessed June 7, 2016.

Chapter 18
1. http://www.brainyquote.com/quotes/quotes/g/georgespa126032.html Accessed June 7, 2016.
2. Yogi Berra. (2016, April 29). *Wikiquote, .* Retrieved 03:18, June 8, 2016 from https://en.wikiquote.org/w/index.php?title=Yogi_Berra&oldid=2121917.
3. Archimedes. (2016, May 3). *Wikiquote, .* Retrieved 03:20, June 8, 2016 from https://en.wikiquote.org/w/index.php?title=Archimedes&oldid=2123249.

Chapter 19
1. http://www.jfklibrary.org/Research/Research-Aids/Ready-Reference/JFK-Quotations.aspx Accessed June 7, 2016.
2. http://www.brainyquote.com/quotes/quotes/y/yogiberra145878.html Accessed June 7, 2016.

3.   Bart Simpson. (2016, June 7). In *Wikipedia, The Free Encyclopedia*. Retrieved 03:27, June 8, 2016, from https://en.wikipedia.org/w/index.php?title=Bart_Simpson&oldid=724213629

Chapter 20
1.   http://www.quotes.net/quote/11056 Accessed June 7, 2016.
2.   http://www.brainyquote.com/quotes/quotes/m/mayaangelo120862.html Accessed June 7, 2016.
3.   http://www.brainyquote.com/quotes/quotes/p/paulgoodma135472.html Accessed June 7, 2016.
4.   Fortune 500 list of largest companies in 2000 were off the list by 2010 ???
5.   The Cask of Amontillado. (2016, June 2). In *Wikipedia, The Free Encyclopedia*. Retrieved 03:42, June 8, 2016, from https://en.wikipedia.org/w/index.php?title=The_Cask_of_Amontillado&oldid=723274490

Chapter 21
1.   https://en.wikiquote.org/wiki/Talk:Samuel_Goldwyn Accessed June 7, 2016.
2.   http://www.brainyquote.com/quotes/quotes/a/alberteins109012.html Accessed June 7, 2016.
3.   Bill Watterson. (2016, March 10). *Wikiquote*, . Retrieved 03:48, June 8, 2016 from https://en.wikiquote.org/w/index.php?title=Bill_Watterson&oldid=2098421.
4.   Gene Kranz. (2016, May 30). In *Wikipedia, The Free Encyclopedia*. Retrieved 03:51, June 8, 2016, from https://en.wikipedia.org/w/index.php?title=Gene_Kranz&oldid=722904763

Chapter 22
1.   http://www.brainyquote.com/quotes/quotes/w/waynedyer384143.html Accessed June 7, 2016.
2.   Yogi Berra. (2016, April 29). *Wikiquote*, . Retrieved 03:56, June 8, 2016 from https://en.wikiquote.org/w/index.php?title=Yogi_Berra&oldid=2121917.
3.   Sun Tzu. (2016, June 5). In *Wikipedia, The Free Encyclopedia*. Retrieved 03:59, June 8, 2016, from https://en.wikipedia.org/w/index.php?title=Sun_Tzu&oldid=723888800

Chapter 23
1.   http://www.brainyquote.com/quotes/quotes/c/carlsagan657452.html Accessed June 7, 2016.
2.   Bill Watterson. (2016, March 10). *Wikiquote*, . Retrieved 04:03, June 8, 2016 from https://en.wikiquote.org/w/index.php?title=Bill_Watterson&oldid=2098421.
3.   May you live in interesting times. (2016, June 2). In *Wikipedia, The Free Encyclopedia*. Retrieved 04:04, June 8, 2016, from https://en.wikipedia.org/w/index.php?title=May_you_live_in_interesting_times&oldid=723412269

Made in the USA
Charleston, SC
30 January 2017